W9-DFM-770

JONATHAN POSTAL / TOWERY PUBLISHING, INC.; POSTER DESIGN: JIM SHERRADEN / HATCH SHOW PRINT

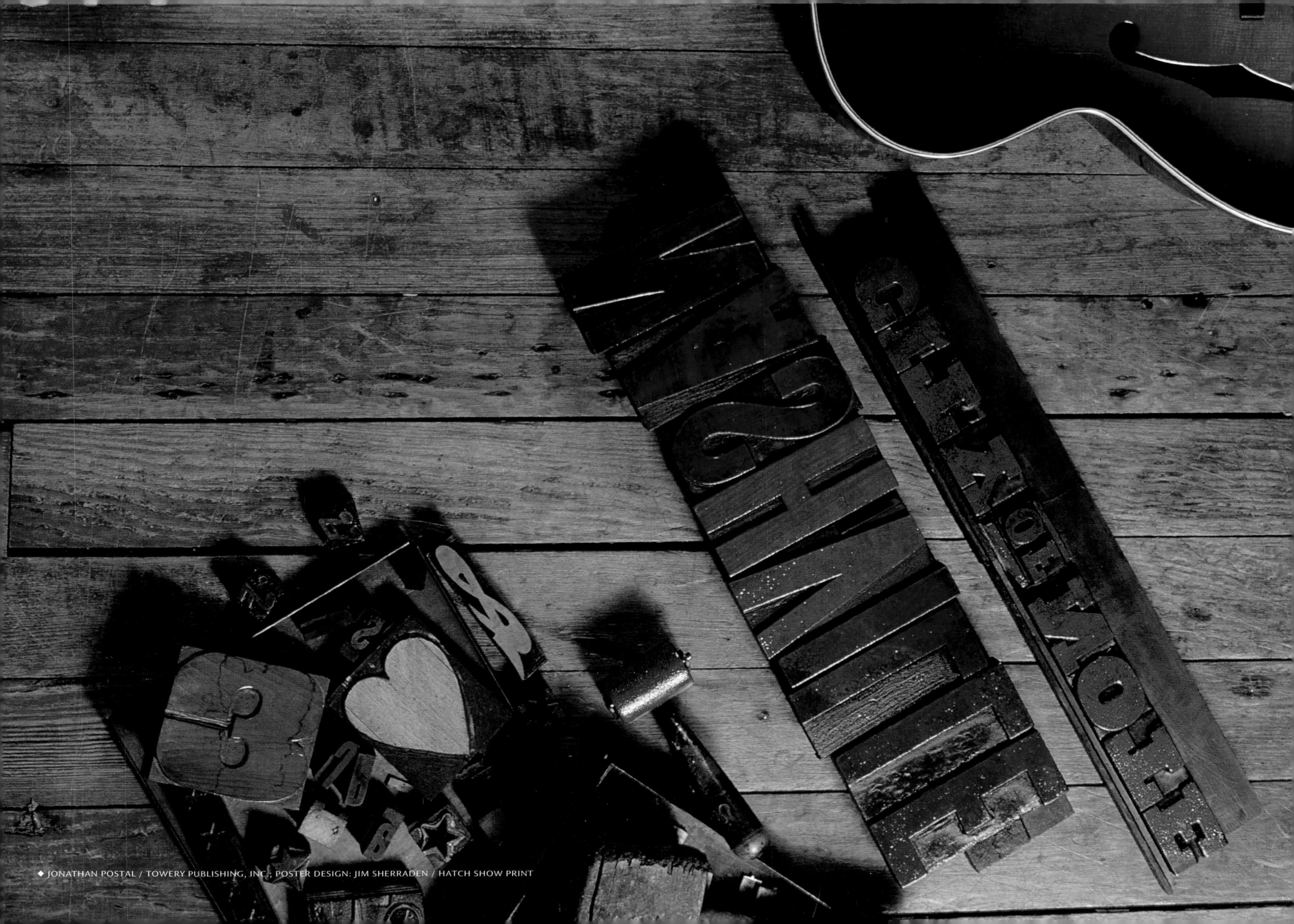

◆ JONATHAN POSTAL / TOWERY PUBLISHING, INC.; POSTER DESIGN: JIM SHERRADEN / HATCH SHOW PRINT

NASHVILLE
CITY OF NOTE

By JOHN M. SEIGENTHALER and CURTIS ALLEN
Profiles in Excellence by HEATHER COCHRAN
Captions by WEB WEBSTER
Art Direction by BRIAN GROPPE and JONATHAN POSTAL

URBAN TAPESTRY SERIES
TOWERY

LIBRARY OF CONGRESS CATALOGING-IN-PUBLICATION DATA

Seigenthaler, John M., 1955-
Nashville : city of note / by John M. Seigenthaler and Curtis Allen ; profiles in excellence by Heather Cochran ; captions by Web Webster ; art direction by Brian Groppe and Jonathan Postal.
p. cm.—(Urban tapestry series)
Includes index.
ISBN 1-881096-43-2
1. Nashville (Tenn.)—Civilization. 2. Nashville (Tenn.)--Pictorial works. 3. Nashville (Tenn.)—Economic conditions. 4. Business enterprises—Tennessee—Nashville. I. Allen, Curtis, 1950- . II. Cochran, Heather, 1961- . III. Title. IV. Series.
F444.N25S43 1997 97-15755
976.8'55—dc21 CIP

Towery Publishing, Inc., 1835 Union Avenue, Memphis, TN 38104

Publisher: J. Robert Towery
Executive Publisher: Jenny McDowell
National Sales Manager: Stephen Hung
Marketing Director: Carol Culpepper
Project Directors: John Lorenzo, Robert Philips

Executive Editor: David B. Dawson
Managing Editor: Michael C. James
Senior Editors: Lynn Conlee, Carlisle Hacker
Editors: Mary Jane Adams, Lori Bond, Jana Files
Assistant Editor: Jennifer C. Pyron
Editorial Contributor: Christopher A. Cunningham

Profile Designers: Jennifer Baugher, Laurie Lewis, Ann Ward
Technical Director: William H. Towery
Digital Color Supervisor: Brenda Pattat
Production Assistants: Jeff McDonald, Robin McGehee
Print Coordinator: Beverly Thompson

Contents

By John M. Seigenthaler

IKE MOST CITIES THAT ARE POPULAR TOURIST DESTINATIONS, there are two versions of Nashville. ★ There's the hometown where I grew up—a city of business and politics, education and culture—that still lives up to its old nickname as the "Athens of the South" (although you rarely hear it anymore).

◀ KARINA

This city is one of learning and commerce, of government and trade—a focal point for Tennessee's cultural life.

For those who know Nashville only from a visitor's perspective, though, it's "Music City," the high-decibel wonderland of country music, an image that tends to mask the rest of what goes on here. The Music City veneer is so pervasive, so powerful, that it's no wonder millions of tourists leave Nashville knowing a completely different city than the people who live here.

There is, of course, nothing wrong with this dichotomy. After all, most of the visitors who make the pilgrimage to hear the Nashville Sound, and to gaze at the stars who create it, go home smiling and happy. I suppose it's the same sort of thing that goes on in Louisville during Derby Week or in New Orleans during Mardi Gras. People are drawn to a place by its predominant events or characteristics, and when they leave, they have an idea that they have somehow experienced all that is important or "real" about it.

And when it comes to Nashville, what's important for the visitors and tourists is, of course, the music. Thankfully, there's plenty to go around. The Nashville Sound has made a distinctive mark and is recognized around the world. It remains our trademark, our calling card, our claim to fame.

▶ JONATHAN POSTAL / TOWERY PUBLISHING, INC.

Naturally, we're proud of our music industry, and most of the folks who live here genuinely enjoy the country tunes that spin forth from the many performers who call Nashville home—from hillbilly innovators like the late Bill Monroe and Minnie Pearl to today's retro-modern artists like BR5-49 and Dwight Yoakam, and every rhinestoned, tuned-up, big-hatted one of them in between. But this image excludes the Athens of the South part of the story, the Nashville where we do most of our real living.

It's important for people to know that there's more to Nashville than the twangy melodies of a country song. We want the world to realize that our hometown is the capital of Tennessee and a regional center for government, health care, communications, transportation, education, and manufacturing. It is a place of rich history and grand culture, of old money and solid traditions that predate the country music that has come to define us.

Here, then, on Middle Tennessee's Cumberland Plateau, a tale of two cities unfolds: one, an enduringly popular tourist destination; the other, a vibrant, progressive, modern megalopolis with an inspiring heritage. Assuredly, it's a tale worth telling. ☛

CITY THAT SUCCESSFULLY combines the arts, music, and dance with business and government, Nashville deserves its distinctions as both Music City and Athens of the South. The artful blending of the two realms is captured during the annual Summer Lights outdoor festival (PAGES 6 AND 7). Grand Ole Opry veteran Grandpa Jones (OPPOSITE) and Gary Bennett of BR5-49 (LEFT) represent the past and the future of the potent Nashville Sound.

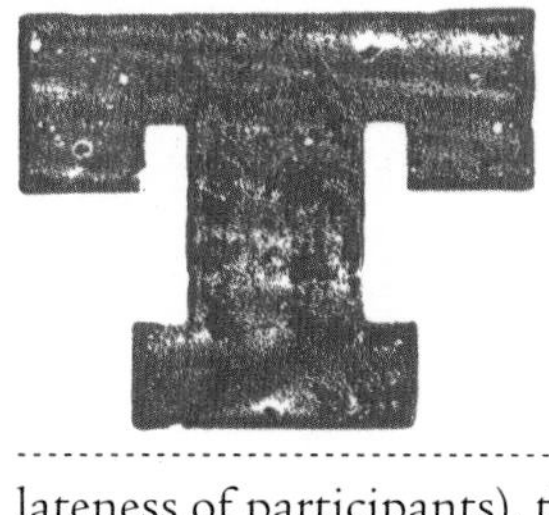

THE MOST ENDURING SYMBOL OF NASHVILLE'S ATHENS PERSONA IS, of course, the replica of the Parthenon in Centennial Park. Originally built in 1897 to serve as the city's entry in the Tennessee Centennial Exposition (which, by the way, was held a year after the actual centennial date due to the overall lateness of participants), the wood and plaster structure was meant to serve only as a temporary exhibit.

Yet this full-scale model was said to be so beautiful—so appropriate—that it was left standing long after the close of the exposition. And in the early 1920s, after the old Parthenon had become decrepit, city engineers began rebuilding the structure using steel and concrete to meet the exact dimensions of its Grecian prototype. Today, the Parthenon, which houses the city's fine arts museum, remains a symbol of refinement, learning, government, statesmanship, and culture. It embodies the "easy-going spirit of the old South," as one guidebook put it, that the Athens moniker has long evoked.

How did Nashville evolve into the Athens of the South? Where did this tradition come from? You have to burrow deep into the city's history to find out. Here, at the intersection of the Cumberland River, the Wilderness Road, and the Natchez Trace (an Indian trail stretching south into Mississippi), came a blend of cultural and social influences that helped to launch and drive Nashville's progress. Nashville's status as the capital of Tennessee was solidified in October 1843, although it had been the state's unofficial center of activity ever since it was settled.

It was here that Andrew Jackson, already a legendary figure in the early 1820s due to his involvement in the War of 1812, received genteel visitors at the Hermitage, his plantation on the eastern side of the city. Today, Jackson's home is a magnet for tourists, and his memory is highly regarded hereabouts. In fact, the oldest (now remodeled) downtown hotel is also called the Hermitage. Other tourist sites are similarly rooted in Nashville's history and reflect the city's heritage of learning and culture, including the home of President James K. Polk; Belle Meade Plantation; the Belmont Mansion; Fort Donelson National Battlefield; and Traveller's Rest Historic House and Grounds, a 1799 Federalist farmhouse built by Judge John Overton, another influential early landowner.

Nashville's character is on permanent display at these and other historic buildings and sites. Culture and refinement, roughness and frontier know-how—they're all blended here. They're all interdependent. And they're all part of what makes up the city as we know it today. ☛

▶ GARY LAYDA
◀ CAROL AND DAN THALIMER / HILLSTROM STOCK PHOTO

ORIGINALLY BUILT AS A temporary structure for Tennessee's Centennial Exhibition, the Parthenon became a permanent part of Nashville's landscape when a concrete version of the structure opened in 1931 (OPPOSITE). Another recognizable city landmark is the statue of Andrew Jackson tipping his hat to the state flag that flies over the Tennessee State Capitol (LEFT).

MARKET STREET EMPORIUM
31 Baskin Robbins
31 Baskin Robbins
Yes! We're
DECADES
Remember When Gallery
MARKET STREET EMPORIUM
Food · Fashion · Gifts & More...

HILE THE PARTHENON EVOKES THE REFINED, CULTURED, and moneyed side of Nashville, the century-old Ryman Auditorium serves as a symbol for its Music City identity. Here, at the Ryman, coalesced the influences that emerged as modern-day country music. Ever since, the city has remained identified with the fiddles, washboards, and moonshine jugs that the Irish and Scottish pioneers who settled the region used when they concocted the hillbilly strains of country music.

▸ BOB SCHATZ

This sound in its many manifestations—bluegrass, rockabilly, country swing, you name it—has its roots in the same melodies that the buckskinned settlers with the raccoon hats hummed as they led their wagons to the Cumberland's fertile valleys. Country music also has deep roots in the dusty Appalachian coal mines, the dirt farms of the lush lands surrounding Nashville, and the honky-tonks that sprang up to serve thirsty factory workers. It is the sound of the region, yet it's also the sound of the nation, a truly American art form born right here in Nashville.

A roster of just a few of country music's luminaries is so evocative that the names themselves tell a good deal of the story: Bill Monroe. Hank Williams (junior and senior). Buck Owens. Faron Young. Loretta Lynn. Lester Flatt and Earl Scruggs. The Judds. Clint Black. Dolly Parton. Alan Jackson. Chet Atkins. The Mandrell sisters. The Oak Ridge Boys. Jim Reeves. Ernest Tubb. Glen Campbell. Mother Maybelle Carter. Conway Twitty. Roy Clark. Porter Wagoner. Patsy Cline. Johnny and June Carter Cash. Bela Fleck. Tammy Wynette. Tom T. Hall. Garth Brooks. Waylon Jennings. Reba McEntire. Amy Grant. Brooks & Dunn. John Hiatt. Travis Tritt. Vince Gill. Little Jimmy Dickens. Grandpa Jones. Charlie Daniels. George Jones. Merle Haggard. Rosanne Cash. Willie Nelson. Marty Robbins. The Statler Brothers. Emmylou Harris.

There. I just left out your favorite, didn't I? Yet my point is not to provide an exhaustive list of country music's brightest stars; such a task would be nearly impossible, certainly beyond the scope of this introduction to my hometown. Instead, my point is to show the breadth of talent that has made it in Nashville. To go further, you'll need to put on your boots, crank up the volume, and let the music tell the rest of that story.

Or come to areas of town like Lower Broad and see the spectacle in action, night after night, year-round.

Lower Broad got its name because it's located where Broadway runs downhill from Second Avenue to the Cumberland River. More than 15 years ago, it was known for its X-rated peep shows and bookstores. At the time, it was a symbol of inner-city decay.

PAYING HOMAGE TO THE dulcimer, guitar, fiddle, and voice, Thomas Hart Benton's *The Sources of Country Music* (BELOW) hangs in the Country Music Hall of Fame, which chronicles the history of the genre. Today's hillbilly tunes find a welcome home throughout Nashville, including the Wildhorse Saloon in the District. The popular watering hole celebrated its grand opening by herding cattle down Second Avenue (OPPOSITE)—much to the dismay of city sanitation workers.

▸ COUNTRY MUSIC HALL OF FAME

NAMED FOR THE REPORTERS and newspapermen who frequented its establishments, Printer's Alley was long home to Nashville nightspots like the Pink Poodle (RIGHT). Tucked in an alley that runs from Commerce to Union streets between Third and Fourth avenues, the area still houses many of the bars and adult dance clubs that made it famous.

Countless superstars have come to Nashville to lay down their piece of music history. Included in the long list of familiar faces and voices are (OPPOSITE, CLOCKWISE FROM TOP LEFT) Buck Owens, Lorrie Morgan, LeAnn Rimes, Roy Acuff, Charlie Daniels, actor/comedian Pee-Wee Herman, Kathy Mattea, Johnny Cash, and Loretta Lynn.

PAGE 15, CLOCKWISE FROM TOP LEFT: COUNTRY MUSIC HALL OF FAME, GARY LAYDA, JOHN CHIASSON, GARY LAYDA, GARY LAYDA, GARY LAYDA, BOB SCHATZ, COUNTRY MUSIC HALL OF FAME, GARY LAYDA

STEPHEN GREENFIELD PHOTOGRAPHY

Today, Lower Broad is a booming entertainment center that has been renamed "the District." It draws in-towners and out-of-towners alike to such exciting locales as the Hard Rock Cafe, the Wildhorse Saloon, Planet Hollywood, and a brand-new, steel-and-glass arena that bears a striking resemblance to a spaceship in a *Star Trek* movie.

The District includes dozens of restaurants and clubs—such as Tootsie's World Famous Orchid Lounge and Robert's Western World (also known as Three Doors Down, because it's, well, three doors down from Tootsie's). These venerable hot spots, and many others, have popped up over the years in the shadow of the history-laden Ryman Auditorium, where W.C. Fields performed his vaudeville act, where Billy Sunday staged spirit-moving revivals, and where the Grand Ole Opry moved its increasingly successful broadcast in 1943. In this music mecca, the Ryman—recently renovated and serving once again as a performance hall for touring classical music ensembles, among other things—has been a shrine for country music fans and performers alike. In the old days, to play the Ryman was tantamount to approaching country music paradise, even if the crowd was less than enthusiastic. And yet, if they liked your song or chuckled at your jokes, you found yourself in hillbilly heaven, and nobody could ever take that sublime moment away.

Today, this bulwark of the country music business has moved to the immense Opryland USA Themepark—where the Grand Ole Opry now holds court in its own special theater. Also at Opryland are a big-time amusement park, the Hangman roller coaster, the General Jackson paddle wheel showboat that transports thousands of visitors up and down the Cumberland, outdoor shows, a convention hotel with three indoor gardens covering more than four acres, and an 18-hole PGA golf course—all located just 15 minutes from downtown Nashville.

Then, you have other mainstays of the country music industry scattered between the Opryland complex and the District, including the studios of The Nashville Network, the Country Music Hall of Fame, Twitty City, Barbara Mandrell Country, the House of Cash, and so many others that there's simply not enough room to include them all. Then, there's Music Row, an area where the major recording companies have offices and where a good many entertainers have their own museums (or where they're likely to be enshrined in the Country Music Wax Museum if they don't). I could go on and on: Nashville is the country music capital of the world, after all. No more elaboration is necessary.

EAST SOUTH
24
65
Nashville
EXIT 86
265
Memphis
EXIT
86

ITH OUR DOWN-HOME IMAGE AND BACKWOODS REPUTATION, people are often surprised to learn that Nashville is a relatively wealthy town. What's more, there's *always* been money here—"old money," as you'll often hear it called. The 37205 zip code, which encompasses a grand old neighborhood west of downtown called Belle Meade, is the home of more millionaires per square foot than most cities in the South can boast.

◄ GARY LAYDA

Yes, music is one of the mainstays of the local economy, an industry that has created a good many fortunes throughout the area. This new money, most of it made by transplants with some connection to the music industry, is plentiful and on full display. The old myths about people arriving in Nashville aboard a Greyhound bus (that deus ex machina of so many country songs) with nothing more than a few dollars, a beat-up guitar, and a head full of dreams is not only an enduring one, but also a proven formula for success for a good many of country music's luminaries. For instance, Johnny Cash, fresh from a WPA-built, Depression-era village in Arkansas, struggled from dirt and poverty to fame and fortune in Nashville. And today, tourists pay money for a bus ride by the impressive compound owned by Cash on Old Hickory Lake east of the city, one of many such estates the stars call home.

In the nice, symbiotic way that has come to symbolize Nashville's method of doing things, it was actually the old money that made possible the new. Well, sort of. National Life, one of the city's established insurance companies that helped populate Belle Meade, actually created the Opry as a radio show broadcast over the company's clear channel station. The idea was to sell insurance to rural folk who loved the music. The Opry founders never dreamed that the show they started would ultimately be the driving force that put Nashville so squarely on the world's musical map.

By the same token, the city's old guard was also very much involved in making Nashville a center of government, commerce, transportation, education, and culture. The Athens of the South. Music City. When it comes to the money that made them possible, the two are perhaps not so different after all.

Which is to say, the city's identity is by no means a static one. Instead, there's a gentle pull and tug between old money and new, between country and urban, between insider Nashville and tourist Nashville. These days, the lines between such worlds are dissolving as the city takes its place as one of the most progressive, forward-thinking communities in the country.

Recent developments—especially those that have occurred in my lifetime—have been dramatic. When I was growing up, some folks used to tell their kids that one of the worst evils that could befall Nashville was to have it grow into a city like Atlanta. "Grow Slow!" was the motto. Today, the unspoken motto in Nashville is "Grow and Go."

The construction of the Nashville Arena is an apt example of that new attitude. It was the brainchild of Phil Bredesen, our first nonnative mayor, who convinced a doubting city council to spend more than $140 million to build the place in hopes of attracting a professional hockey or basketball team. A 20,000-seat arena now stands downtown. Amy Grant filled it when she held a concert for the grand opening, but what about those teams? Well, it pays to have faith. In June 1997, the National Hockey League announced that a franchise will start play in Nashville in 1998.

In a left-handed way, though, the arena had already brought us professional sports. During its construction, Bud Adams, owner of the Houston Oilers, announced that he would move his team to Nashville if the city matched its effort in constructing the arena by building a new stadium. Adams' lease with the Astrodome in Houston was running out, and true to the spirit of the times in pro football, he was looking for a sweeter deal. So, again thanks to a Bredesen leap of faith, a new stadium is under construction, just across the river from Lower Broad, and the Oilers are expected to start playing in Tennessee in 1997. ☛

NASHVILLE'S RAPIDLY GROWing business district provides a spectacular greeting to drivers heading into the city on I-65. The recently completed Nashville Arena (BELOW) is the newest jewel in this sparkling skyline.

► METRO GOVERNMENT OF NASHVILLE / GARY LAYDA

HE ANNOUNCEMENT OF THE PENDING NFL TEAM SEEMED TO provide the culmination—the acknowledgment of success—of a long series of changes and transformations that have helped reshape modern Nashville. ★ It is perhaps the downtown skyline that has seen the most dramatic change. When I was a child, the city was framed primarily by two lone skyscrapers that were clearly visible as you drove toward town on West End Avenue. They were known as the Life and Casualty and the National Life buildings, headquarters of the companies for which they were named. As the years have passed, what was once plenty of open space, with squatty buildings between the two insurance towers, has been filled with tall, gleaming structures. The most notable is probably the BellSouth Tower, which has attracted unexpected national attention because it looks like something out of a Batman movie.

The city's attitudes toward race have also undergone substantial change. Areas where sit-ins once occurred now boast racially mixed office buildings and stores. Despite being a thoroughly southern city—with all of what that distinction entails regarding race—Nashville has indeed made remarkable progress.

Other attitudes have remained steadfast. Nashville is, and always has been, a religious town, one of the many in the South that people have dubbed the buckle of the Bible Belt. Steeples seem to grow out of every neighborhood in this town of more than 800 churches. But what *has* changed is the growing diversity of the religious community. Once almost exclusively Christian, the landscape is now dotted with an array of synagogues, mosques, and temples.

In addition to the practice of worship, Nashville is home to the business side of religion. The United Methodist Publishing House; the Southern Baptist Convention; the Baptist Sunday School Board; the National Baptist Convention USA; and Thomas Nelson, Inc., the world's largest publisher of Bibles, are all based here.

Another notable change has been Nashville's emergence during the past couple of decades as an industrial center. Although there has always been a smattering of industry here, Nashville became an automotive town back when Lamar Alexander (the plaid-shirted 1996 presidential contender) was governor. Alexander enticed Japanese businesses to invest in Middle Tennessee. One of them, Nissan, moved in and launched a giant auto manufacturing business in the outlying city of Smyrna. A few years later, state industry recruiters challenged General Motors to build their new Saturn car plant in Spring Hill, just 40 miles away from the Nissan facility. With these new industrial tenants came a host of automotive supply companies, helping to establish the area as a car making hub.

Ascending along a different trajectory has been Nashville's emergence as a world-renowned medical center. Vanderbilt University Medical Center has maintained a strong presence here for 125 years. Recently, though, Nashville became home to the nation's largest owner and operator of for-profit hospitals when Columbia Healthcare and Hospital Corporation of America (HCA) merged. The original HCA was born in Nashville in 1968 when the late Jack Massey teamed up with Dr. Thomas F. Frist Sr. and his son Dr. Thomas F. Frist Jr. to launch the hospital chain. Today, Dr. Thomas Frist Jr. serves as CEO and chairman of the board for the giant Columbia/HCA Healthcare Corporation. (His brother, Dr. Bill Frist, a cardiac transplant surgeon, was elected to the U.S. Senate in 1994.) After the Columbia/HCA merger secured Nashville as the headquarters for the company, Nashville began accumulating the largest concentration of health care management firms in the nation.

The city's array of arts organizations, museums, theaters, and parks have also flourished in recent years. At the beautiful Tennessee Performing Arts Center, you can catch everything from the latest Broadway show to performances by the

◀ GARY LAYDA

▶ GARY LAYDA

WHEN THE NEW BELLSouth headquarters was completed in Nashville in 1994 (OPPOSITE), a local journalist suggested that it bore an uncanny resemblance to a hooded superhero with an affinity for bats. The name Bat Building was soon coined and remains a popular nickname today.

Although separated by several city blocks, church and state make better neighbors than you'd think in downtown Nashville. St. Mary's Catholic Church, with its gold dome and cross, and the Tennessee State Capitol were both designed by architect William Strickland.

◀ METRO GOVERNMENT OF NASHVILLE / GARY LAYDA
◀ BOB SCHATZ

Nashville Ballet, Nashville Opera, or Nashville Symphony Orchestra. In addition to the Tennessee Repertory Theater and Actor's Playhouse, considered one of the best around, the natural-environment Nashville Zoo is always a popular retreat, as is the Cumberland Science Museum, complete with a planetarium. The Tennessee State Museum chronicles the state's historical heritage from precolonial times to today. And the State Capitol, in addition to its important governmental function, is an outstanding place to visit and learn a whole semester's worth of civics lessons just by touring its historic halls.

Although outright change is perhaps not so apparent in Nashville's colleges and universities, progress at the city's 17 institutions of higher learning continues at a steady pace. Vanderbilt, endowed by Commodore Cornelius Vanderbilt in 1873, remains the dominant institution, with a reputation as one of the finest private universities in the country. Its law and medical schools, specifically, have long held national rank. The city's three predominantly African-American schools—Fisk University (home of the Carl Van Vechten Gallery, containing priceless works of art by Cézanne, Picasso, Renoir, Toulouse-Lautrec, and O'Keeffe), Meharry Medical College (which has produced 40 percent of the African-American doctors and dentists in the nation), and Tennessee State University (where Olympic gold medalist Wilma Rudolph was a track star)—provide unlimited opportunities for students to gain the knowledge and professional skills they desire.

And that's just scratching the surface. Clearly, the Athens of the South fosters one of the most dynamic business, cultural, social, and educational environments in America, thanks to a varied economic base that includes, of course, lots of country music.

So, whether you prefer Athens of the South or Music City, it doesn't really matter. By any name at all, Nashville is a place of distinction. It's a place that I am proud to call home. ★

NASHVILLE'S ANSWER TO the National Cherry Blossom Festival in Washington, D.C., comes all too briefly during early spring when dogwoods explode into bloom in Legislative Plaza (OPPOSITE) and throughout the city.

Downtown skyscrapers create an unusual backdrop for this graceful dancer—a metaphor for the role the business community plays in the area's thriving performing arts scene.

◆ GARY LAYDA

WKDF
MISSISSIPPI
JACKSON

NASHVILLE WAS FOUNDED in 1779 when a band of pioneers, led by John Robertson, stopped at a quiet crook in the Cumberland River and built Fort Nashborough. From that wooden stockade, the city grew up, around, and out from its river roots into today's skyscraping center of commerce.

▼ D.R. PRODUCTIONS

▲ STEPHEN GREENFIELD PHOTOGRAPHY

▶ KARINA
◀ AUBREY WATSON

A WREATH OF DOGWOOD blooms around the Tennessee State Capitol signals spring and the beginning of another session of the state legislature.

▼ METRO GOVERNMENT OF NASHVILLE / GARY LAYDA ▲ KARINA

▲ METRO GOVERNMENT OF NASHVILLE / GARY LAYDA

THE WHEELS AND WINGS of commerce converge in Tennessee's capital, a popular destination city that draws millions of tourists and conventioneers each year. The Nashville International Airport offers first-class passenger and air cargo facilities (BOTTOM RIGHT), while the Nashville Convention Center features a 118,675-square-foot exhibit hall; an 11,000-square-foot ballroom; 22 additional meeting rooms; and full-service, in-house catering (OPPOSITE, BOTTOM LEFT).

▲ METRO GOVERNMENT OF NASHVILLE / GARY LAYDA

▼ GARY LAYDA

SUNRISE OVER THE *Music City Queen*'s twin stacks burns fog off the Cumberland River (PAGES 30 AND 31).

BOB SCHATZ

▼ METRO GOVERNMENT OF NASHVILLE / GARY LAYDA

▼ METRO GOVERNMENT OF NASHVILLE / GARY LAYDA

PROGRESS IS DRIVEN BY man and machine. The Nashville Arena, before punching skyward, takes out a building standing in its way (ABOVE).

▲ TIM CAMPBELL

▼ METRO GOVERNMENT OF NASHVILLE / GARY LAYDA

▼ METRO GOVERNMENT OF NASHVILLE / GARY LAYDA

▲ METRO GOVERNMENT OF NASHVILLE / GARY LAYDA

▲ METRO GOVERNMENT OF NASHVILLE / GARY LAYDA

▲ METRO GOVERNMENT OF NASHVILLE / GARY LAYDA

An army of construction workers transform the raw materials of wood, cement, and steel into a world-class entertainment venue. The much anticipated Nashville Arena, opened in December 1996, seats some 20,000 people.

CHIEF OF POLICE EMMETT H. Turner strives to keep Nashville's citizens safe and sound (TOP). Not only do his officers drive the beat, but they also use bicycles and motorcycles to chase away crime. Increased motorcycle patrols have also resulted in tightened enforcement of the city's speed laws—a blessing for most, but a curse for those who fail to see the custom-built Harleys in time.

▼ JONATHAN POSTAL / TOWERY PUBLISHING, INC.

▼ METRO GOVERNMENT OF NASHVILLE / GARY LAYDA

▲ JONATHAN POSTAL / TOWERY PUBLISHING, INC.

▲ JONATHAN POSTAL / TOWERY PUBLISHING, INC.

▼ JONATHAN POSTAL / TOWERY PUBLISHING, INC.

▶ METRO GOVERNMENT OF NASHVILLE / GARY LAYDA

Located in the historic Lockeland Springs neighborhood, Engine Co. 14 is home to the city's only operative brass fire pole. The department joins with 34 others to provide fire safety to more than 500,000 Nashvillians inside the city's 533 square miles.

STEVE BAKER / HIGHLIGHT PHOTOGRAPHY

THE BROADWAY DINNER Train combines a four-course meal with a 2.5-hour train ride—serving up portions of stunning scenery with its tasty prime rib (ABOVE). For a different kind of adventure, there's the "otherworldly" Nashville Arena, which hosts the Nashville Kats arena football team and brings top-notch entertainment and sporting events to town, including the 1997 U.S. Figure Skating Championships.

▲ METRO GOVERNMENT OF NASHVILLE / GARY LAYDA

ONCE A CROWN JEWEL OF the Union-Pacific Railroad Company, the recently restored Union Station sparkles once again as a grand hotel and restaurant (PAGES 42 AND 43).

◆ BOB SCHATZ

▲ JONATHAN POSTAL / TOWERY PUBLISHING, INC.
▼ STEVE BAKER / HIGHLIGHT PHOTOGRAPHY

REMINDERS OF NASHVILLE'S musical heritage permeate the city, from sewer grates underfoot to an old advertisement on the side of a building.

RUSTY

▲ TIM CAMPBELL

James Hall knew you don't have to sing, write, or play an instrument to be a part of the Nashville scene. You just have to love country music. Hall drove down from Rhode Island and stayed until his death a few years ago. His eye-catching car was a Music Row fixture.

▲ STEPHEN GREENFIELD PHOTOGRAPHY

▲ METRO GOVERNMENT OF NASHVILLE / GARY LAYDA

▼▲ JONATHAN POSTAL / TOWERY PUBLISHING, INC.

Downtown Nashville has long been known for its variety of entertainment options. Both Lower Broad and Printer's Alley are still home to their share of honky-tonks, strip clubs, and other colorful nightspots.

▼ METRO GOVERNMENT OF NASHVILLE / GARY LAYDA

▲ STEVE JONES

▲ GARY LAYDA

▲ METRO GOVERNMENT OF NASHVILLE / GARY LAYDA

LOWER BROAD, NOW KNOWN as the District, is one of the best examples of downtown's rebirth. Stretching from Second Avenue to the river, the area has recently been "cleaned up" (some would say "sterilized"), with the clubs of old replaced by such high-profile tourist draws as Planet Hollywood and the Hard Rock Cafe.

▼ JONATHAN POSTAL / TOWERY PUBLISHING, INC.

▼ JONATHAN POSTAL / TOWERY PUBLISHING, INC.

▼▲ JONATHAN POSTAL / TOWERY PUBLISHING, INC.

LOWER BROAD ATTRACTS its fair share of interesting visitors, including a well-known fast-food clown, a costumed elephant, and a patchwork cowboy (PAGE 55). The District also draws country music performers from the Ryman Auditorium, who occasionally seek refuge at Tootsie's World Famous Orchid Lounge (PAGE 54). Thousands of autographed photos grace the walls and ceilings of this renowned club.

GUITARS
Hats
4-1897
ROBIN

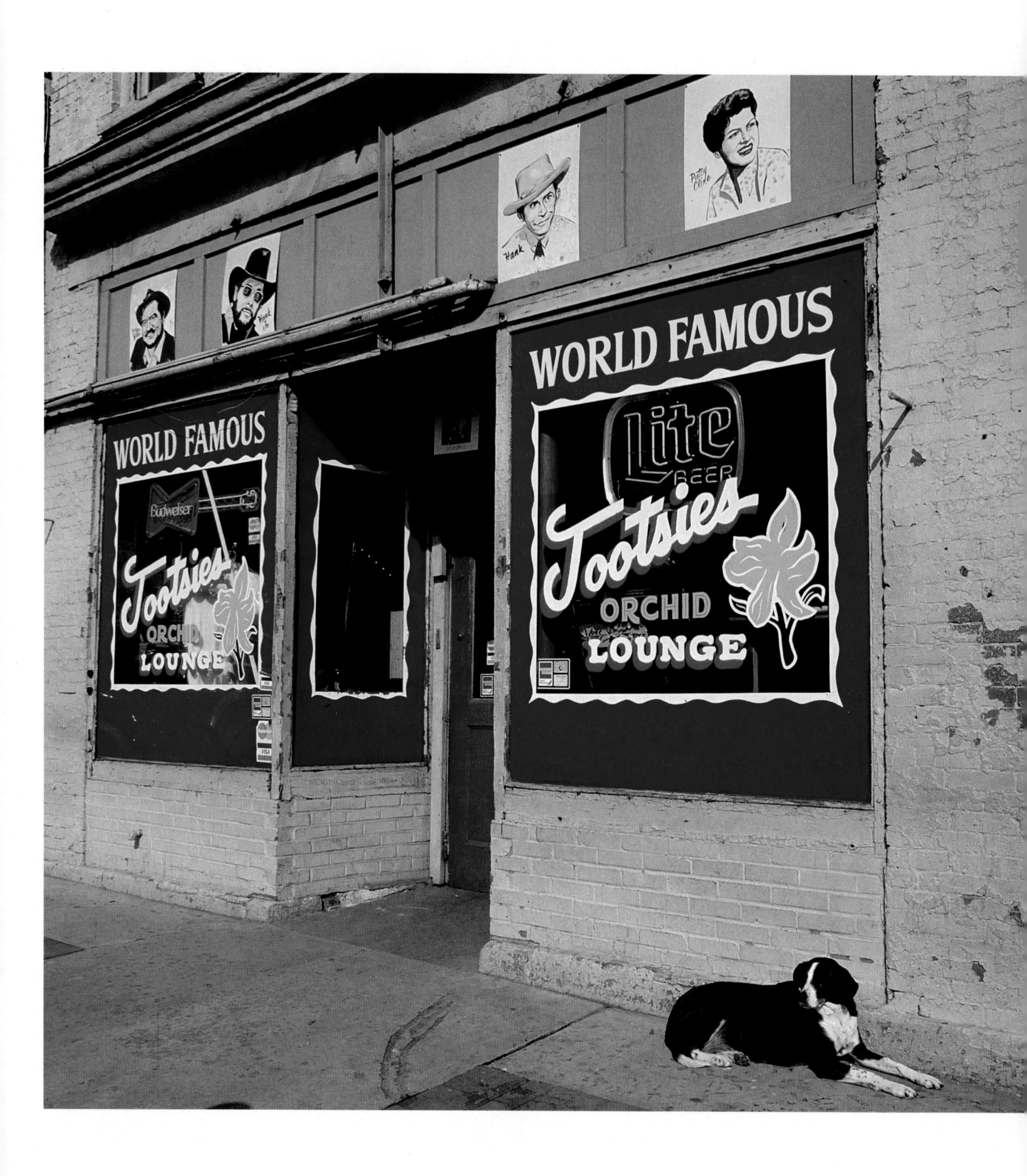
WORLD FAMOUS
Tootsies
ORCHID
LOUNGE
Budweiser
WORLD FAMOUS
Lite
BEER
Tootsies
ORCHID
LOUNGE
Hank
Patsy Cline

▼▲ STEPHEN GREENFIELD PHOTOGRAPHY

▼ JONATHAN POSTAL / TOWERY PUBLISHING, INC.

▼ JONATHAN POSTAL / TOWERY PUBLISHING, INC.

▼ JONATHAN POSTAL / TOWERY PUBLISHING, INC.

▲ TIM CAMPBELL

WITH A NAME LIKE Music City, it's no surprise that Nashville is home to plenty of record stores. You can pay any way you want at the Lawrence Brothers Record Shop, as long as it's in cash. For more than three decades, Ted Lawrence has been selling country, rock, jazz, and classical on vinyl, 45s, and even some 8-Tracks from his location on Broadway (OPPOSITE).

In 1947, Country Music Hall of Famer Ernest Tubb opened the Texas Troubadour Theatre—along with his own record shop—as a stage for rising talent (LEFT). Still broadcast from the theater, the *Midnight Jamboree* radio show reaches 28 states via clear channel WSM-AM 650 and can be heard as far away as Alaska and Canada.

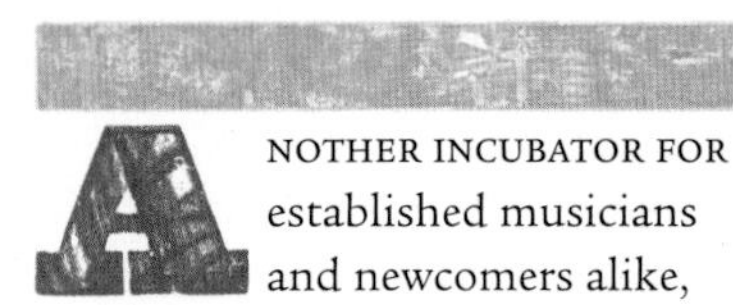

ANOTHER INCUBATOR FOR established musicians and newcomers alike, Robert's Western World in the District has showcased such rockabilly sensations as BR5-49, and is the only place in town where you can buy an ice-cold beer and a pair of boots under one roof (RIGHT AND OPPOSITE TOP).

▼ JONATHAN POSTAL / TOWERY PUBLISHING, INC.

▲ JONATHAN POSTAL / TOWERY PUBLISHING, INC.

IN NASHVILLE, FAME STARTS with a song, an agent, and a head shot, and most every bar and honky-tonk in town is plastered with autographed photos. Here, Reba McEntire's mug rubs shoulders with those of Japanese fiddle sensation Shoji Tabuchi and countless others (BOTTOM).

▲ JONATHAN POSTAL / TOWERY PUBLISHING, INC.

ROBERTSON COUNTY
FAIR
SPRING-
FIELD
THE ROOTS OF COUNTRY
Nashville Celebrates
JUNE 1
1994
THE RYMAN
SKINNER BLUES

▼▲ JONATHAN POSTAL / TOWERY PUBLISHING, INC.

▲ JONATHAN POSTAL / TOWERY PUBLISHING, INC.

WOOD BLOCKS, INK, and an eye for color are Jim Sherraden's tools in the subtle art of persuasion. Since 1879, Hatch Show Print has been producing posters and handbills for the stars—from Hank Williams Sr. to Bruce Springsteen, and everyone in between.

IN PERSON
BR5-49
HILLBILLY BEATNIK MUSIC
WED.-SAT. NIGHTS
9PM-2AM
ROBERT'S WESTERN WORLD
416 BROADWAY
12th & PORTER
A TUESDAY EVENING WITH
"GUIDDY UP GO DADDY, GUIDDY UP GO"
HELL BILLY
CANNERY★FRI. JAN. 6★10PM $5
Something To Crow About
DELEVANTES
9:30 P.M.
& PORTER
SHAVER
TIM FERGUSON
BR5-49
THE DELTA MUDCATS
THURS. FEB. 2

JONATHAN POSTAL / TOWERY PUBLISHING, INC.

TMY 19 KODAK 5053 TMY 20 KODAK 5053

19 19A 20 20A

DRESSING FOR SUCCESS starts at Katy K Designs on 17th Avenue. A New Yorker who relocated to the Music

bunch of sequins, a few rhinestones, and a little red fringe can make the difference between the audience liking and loving you.

shows off one of Katy's designs—a 1950s cowgirl ensemble—in a dressing room plastered with Hatch Show Prints (OPPOSITE).

▼ JONATHAN POSTAL / TOWERY PUBLISHING, INC.

▲ JONATHAN POSTAL / TOWERY PUBLISHING, INC.

▲ JONATHAN POSTAL / TOWERY PUBLISHING, INC.

A HAND-TAILORED JACKET by Manuel Exclusive Clothier has been a necessary wardrobe addition for superstars ranging from Johnny Cash and Bob Dylan to Dwight Yoakam and Opry luminary Porter Wagoner. From initial consultation to final fit, Manuel (TOP) and his son Manny (BOTTOM) spend up to six weeks crafting each jacket and outfit.

▲ JONATHAN POSTAL / TOWERY PUBLISHING, INC.

BY HIS OWN ESTIMATE, Bo Riddle designs and handcrafts only 50 pairs of boots each year. And it's no wonder: Bo's boots take between 30 and 130 hours per pair to sew, and each boot can consist of up to 200 individual pieces of material.

Born Rubye Blevins in Hot Springs, Arkansas, Patsy Montana was only 21 years old when she yodeled her way into history with "I Want to Be a Cowboy's Sweetheart" in 1935 (OPPOSITE). The song was the first country record by a woman to sell more than a million copies.

▼ COUNTRY MUSIC HALL OF FAME

▼ JONATHAN POSTAL / TOWERY PUBLISHING, INC.

▲ JONATHAN POSTAL / TOWERY PUBLISHING, INC.

▲ JONATHAN POSTAL / TOWERY PUBLISHING, INC.

TEACHER AND STUDENT come together at the Blair School of Music, established in 1964 and merged with Vanderbilt University in 1981. Here, Emelyne Bingham indoctrinates students into the arcana of conducting, while Lawrence Borden, assistant professor of trombone, coaches a student through a difficult passage.

NASHVILLIANS FIND DIVERSE ways to express themselves through dance. Established in 1981, the Nashville Ballet offers a variety of classical and contemporary programs, including *Footage* (TOP LEFT) and *Carousel* (BOTTOM). The UHURU Dance Company celebrates African cultural traditions through dance, music, theater, and story telling (TOP RIGHT AND OPPOSITE).

▼ MARIANNE LEACH

▼▲ JONATHAN POSTAL / TOWERY PUBLISHING, INC.

▼ MARIANNE LEACH

▼ METRO GOVERNMENT OF NASHVILLE / GARY LAYDA

▼▲ METRO GOVERNMENT OF NASHVILLE / GARY LAYDA

▼ BOB SCHATZ

▼ METRO GOVERNMENT OF NASHVILLE / GARY LAYDA

Summer Lights, an arts festival held downtown, presents the eclectic best of Nashville music—from rock and reggae to brass and strings. On the quieter side, a group of guitarists at the Bluebird Cafe offer an intimate glimpse into the art of making music during Songwriter's Night, held each Sunday.

▼ JONATHAN POSTAL / TOWERY PUBLISHING, INC.

JONATHAN POSTAL / TOWERY PUBLISHING, INC.

JONATHAN POSTAL / TOWERY PUBLISHING, INC.

JONATHAN POSTAL / TOWERY PUBLISHING, INC.

EVEN IN THE MUSIC CITY, the brush and pen are sometimes mightier than the guitar. No matter the "weapon," Nashville boasts its fair share of talent, including (CLOCKWISE FROM OPPOSITE) James Threalkill, who uses oil and canvas to capture the city's spirit and her people; Myles Maillie, pictured in front of his work at the Museum of Maillie; the multitalented R.S. Field, who was awarded Best Producer Who's Not on Music Row by the *Nashville Scene* in 1997; Andrée Aleers LeQuire, chair of the Metropolitan Arts Commission; and songwriter, music publisher, and entertainment lawyer Dan Tyler, who wove a tale of intrigue, murder, and music in his novel *Music City Confidential*.

▼ JONATHAN POSTAL / TOWERY PUBLISHING, INC.

▶ TIM CAMPBELL

▶ METRO GOVERNMENT OF NASHVILLE / GARY LAYDA

Reminders of Nashville's Athens of the South veneer can be found throughout the city. Alan LeQuire's Athena, honoring the Greek goddess of arts, wisdom, and prudent warfare, is a replica of the original found in Athens. The 42-foot-tall work is the largest indoor sculpture in the world (top right and bottom).

In the early 1920s, after Nashville's version of the Parthenon had fallen into a state of disrepair, city officials began a reconstruction effort that resulted in a more permanent match to the original structure in Athens—exact in size and layout to within 1/16 of an inch (pages 82 and 83).

▶ METRO GOVERNMENT OF NASHVILLE / GARY LAYDA

GARY LAYDA

▼ DAN BALL / TOWERY PUBLISHING, INC.

▼ STEVE BAKER / HIGHLIGHT PHOTOGRAPHY

▲ DAN BALL / TOWERY PUBLISHING, INC.

▲ GARY LAYDA

A pedestrian's-eye view of downtown Nashville's buildings and statuary reveals the city's larger-than-life side.

AND DAVIDSON

▼▲ JONATHAN POSTAL / TOWERY PUBLISHING, INC.

▲ JONATHAN POSTAL / TOWERY PUBLISHING, INC.

ITH THE HELP OF William Dunavant (TOP) and Sami Dietrich (BOTTOM)—state commissioner and state deputy commissioner of economic and community development, respectively—Mayor Phil Bredesen (OPPOSITE) has ably led the city to the threshold of a new century. A former Boston businessman, Bredesen has overseen the rebirth of downtown, the construction of two world-class sporting facilities, and the relocation of countless businesses to Nashville.

▼ RICH MAYS ▲ DAVID WRIGHT PHOTOGRAPHY

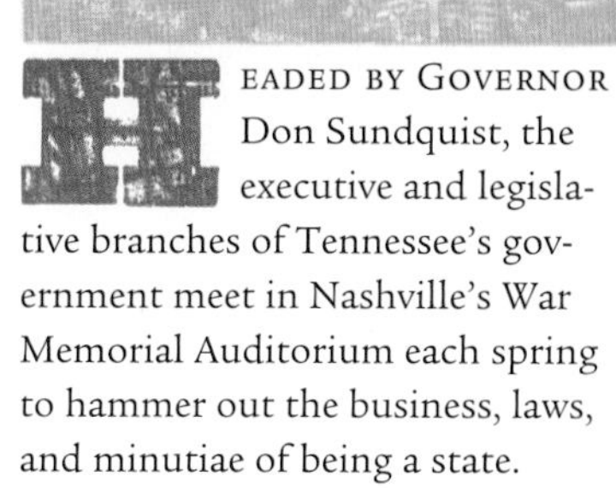

HEADED BY GOVERNOR Don Sundquist, the executive and legislative branches of Tennessee's government meet in Nashville's War Memorial Auditorium each spring to hammer out the business, laws, and minutiae of being a state.

A DEPICTION OF BLIND justice with her proverbial scales (TOP), housed in the Metro Courthouse, provides inspiration to general sessions court judges Penny Harrington (BOTTOM) and Bill Higgins (OPPOSITE). Along with seven other justices, they hear more than 400,000 criminal, civil, traffic, and environmental cases every year.

▲ JONATHAN POSTAL / TOWERY PUBLISHING, INC.
◀ METRO GOVERNMENT OF NASHVILLE / GARY LAYDA

▼ JONATHAN POSTAL / TOWERY PUBLISHING, INC.

AGRICULTURE
JUDGE BILL HIGGINS

▼ STEPHEN GREENFIELD PHOTOGRAPHY

▲ D. R. PRODUCTIONS

THE CUMBERLAND RIVER symbolizes the past, present, and future of Nashville. The site where John Robertson built his fort in 1779, the riverfront today serves not only as a distribution port but also as the site of concerts and festivals, as well as the future home of a brand-new stadium for the city's NFL team. A crossroads of commerce and culture, Nashville is indeed a city where it all comes together.

METRO GOVERNMENT OF NASHVILLE / GARY LAYDA

L&C
WKDF

▲ JONATHAN POSTAL / TOWERY PUBLISHING, INC.

As the familiar saying goes, don't judge a book by its cover. What some would dismiss as an ugly pile of trash or a beat-up old truck often exudes unexpected character.

▼ STEVE BAKER / HIGHLIGHT PHOTOGRAPHY

STEVE BAKER / HIGHLIGHT PHOTOGRAPHY

THE PAINT MAY BE peeling and the leather cracking, but the aesthetic value of unintentional art can be tremendous.

LIKE RUNNING ACROSS Dolly Parton at the supermarket or standing in line at the bank behind Reba McEntire, found art means the difference in merely residing in Nashville and really living here. Displays range from an outdoor mosaic in Fanny Mae Dees Park to a festive scene outside a local bar. This pair of snowball-throwing polar bears stand in stony silence on Edgehill Avenue.

▼ JONATHAN POSTAL / TOWERY PUBLISHING, INC.

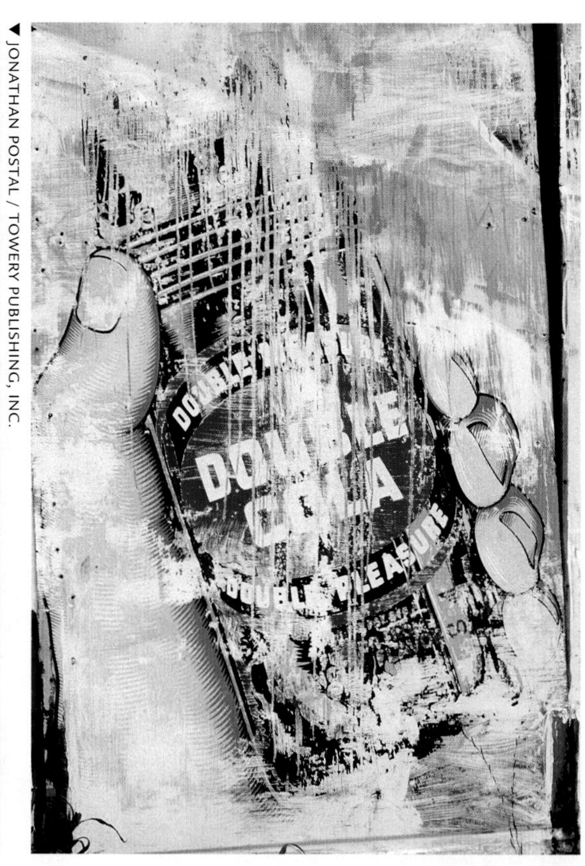

▼ JONATHAN POSTAL / TOWERY PUBLISHING, INC.
▼ GARY LAYDA

▼ JONATHAN POSTAL / TOWERY PUBLISHING, INC.

Lite
Official Beer Sp
Of Super Bowl
Tide
FREE

▲▲ JONATHAN POSTAL / TOWERY PUBLISHING, INC.

▲ JULIE GREEN

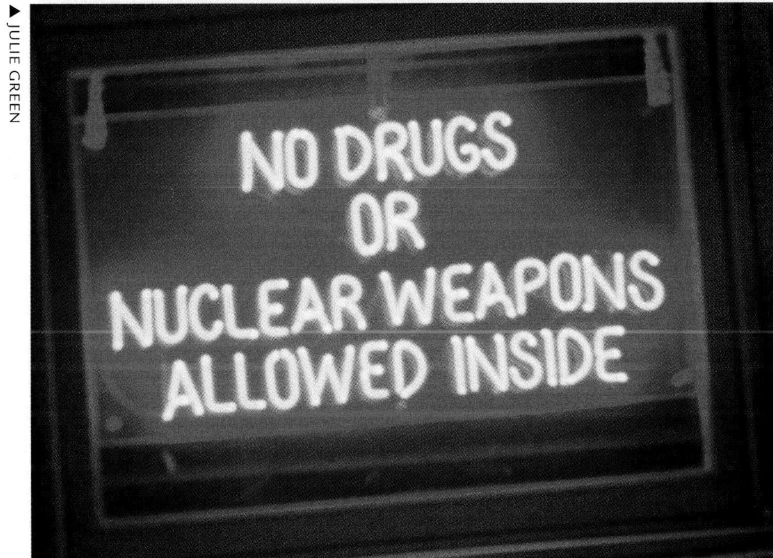

▲ JONATHAN POSTAL / TOWERY PUBLISHING, INC.

NEON LIGHTS AND PSYCHEdelic colors brighten views throughout Music City. Sometimes, the message is as colorful as the medium.

EACH YEAR, THE WHISPERED promise of success and fame draws thousands to Music City, with their guitar cases full of dreams and aspirations. Although many will be forgotten before they are even known, a few will pen the next generation of country hits, thereby fueling the dream that lures aspiring musicians to the bright lights and the rhinestone glitter of Nashville.

▼ JONATHAN POSTAL / TOWERY PUBLISHING, INC.

▼ JONATHAN POSTAL / TOWERY PUBLISHING, INC.

▼ JONATHAN POSTAL / TOWERY PUBLISHING, INC.

▲ JONATHAN POSTAL / TOWERY PUBLISHING, INC.

▼▲ BOB SCHATZ

UTABAGAS, SUMMER squash, and tons of other fruits and vegetables fill the stalls at Nashville's Farmer's Market. With the construction of a pedestrian mall to celebrate Tennessee's bicentennial in 1996, the Farmer's Market moved to within spitting distance of the State Capitol, bringing fresh produce, meat, seafood, and Ms. Maxwell's trademark geraniums downtown.

TABLE GRAPES
KALE
MUSTARD
COLLARDS
TURNIPS

At the Loveless Cafe just outside Nashville, breakfast is the most important meal of the day. And it's smiles all around, thanks to the hot coffee, fried eggs, country ham, and biscuits that are legendary throughout the city.

▼ JONATHAN POSTAL / TOWERY PUBLISHING, INC.

▼ JONATHAN POSTAL / TOWERY PUBLISHING, INC.

▲ JONATHAN POSTAL / TOWERY PUBLISHING, INC.

▲ JONATHAN POSTAL / TOWERY PUBLISHING, INC.

▼ JONATHAN POSTAL / TOWERY PUBLISHING, INC.

IN A CITY WHERE RESTAURANTS seem to come and go weekly, Jody Faison (BOTTOM) has managed to tap into the culinary psyche of Nashville, offering at his seven establishments something for everyone, from down-at-the-wallet college students to well-heeled executives. For discerning palates, Vito D. Randazzo, chef at Faison's Cafe 123 (TOP), has created such delicious entrées as herb-crusted Australian rack of lamb (OPPOSITE).

▲ JONATHAN POSTAL / TOWERY PUBLISHING, INC.

▼ JONATHAN POSTAL / TOWERY PUBLISHING, INC.

▼ JONATHAN POSTAL / TOWERY PUBLISHING, INC.

FOLKS FROM AROUND Nashville go to Brown's Diner on Blair Avenue for one of the best hamburgers in the city. The front of the café is part of an old converted trailer, adding a degree of ambience to this popular greasy spoon.

▲ GARY LAYDA

Its close proximity to Vanderbilt, downtown, Music Row, and Baptist Memorial Hospital has made the Elliston Place Soda Shop (above and pages 114 and 115) a haven for students, professors, doctors, lawyers, businessmen . . . you name it. Nearly every man, woman, and child who has lived in Nashville for more than 10 minutes has eaten at the diner, whose burgers, fries, and milk shakes have made their mark on many a waistline.

▼ JONATHAN POSTAL / TOWERY PUBLISHING, INC.

▼ JONATHAN POSTAL / TOWERY PUBLISHING, INC.

▼ JONATHAN POSTAL / TOWERY PUBLISHING, INC.

▲ JONATHAN POSTAL / TOWERY PUBLISHING, INC.

▲ JONATHAN POSTAL / TOWERY PUBLISHING, INC.

▼ JONATHAN POSTAL / TOWERY PUBLISHING, INC.

GARY LAYDA

GARY LAYDA

WHETHER YOU SING like Marty Stuart (OPPOSITE) or pick guitar like Chet Atkins (LEFT), the road to the Grand Ole Opry is paved with hard work, tireless self-promotion, and a somewhat indefinable quality known as crowd appeal. No one knows crowd appeal better than the legendary Garth Brooks, whose songs and showmanship helped vault country music back into the mainstream in the early 1990s (RIGHT).

▼ GARY LAYDA

▼ GARY LAYDA

▼▲ GARY LAYDA

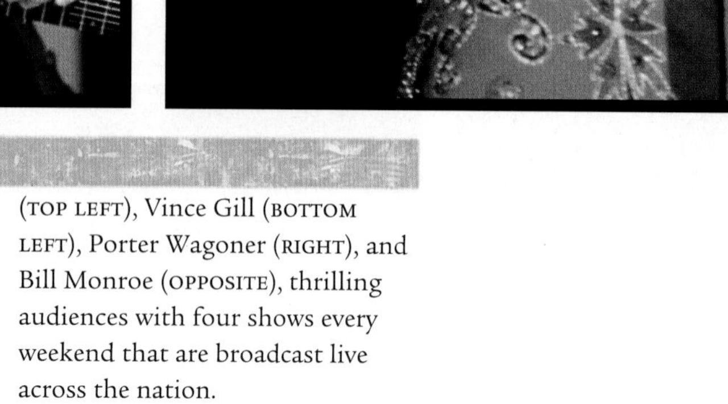

COUNTRY'S STARS ARE FLUNG across a constellation of styles—from bluegrass and Texas swing to hot country. The longest-running radio show in history, the Grand Ole Opry features such legends as Charley Pride (TOP LEFT), Vince Gill (BOTTOM LEFT), Porter Wagoner (RIGHT), and Bill Monroe (OPPOSITE), thrilling audiences with four shows every weekend that are broadcast live across the nation.

In recent years, country music has become one of the nation's most popular radio formats, thanks to such bright stars as (clockwise from top left) neon-rainbow-chaser Alan Jackson, who won Male Vocalist of the Year in 1995; familiar fixture and perennial nice guy Clint Black; Kentucky-born Wynonna; the ever popular Aaron Tippin; and Grammy Award-winner Emmylou Harris, who has entertained audiences for more than two decades.

GARY LAYDA

METRO GOVERNMENT OF NASHVILLE / GARY LAYDA

GARY LAYDA

BOB SCHATZ

GARY LAYDA

WSM

▲▼ COUNTRY MUSIC HALL OF FAME

NASHVILLE'S OLDEST remaining recording studio is appropriately located in the Country Music Hall of Fame and Museum on Music Row. RCA's Studio B has hosted countless legends, including Elvis Presley and Dolly Parton, as well as Hank Williams Sr., one of the fathers of country music (OPPOSITE).

▼ JONATHAN POSTAL / TOWERY PUBLISHING, INC.

▼ JONATHAN POSTAL / TOWERY PUBLISHING, INC.

▼ JONATHAN POSTAL / TOWERY PUBLISHING, INC.

▼ JONATHAN POSTAL / TOWERY PUBLISHING, INC.

▲ JONATHAN POSTAL / TOWERY PUBLISHING, INC.

EVERYTHING OLD SEEMS new again when groups like Blackhawk, led by singer Henry Paul, take to the studios to record what's known in the industry as new country or hot country (THIS PAGE). Mixed to compete on the radio with Top 40 hits, the music pairs the twang of the Nashville Sound with a slicked-up, bass-heavy beat that makes it great for dancing.

▲ JONATHAN POSTAL / TOWERY PUBLISHING, INC.

▲ JONATHAN POSTAL / TOWERY PUBLISHING, INC.

▼ COUNTRY MUSIC HALL OF FAME / LES LEVERETT

GARY LAYDA

GARY LAYDA

GARY LAYDA

IN THE SPRING OF 1885, shortly after hearing a sermon by the Reverend Sam Jones, riverboat captain Thomas Ryman had the Union Gospel Tabernacle built. Upon Ryman's death some years later, Jones recommended that the building be renamed the Ryman Auditorium, a suggestion that brought the entire congregation to its feet in a roar of assent. The Mother Church of Country Music, as it came to be called, hosted the Grand Ole Opry from 1943 to 1974 and helped make stars of personalities like the late Minnie Pearl, whose popularity lives on in today's fans. Reopened in 1995, the restored Ryman has come back into its own as a performance venue, hosting the likes of Bruce Springsteen, James Brown, and Mary Chapin Carpenter.

▼ DAVID WRIGHT PHOTOGRAPHY

▼ GARY LAYDA

▲ GARY LAYDA

COUNTRY MUSIC COMMERCE meets country music history along Music Row, home to the Hall of Fame, RCA Studio B, and many museums honoring individual stars. Specially marked trolleys ferry droves of tourists around downtown in hopes of spotting someone famous. If the stars themselves elude you, Nashville's three automobile museums offer a glimpse at plenty of famous cars, including Roy Acuff's shiny white ride.

▼ COUNTRY MUSIC HALL OF FAME

▼▲ JONATHAN POSTAL / TOWERY PUBLISHING, INC.

STEVE JONES

NASHVILLE'S LARGEST guitar dealer is Gruhn Guitars, located on Lower Broad within spittin' distance of the Ryman Auditorium. In addition to stocking more guitars, Dobros, mandolins, and banjos than just about any other store in the world, the shop is home to numerous rare and one-of-a-kind instruments. Here, owner George Gruhn (OPPOSITE), proudly shows off his B&D Silverbell Montana Special #1 banjo, custom-made circa 1930 for entertainer Frank Webb.

Building the instruments that have launched innumerable careers, Gibson Musical Instruments has been handcrafting guitars in Nashville since 1974. Chairman and CEO Henry Juszkiewicz, who took control of the company in 1986, has helped secure Gibson's future as a major player in the worldwide market.

A FIVE-MEMBER BAND THAT blends honky-tonk and rockabilly, BR5-49 has taken Nashville and the entire country by storm. Established in 1994, the group took its name from a *Hee Haw* sketch and is known for its five- and six-hour live performances.

▼▲ JONATHAN POSTAL / TOWERY PUBLISHING, INC.

▼ BOB SCHATZ

▶ METRO GOVERNMENT OF NASHVILLE / GARY LAYDA

▶ METRO GOVERNMENT OF NASHVILLE / GARY LAYDA

OFFERING AN OPPORTUNITY for worship and a sense of community to people of all faiths, Nashville is home to more than 800 churches, temples, synagogues, and mosques, including (CLOCKWISE FROM OPPOSITE) Holy Trinity Greek Orthodox Church, Christ Episcopal Church, Temple Ohabai Sholom, and Tulip Street Methodist Church.

▶ METRO GOVERNMENT OF NASHVILLE / GARY LAYDA

▼ GARY LAYDA

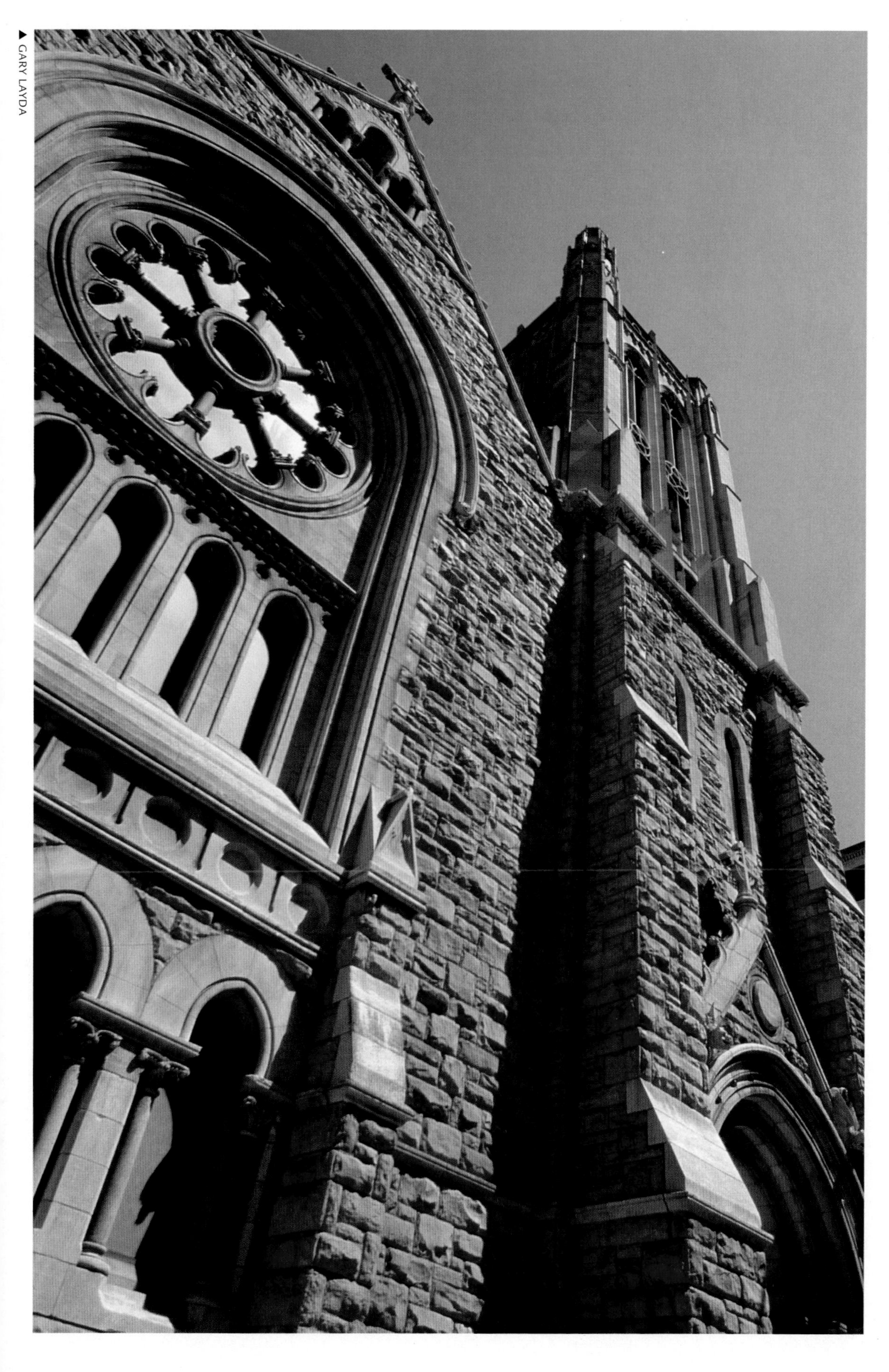

▲ GARY LAYDA

COMPLETED IN 1892, CHRIST Episcopal Church features working gargoyles and original Tiffany stained glass windows. The landmark church is also the seat of the Episcopal Diocese of Middle Tennessee.

BOB SCHATZ

The grand staircase at the Belmont Mansion gives the promise of further delights in this 1850s home, which features a myriad of rooms filled with original and period furnishings and artwork.

▲ CAROL THALIMER

▲ BOB SCHATZ

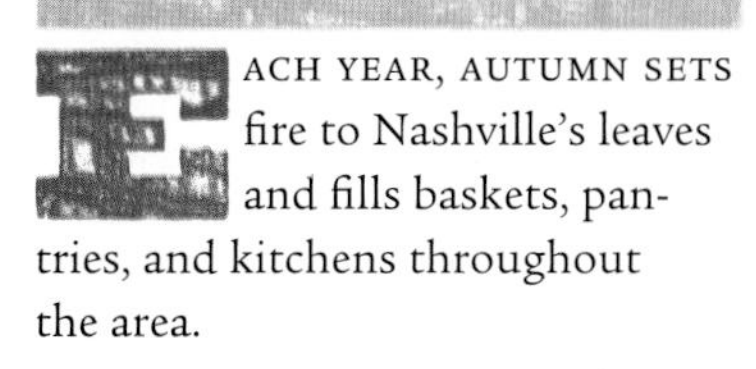

EACH YEAR, AUTUMN SETS fire to Nashville's leaves and fills baskets, pantries, and kitchens throughout the area.

▲ METRO GOVERNMENT OF NASHVILLE / GARY LAYDA

ASK MOST TRANSPLANTED parents what they like about Nashville and you'll hear a familiar refrain—"It's a great place to raise a family." Local youngsters would add that it's also a great place to watch a parade (BELOW), hang out in a tire swing (OPPOSITE), or snag a cold drink with a four-legged friend (PAGES 156 AND 157).

▲ STEPHEN GREENFIELD PHOTOGRAPHY

▼ STEVE BAKER / HIGHLIGHT PHOTOGRAPHY

Thank You... Please Call Again
LEVI

◆ TIM CAMPBELL

▼ BOB SCHATZ

▲ BOB SCHATZ

THESE CUB SCOUTS, attending Twilight Camp at Elmington Park, have found the best way to beat the summer heat.

▼ RON VOLPE

▲ METRO GOVERNMENT OF NASHVILLE / GARY LAYDA

▲ RICH MAYS

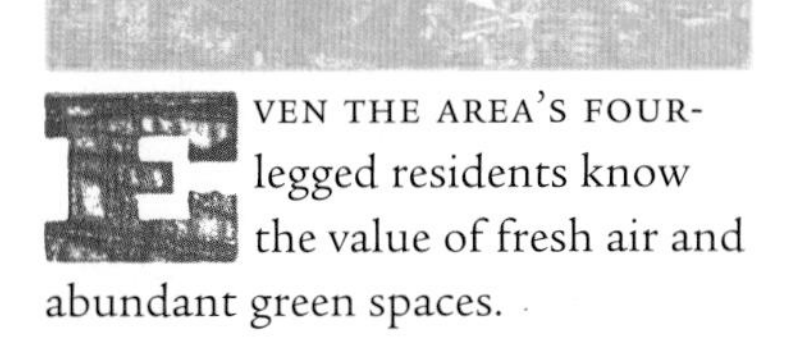

EVEN THE AREA'S FOUR-legged residents know the value of fresh air and abundant green spaces.

NATURE'S BEAUTY FINDS diverse expression in and around Nashville, which boasts more than 40 parks and recreation areas, in addition to plenty of serene, tree-lined neighborhoods.

▼ BOB SCHATZ

▼ DAVID DUHL

▲ STEVE BAKER / HIGHLIGHT PHOTOGRAPHY

BATHED IN A LATE FALL fog, the Shelby Street Bridge connects downtown to East Nashville (PAGES 164 AND 165). As the riverfront is revitalized by the construction of a stadium for professional football, the fate of the bridge is in question. Redevelopment plans call for a new trans-Cumberland viaduct to be built, and the Shelby Street Bridge to be recast as a pedestrian walkway.

▲ STEVE BAKER / HIGHLIGHT PHOTOGRAPHY

▲ DAVID WRIGHT PHOTOGRAPHY

METRO GOVERNMENT OF NASHVILLE / GARY LAYDA

ANDREW JACKSON'S HERMITAGE started as a one-room log cabin situated in northeastern Davidson County (RIGHT). Dusted with a layer of snow, the simple structure belies the grandeur of the nearby mansion, which was added in 1821.

A mother goose watching her goslings is just one of the many treats that await visitors to Centennial Park, which is also home to Nashville's replica of the Parthenon (OPPOSITE).

▼ KARINA

▲ METRO GOVERNMENT OF NASHVILLE / GARY LAYDA

▲ DAN BALL / TOWERY PUBLISHING, INC.

▲ DAN BALL / TOWERY PUBLISHING, INC.

NASHVILLE'S PARKS OFFER something for everyone, from teens who want to enjoy a warm day in Shelby Park to golfers who want to chase little white balls to those who simply want to walk in the green silence of the Radnor Lake State Natural Area.

▼ DAN BALL / TOWERY PUBLISHING, INC.

▼ BOB SCHATZ

▼ DAN BALL / TOWERY PUBLISHING, INC.

To the delight of local elementary school students, Nashville is graced with two zoos. Grassmere Wildlife Park features species native to Tennessee, including bison, elk, and black bears (BOTTOM), while the 135-acre Nashville Zoo just outside the city is home to more exotic animals, including pythons, pandas, and white tigers (TOP).

▲ STEVE BAKER / HIGHLIGHT PHOTOGRAPHY
▼ JONATHAN POSTAL / TOWERY PUBLISHING, INC.

On spring evenings, the crack of the bat fills the air at Greer Stadium. The Nashville Sounds, a Class AAA farm team for the Chicago White Sox, plays more than 72 home games there every season (opposite).

Nashville's baseball tradition also includes native-born Clinton "Butch" McCord Jr., who played outfield for the Baltimore Elite Giants and the Chicago American Giants in the Negro National League from 1948 to 1950 (above). A former football player at Tennessee State University, McCord is the namesake of a baseball stadium at his alma mater.

SPRING ALSO STIRS THE smells of horseflesh, leather, and turf. In one afternoon, you can catch equestrian feats at the horse show to benefit Oak Hill School, the thunder of rider and horse at the Iroquois Steeplechase, and a polo match at Percy Warner Park. For quieter outdoor pursuits, a round of golf at one of the area's numerous courses provides a relaxing alternative.

▼ BOB SCHATZ

▲ METRO GOVERNMENT OF NASHVILLE / GARY LAYDA

▲ BOB SCHATZ

▲ METRO GOVERNMENT OF NASHVILLE / GARY LAYDA

▲ BOB SCHATZ

DAWN BREAKS AS HUNT master Henry Hooker leads the Hillsboro Hounds, Nashville's only hunt club, to flush a fox.

▼ METRO GOVERNMENT OF NASHVILLE / GARY LAYDA

▼ METRO GOVERNMENT OF NASHVILLE / GARY LAYDA

▲ BOB SCHATZ

▲ METRO GOVERNMENT OF NASHVILLE / GARY LAYDA

NASHVILLE'S FINEST CHASE the elusive high that comes from pushing the limits of feet, wheels, and hooves.

▼ RON VOLPE

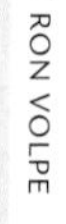

▲ BOB SCHATZ

NASHVILLE'S LOCATION—convenient to river, road, and rail—made it a primary site for battles during the Civil War, the scars of which are remembered today in area reenactments. The bloody Battle of Franklin in 1864 saw thousands of troops killed and four Confederate generals laid out to die on the porch of Carnton Mansion, owned by former Nashville Mayor Randal McGavock. Two years later, in 1866, the McGavock family donated two acres of the plantation to serve as the final resting spot for some 1,500 soldiers who died in the battle.

▼ METRO GOVERNMENT OF NASHVILLE / GARY LAYDA

▼ METRO GOVERNMENT OF NASHVILLE / GARY LAYDA

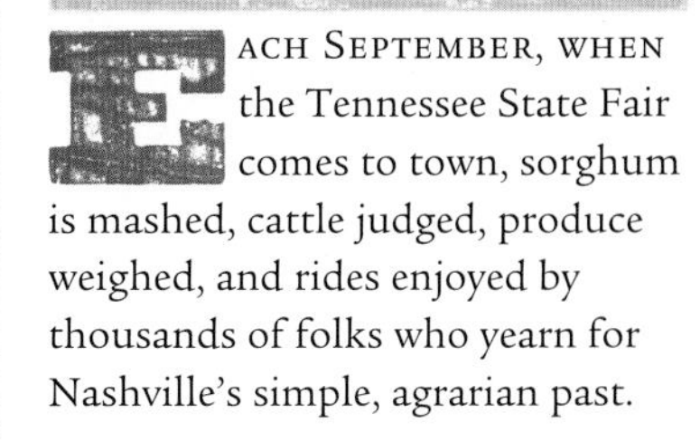

ACH SEPTEMBER, WHEN the Tennessee State Fair comes to town, sorghum is mashed, cattle judged, produce weighed, and rides enjoyed by thousands of folks who yearn for Nashville's simple, agrarian past.

▲ METRO GOVERNMENT OF NASHVILLE / GARY LAYDA

▲ METRO GOVERNMENT OF NASHVILLE / GARY LAYDA

AT THE TENNESSEE State Fair, larger-than-life produce and newfound furry friends bring out the kid in all of us.

METRO GOVERNMENT OF NASHVILLE / GARY LAYDA

METRO GOVERNMENT OF NASHVILLE / GARY LAYDA

▲ METRO GOVERNMENT OF NASHVILLE / GARY LAYDA

▼ METRO GOVERNMENT OF NASHVILLE / GARY LAYDA

▼ METRO GOVERNMENT OF NASHVILLE / GARY LAYDA

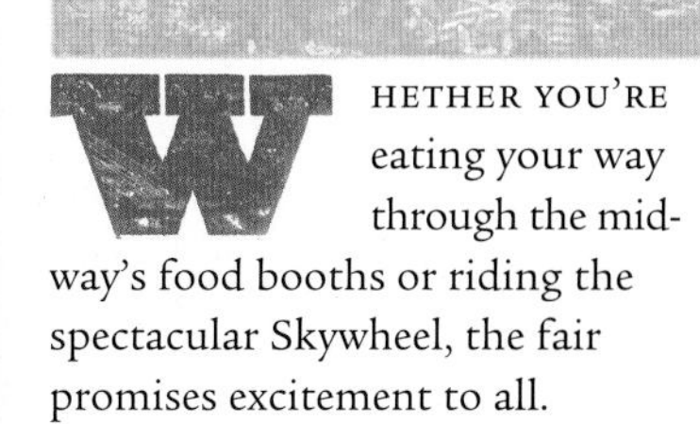

HETHER YOU'RE eating your way through the midway's food booths or riding the spectacular Skywheel, the fair promises excitement to all.

◀ STEPHEN GREENFIELD PHOTOGRAPHY

BOB SCHATZ

GARY LAYDA

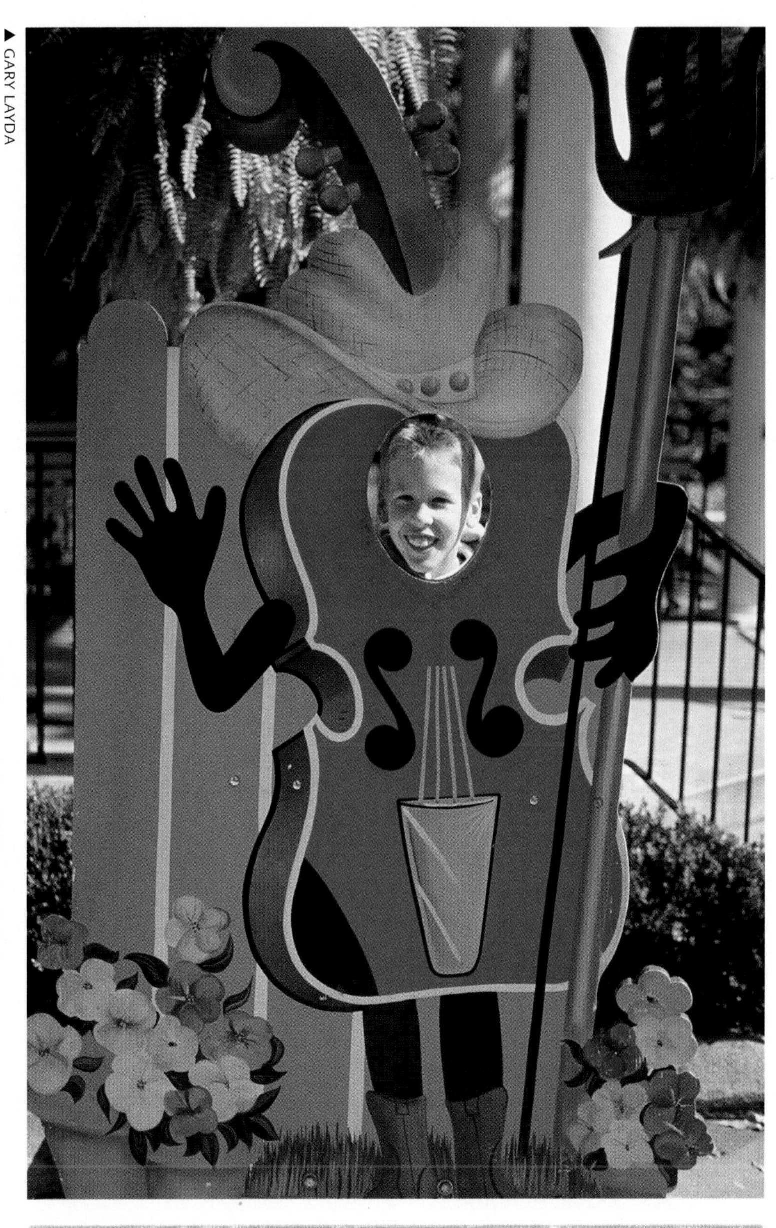

The Opryland Hotel Convention Center must be seen to be believed. The expansive property has 2,883 rooms, 222 suites, 15 restaurants, and more convention and meeting space than any other venue east of the Mississippi River. Guests at the hotel can enjoy a day at nearby Opryland USA Themepark, which features exciting rides, music, and shows that celebrate American music.

▼ TIM CAMPBELL

▼ TIM CAMPBELL

▲ GARY LAYDA

▲ BOB SCHATZ

▲ TIM CAMPBELL

EACH JUNE, THOUSANDS OF country music fans hit Nashville for the International Country Music Fan Fair—a sprawling mix of concerts, celebrity appearances, and autograph sessions featuring such stars as Vince Gill, Johnny Cash, and John Michael Montgomery. Also part of the festivities is the Grand Master Fiddling Championship, where lucky participants can meet the likes of Charlie Daniels.

The Wildhorse Saloon was built for line dancing, two-stepping, and everything in between. From a top-notch sound system to professional dance instructors to a television show broadcast nationally each week on cable's TNN, the Wildhorse may very well be Music City's answer to *American Bandstand*.

▼ Jonathan Postal / Towery Publishing, Inc.

▼ Jonathan Postal / Towery Publishing, Inc.

▼ Jonathan Postal / Towery Publishing, Inc.

▲ JONATHAN POSTAL / TOWERY PUBLISHING, INC.

◆ METRO GOVERNMENT OF NASHVILLE / GARY LAYDA

▼▲ METRO GOVERNMENT OF NASHVILLE / GARY LAYDA

SPEED BUMPS FOR THE summer: Metropolitan Nashville/Davidson County school buses wait patiently for fall and their return to active duty (PAGES 192 AND 193).

NASHVILLE EDUCATES ITS children with a comprehensive system of nearly 300 public, private, and parochial schools. From church-affiliated institutions to innovative magnet programs, local schools strive to be the best in the state.

▼ BOB SCHATZ

▼ BOB SCHATZ

▲ METRO GOVERNMENT OF NASHVILLE / GARY LAYDA

▲ BOB SCHATZ

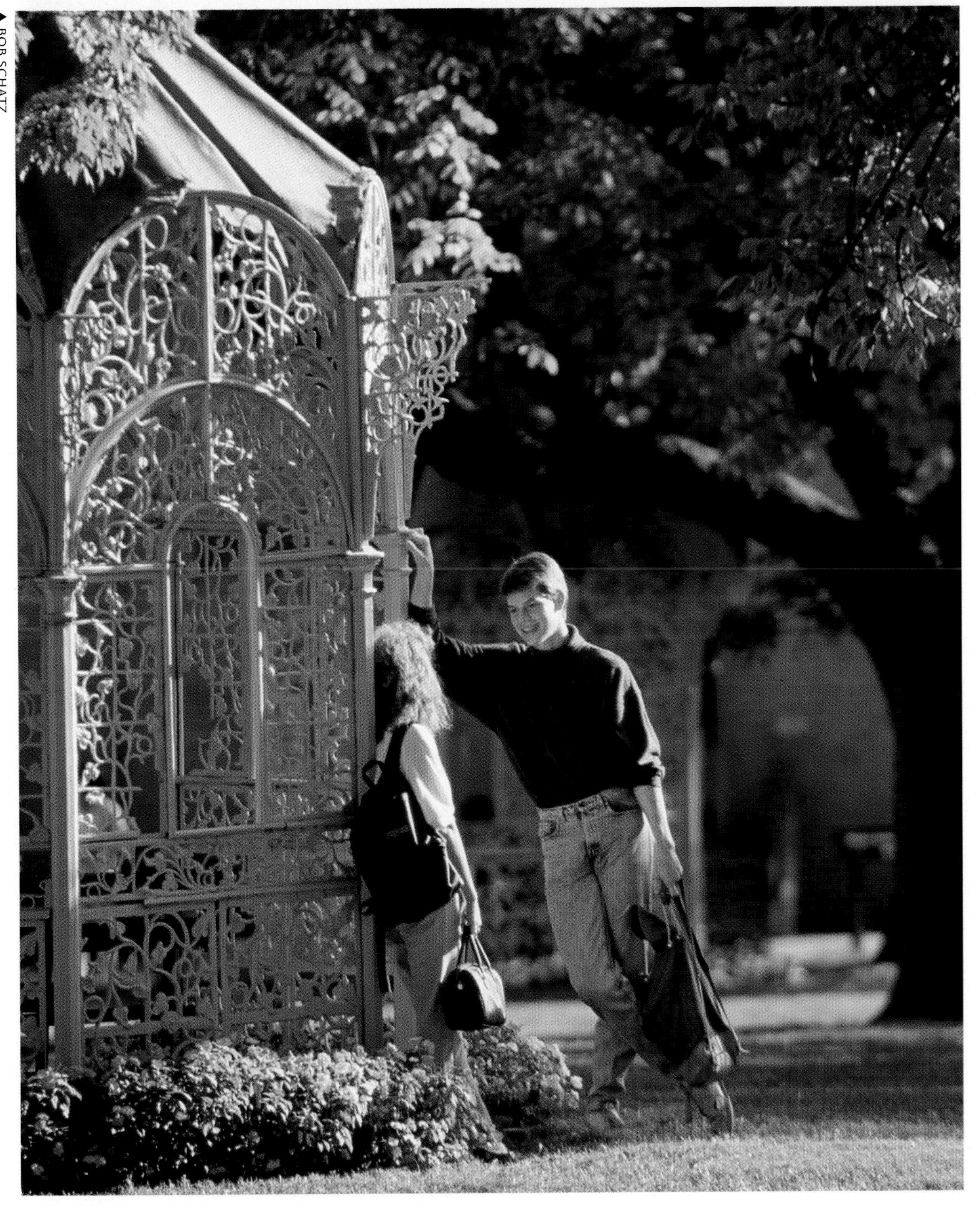

NASHVILLE IS A HOTBED of higher education, boasting such options as Vanderbilt University, which balances academic excellence with a well-rounded athletic program (TOP), and the church-affiliated Belmont University, which combines a picturesque campus with outstanding opportunities for learning (BOTTOM).

THE CITY'S INSTITUTIONS of higher learning are key to its reputation as the Athens of the South. Each year, hundreds of students earn degrees from Vanderbilt's undergraduate and postgraduate programs (TOP). Fisk University boasts not only the world-class Carl Van Vechten Gallery, but also the distinction of long having a place on *Money* magazine's list of best education buys (BOTTOM AND OPPOSITE).

▼ METRO GOVERNMENT OF NASHVILLE / GARY LAYDA

▲ BOB SCHATZ

▼ METRO GOVERNMENT OF NASHVILLE / GARY LAYDA

CLASS
OF
95

JOBS,
PEACE

▲ METRO GOVERNMENT OF NASHVILLE / GARY LAYDA

COMMUNITYWIDE GOALS like jobs and peace start with a decent place to live, and Nashville has been a pioneer in the way it houses its residents. Here, Hands on Nashville volunteers scrape and paint a house, giving someone a new chance at a better life (TOP). Aggressive programs aimed at putting citizens into homes have resulted in the rebirth of many of Nashville's neighborhoods.

▼ DAN BALL / TOWERY PUBLISHING, INC.

▶ DAN BALL / TOWERY PUBLISHING, INC.

AS THE SUN SETS BEHIND the Tennessee State Capitol, whispers of Nashville's historical beginnings can be heard throughout War Memorial Plaza.

NASHVILLE'S HOTELS OFFER more than just a good night's rest. The Union Station Hotel, listed on the National Register of Historic Places, has provided visitors an elegant escape since 1890 (RIGHT). One of the many amenities at the Loews Vanderbilt Plaza Hotel is the Famous Flame Shoe Shine by Henry Adams, who's guaranteed to give you a smile with his spit and polish (OPPOSITE).

▼ BOB SCHATZ ▲ JONATHAN POSTAL / TOWERY PUBLISHING, INC.

THE
FAMOUS
FLAME SHINE

On a clear day in Nashville, the setting sun reveals a city where government and commerce drive glass and steel skyward.

▼ STEPHEN GREENFIELD PHOTOGRAPHY

▶ RICH MAYS

▲ METRO GOVERNMENT OF NASHVILLE / GARY LAYDA

◆ D R PRODUCTIONS

WHETHER AT THE annual Summer Lights Festival (PAGES 208 AND 209) or a festive fireworks display on the river, people, arts, music, and dance all come together in this true city of note.

THE GREATEST

Profiles in Excellence

LOOK AT THE CORPORATIONS, BUSINESSES, PROFESSIONAL groups, and community service organizations that have made this book possible. Their stories—offering an informal chronicle of the local business community—are arranged according to the date they were established in Nashville.

ADT Automotive, Inc. ★ Aegis, Inc. ★ Akersloot, DePriest, Wall & Associates, PLLC ★ Alley-Cassetty Coal Company, Inc. ★ American Fabricators, Inc. ★ American Transitional Hospitals, Inc. ★ Baker, Donelson, Bearman & Caldwell ★ Baptist Sunday School Board ★ Barnes Real Estate Services, Inc. ★ BellSouth ★ Bridgestone/Firestone, Inc. ★ Cambridge Equity Advisors ★ Castner Knott Co. ★ Caterpillar Inc. ★ Charles Hampton A-1 Signs ★ Columbia/HCA ★ Comdata Corporation ★ Cooper, Love & Jackson ★ Curb Records ★ Cytometry Associates, Inc. ★ Davis-Kidd Booksellers, Inc. ★ DuPont Old Hickory ★ Earl Swensson Associates, Inc. ★ Electric Picture Company ★ ENVOY Corporation ★ Equitable Securities Corporation ★ Film House ★ First Union National Bank of Tennessee ★ Fleetguard, Inc. ★ Fox Ridge Homes Inc. ★ Francis & Lusky Co., Inc. ★ French, Clayton, Johnson & Assoc. ★ Gold Skin Care Center ★ Gould Turner Group, P.C. ★ Hermitage Lighting Gallery ★ H.G. Hill Realty Co. ★ H.G. Hill Stores, Inc. ★ InterMedia Partners ★ IPN Network ★ Jamison Bedding, Inc. ★ J.C. Bradford & Co. ★ Kraft Bros., Esstman, Patton & Harrell, PLLC ★ Kyzen Corporation ★ Lankford Hardware & Supply Co., Inc. ★ LifeView Resources ★ Loews Vanderbilt Plaza Hotel ★ Logan's Roadhouse Restaurants ★ Lovell Communications Inc. ★ MagneTek, Inc. ★ The Mall at Green Hills ★ The Mathews Company/R.C. Mathews Contractor ★ Metropolitan Nashville Airport Authority ★ Middle Tennessee Motor Cars, Inc. ★ Murray, Inc. ★ Nashville Area Chamber of Commerce ★ Nashville Electric Service ★ Nashville Gas ★ Nashville Speedway ★ NationsBank ★ Nissan Motor Manufacturing Corporation U.S.A. ★ O'Charley's, Inc. ★ Olsten Staffing Services ★ PMT Services, Inc. ★ Reemay, Inc. ★ Renaissance Nashville Hotel ★ Saturn Corporation ★ Sheraton Music City Hotel ★ Southern Baptist Convention ★ Speer Communications, Ltd. ★ SunTrust ★ Tennessee Managed Care Network ★ Tennessee Orthopaedic Alliance, P.A. ★ Thomas Nelson, Inc. ★ Tractor Supply Company ★ Vanderbilt University Medical Center ★ Whirlpool Corporation ★ Willis Corroon

▼ JONATHAN POSTAL / TOWERY PUBLISHING, INC.; POSTER DESIGN: JIM SHERRADEN / HATCH SHOW PRINT

HANK
WILLIAMS

▼ JONATHAN POSTAL / TOWERY PUBLISHING, INC.; POSTER DESIGN: JIM SHERRADEN / HATCH SHOW PRINT

★

1847
Nashville Area Chamber of Commerce

1851
Nashville Gas

1867
Willis Corroon

1874
Vanderbilt University Medical Center

1879
Alley-Cassetty Coal Company, Inc.

1879
BellSouth

1883
Jamison Bedding, Inc.

1885
Cooper, Love & Jackson

1889
First Union National Bank of Tennessee

1891
Baptist Sunday School Board

1891
Nashville Speedway

1895
H.G. Hill Realty Co.

1895
H.G. Hill Stores, Inc.

1898
Castner Knott Co.

1916
NationsBank

1918
DuPont Old Hickory

1919
Francis & Lusky Co., Inc.

1926
Tennessee Orthopaedic Alliance, P.A.

1927
J.C. Bradford & Co.

1927
Southern Baptist Convention

1927
SunTrust

1930
Equitable Securities Corporation

1937
Metropolitan Nashville Airport Authority

1938
The Mathews Company/R.C. Mathews Contractor

1939
Nashville Electric Service

Nashville Area Chamber of Commerce

N 1847, THE SOUNDS OF NASHVILLE'S COMMERCE INCLUDED HORSE-drawn wagons on the bricks of Market Street, the ping of a blacksmith's hammer, the staccato precision of the *Republican Banner*'s printing press, and the gentle sounds of keelboats cutting through the Cumberland River. It was in that year that the Nashville Area Chamber of Commerce formed the organization that today conducts the Music City's medley of thriving industries and economic growth.

With a macroscopic view of the future of Nashville, the Chamber creates an array of programs to fine-tune business and livability quotients and ensure an attractive quality of life. Under the direction of a board of governors that is comprised of leaders in the community, the Chamber has spearheaded relocation efforts for professional sports teams, programs to bolster the vitality of downtown, improvements in education, and efforts to ensure quality growth in the future.

The Nashville Convention & Visitor's Bureau, working under the purview of the Chamber, strives to communicate the area's distinctive historical and entertainment features, and to promote the city's convention and meeting facilities to a national and international audience.

JONATHAN POSTAL/TOWERY PUBLISHING

A STATE-OF-THE-ART FACILITY KNOWN AS THE NASHVILLE ARENA WAS BUILT BY THE CITY FOLLOWING A SUCCESSFUL LOBBYING CAMPAIGN IN WHICH THE CHAMBER PLAYED A ROLE.

Getting Down to Business

ith more than 4,000 member companies, the Nashville Area Chamber of Commerce basks in a groundswell of membership participation.

Chanting its "return on investment" mantra, the Chamber challenges its members to invest time in its initiatives, which benefit Nashville's business economy and quality of life. The results are best seen in the Nashville area's projected population growth rate of 19.5 percent for 1990-2000, which is twice that of the national average. The Chamber attributes this growth to the addition of more than 100,000 new jobs created by new or expanded business since 1990.

A stellar example of Chamber initiatives includes PARTNERSHIP 2000, established in 1990. Dedicated to the area's economic development, the program focuses on such factors as air transportation, education, quality workforce, and workforce development, all of which are critical in keeping Nashville competitive with and marketable to the rest of the world. While working to strengthen existing businesses, PARTNERSHIP 2000 also strives to attract new industry. In 1996 alone, the initiative played a part in 36 business relocations and 60 major business expansions in the Nashville area.

The Music City is frequently ranked as a hot spot for entrepreneurial and small-business activity. In fact, 86 percent of the Chamber's membership is comprised of companies with fewer than 40 employ-

▲ JONATHAN POSTAL/TOWERY PUBLISHING

ees, and the Chamber's Small Business Council is dedicated to the growth and prosperity of these small businesses. For example, the Small Business Council coordinates ACCE$$, a business financing program brought together by the SBA; the Music City Future 50, which spotlights the 50 fastest-growing privately held companies in Middle Tennessee; and Partners in Prosperity, which assists women- and minority-owned businesses.

Nashville's downtown has enjoyed a renaissance in recent years and the Nashville Downtown Partnership, created by the Chamber in 1994, strives to ensure that the area remains a clean, vibrant, and safe center. More than 100 businesses in the downtown area have joined the Downtown Partnership.

The Chamber also works to support and enhance Nashville's well-deserved reputation as the music/entertainment and health care capital of the country. The Nashville Health Care Council was established in 1995 as part of the Chamber to further Nashville's leadership role in the nation's health care business.

Quality of Life

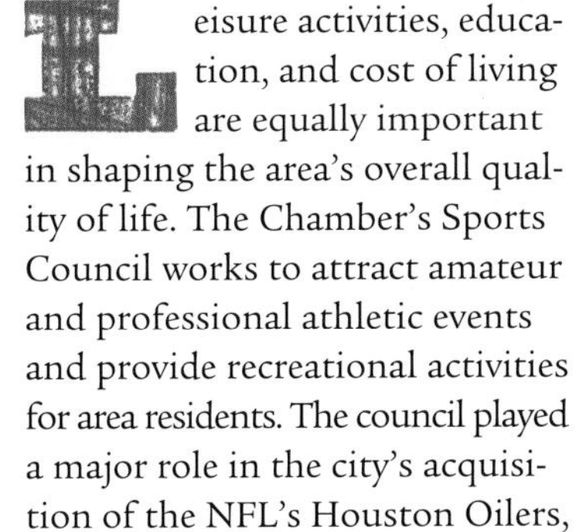

Leisure activities, education, and cost of living are equally important in shaping the area's overall quality of life. The Chamber's Sports Council works to attract amateur and professional athletic events and provide recreational activities for area residents. The council played a major role in the city's acquisition of the NFL's Houston Oilers, an effort that captured the attention of numerous sports fans.

The Chamber is making its most important investment in tomorrow's leaders, having initiated an ambitious School to Career Program. The Chamber's goal is for 100 percent of Metro students to successfully complete their high school education by the year 2010, thereby allowing them to make a successful transition from school to both career and further education.

Due to the tremendous growth of Nashville in the early 1990s, the Chamber launched a Livability Index in 1995 that serves to measure and monitor quality-of-life progress and change. The index serves as an early warning system in the identification of any deterioration in quality-of-life attributes.

Strengthening Nashville for the Future

The Chamber's focus on the future encompasses a number of key issues that are critical to the Nashville region's future success. Those issues include workforce availability and quality, improving the quality of the area's public education system, strengthening the region by improving the core city, and assessing the effect of rapidly changing electronic communication on businesses and lifestyles.

With a strong track record of getting in front of issues, taking a stand, and articulating clear goals that generate results, the Nashville Area Chamber of Commerce will no doubt blaze a trail into the future, furthering its mission "to provide leadership that will help create the best possible place in which to operate a business while enhancing the Music City region as a desirable place to live, work, and visit."

THE 2ND AVENUE ENTERTAINMENT DISTRICT DEMONSTRATES THE CHAMBER'S ONGOING EFFORTS TO REDEFINE NASHVILLE'S DOWNTOWN AREA AS A PLACE TO LIVE, WORK, SHOP, PLAY, AND VISIT.

AS A CHAMPION OF PUBLIC EDUCATION IMPROVEMENT, THE CHAMBER IS INVOLVED IN ACTIVITIES THAT ALLOW BUSINESS AND GOVERNMENT LEADERS TO INTERACT WITH METRO NASHVILLE PUBLIC SCHOOLS.

Nashville Gas

OFFERING A BEAUTIFUL SILK DRESS TO THE FIRST LADY IN NASHville who would agree to have her home illuminated with gas was quite an intriguing promotion by the newly formed Nashville Gas & Light Company. The offer by company president Washington Barrow in 1851 stirred civic interest, and, by year's end, 285 customers were using gas in their homes.

Today, Nashville Gas prides itself on being the city's Energy Partner, servicing 125,000 residential, commercial, and industrial customers, and taking a high-profile role in civic and charitable causes.

Nashville's Oldest Company

As the first gas company in operation in Tennessee and the oldest business in Nashville, the Nashville Gas & Light Company was founded by a group of businessmen who recognized the need to better light the streets and homes in Nashville.

The lighting of the first gas street lamp on the evening of February 13, 1851, marked the official opening of Nashville Gas & Light. A century later, in 1951, the company changed its name to the Nashville Gas Company and was serving 33,000 customers with 451 miles of main. In 1985, Piedmont Natural Gas in Charlotte, North Carolina, purchased Nashville Gas, providing the financial muscle for the company to extend its mains and furnish more gas than ever before to Nashvillians and residents of seven surrounding counties.

Energy Partner

Traditionally a lower-cost energy alternative, natural gas provides customers with the benefits of comfort, economy, and efficiency. Providing natural gas and gas appliances—logs, ranges, grills, lights, space heaters, and water heaters—is the cornerstone of the company. Its foundation, however, is its service. "Nashville Gas is a service company that just happens to sell natural gas," says J. William Denny, president.

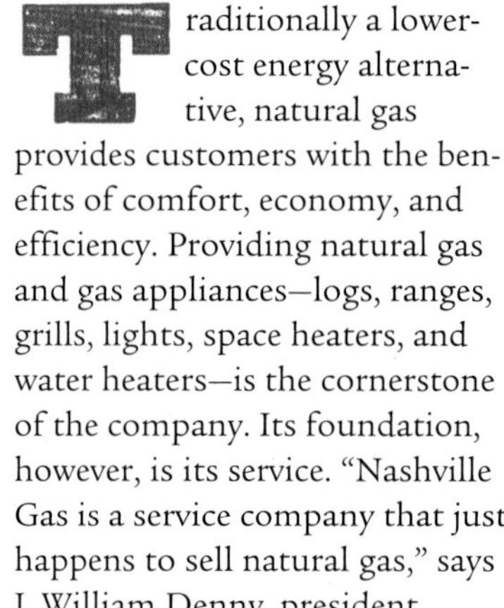

Backing up Nashville Gas' customer-service-oriented focus are programs and services such as the Equal Payment Plan (EPP), which allows customers to make equal payments throughout the year toward their natural gas bills; the Telecommunications Device for the Deaf, which allows hearing-impaired customers to communicate more effectively with Nashville Gas; a 24-hour emergency line that consumers can call 365 days a year to report safety concerns; and the availability of financing for customers who wish to purchase natural gas appliances from the company or central heating systems from qualified natural gas heating contractors.

Rousing Civic Pride

Nashville Gas has earned a reputation for taking its commitment to service into the community as well. "Our employees are involved in more than 100 community and civic organizations," notes Denny. The company and its employees are responsible for bringing the Christmas Parade to Nashvillians for 44 years, as well as the colorful Rudolph's Red Nose Run, which benefits Big Brothers of Nashville.

Nashville Gas' dramatic, award-winning office building in the MetroCenter complex reflects the company's commitment of service to its customers and its competitive positioning for the future. The firm's future, not surprisingly, rests on developing both new services and new uses for natural gas for its customers, such as power generation and alternative fuels for vehicles; new natural gas equipment, including the Triathlon heating and cooling unit that can reduce residential energy consumption and energy bills significantly; and, through the company's home page on the Internet, up-to-date information on all of the company's available products and services. With tremendous equity in its past, Nashville Gas is lighting the way for Middle Tennessee's future.

Nashville Gas is proud to be Middle Tennessee's energy partner (top).

Established in 1851, Nashville Gas today services 125,000 residential, commercial, and industrial customers, and takes a high-profile role in civic and charitable causes (bottom).

Willis Corroon

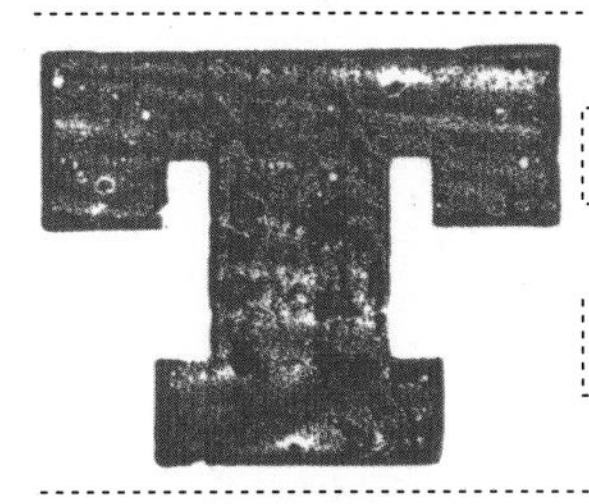

Tennessee's early pioneers followed the course of rivers seeking permanent settlements. Calculated risks and bold moves were an integral part of everyday life: staking land, taming the wilderness, charting waterways—undaunted by the perils of ever present dangers.

A Leading North American Broker

Managing risk is what Willis Corroon is all about. Its Tennessee history goes back for more than a century to 1867, a time when insuring crops and goods traveling up and down the Tennessee and Cumberland rivers instilled confidence in a brighter future.

Today, Willis Corroon is continuing the tradition and heritage of its founders, insuring bold moves of business and industry in the United States and around the world. Whether from its North American headquarters in Nashville or from ports in New York, Seattle, or New Orleans, Willis Corroon is recognized as one of the leading insurance brokers in North America. The company's roots are firmly entrenched in hometown America but its reach spans the globe with representation in some 70 countries from 300 offices.

Through retail offices in Nashville, Knoxville, Chattanooga, and nearly 100 other U.S. and Canadian cities, Willis Corroon serves government, industrial, commercial, and other clients, corporate and individual, in every form of business or economic activity in the management, control, and transfer of every form of risk. The range of services offered extends beyond traditional insurance broking with risk management as its basis. Services include captive company design and management, self-insurance consulting, actuarial services, and third-party administrative and claims management services for both life and health programs and property and casualty programs.

In addition to being the largest construction broker in North America, Willis Corroon has earned a reputation for its global specialties of aerospace, energy, marine, global non-marine reinsurance, and global non-marine broking services. Willis Corroon's U.S. operations also include a number of companies marketing a variety of specialized insurance programs on a wholesale basis through retail brokers and agents.

Willis Corroon's benefits operations provide services to corporations and individuals. The benefits program and related services include pensions and retirement plans; executive compensation; life, health, and accident insurance; expatriate and other executive financial planning; and investment advice and management.

What Makes Willis Corroon Different

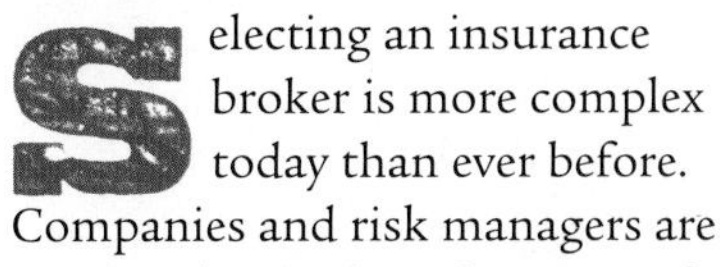

Selecting an insurance broker is more complex today than ever before. Companies and risk managers are viewing the total implications of risk, not merely insurance, as part of their overall corporate strategy.

Willis Corroon's worldwide presence gives it special access to global insurance markets with capacity to underwrite the most difficult risks. The company is able to use its considerable buying power, as well as unique relationships in the insurance markets and with insurers worldwide, to negotiate on behalf of its clients.

Willis Corroon is prepared for the challenges of the next century. Through global operations, Willis Corroon offers a wealth of experience and insight into the risk management process for thousands of companies doing business—whether in Tennessee or around the world.

After more than 100 years of meeting and exceeding the expectations of its clients, Willis Corroon is proud to be regarded as the broker of choice.

▶ Architectural Photography

From top:

Kenneth H. Pinkston is chairman and CEO of Willis Corroon Corporation.

Willis Corroon's Tennessee roots go back more than a century to a time when the company arranged for the insurance of crops and goods traveling up and down the Tennessee and Cumberland rivers.

Willis Corroon was selected to provide risk management and insurance brokerage services for the construction of Nashville's NFL stadium.

Vanderbilt University Medical Center

LifeFlight helicopter transports an accident victim for emergency care. Researchers refine a low-cost imaging technology to allow doctors to see how a living organ is functioning. Parents take home a baby born three months early, her survival a modern miracle. ★ For patients and their loved ones, moments like these are life-changing and, sometimes, life-saving events. For Vanderbilt University Medical Center, they are daily occurrences.

A Legacy of Caring

Throughout its history, Vanderbilt University Medical Center (VUMC) has combined the missions of patient care, medical and nursing education, and biomedical research for the benefit of people in Middle Tennessee.

Indeed, the Medical Center's precursor institution actually predates Commodore Cornelius Vanderbilt's establishment of a university in Nashville; the Nashville Medical College, founded in 1850, merged into the new Vanderbilt University in 1874. Since those early days, when the entire school was housed in a building at the corner of Franklin Street and Second Avenue on Rutledge Hill, VUMC has grown to become an institution that touches thousands of lives throughout the nation every day.

Clockwise from top:
Vanderbilt University Medical Center's emergency air transport system, unique to Middle Tennessee, has carried more than 8,500 patients to Vanderbilt and other hospitals in the past decade.

Surgeons perform a liver transplant at VUMC, one of the only hospitals in the region with a liver transplant program.

Throughout its history, VUMC has combined the missions of patient care, medical and nursing education, and biomedical research for the benefit of people in Middle Tennessee.

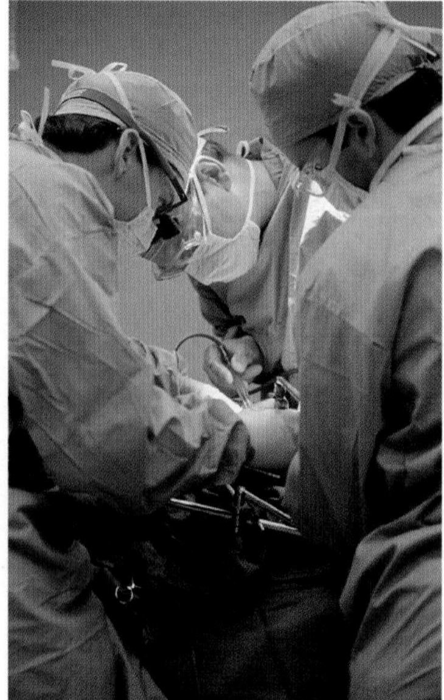

Today, the Medical Center leads the way among academic health centers in developing new approaches to managed care—medicine's new paradigm for the 21st century. "Academic health centers are about investment—investment in our future," says Roscoe R. Robinson, M.D., Vice Chancellor for Health Affairs. "They will prepare the next generation of doctors, nurses, and other health care professionals and provide much of the next generation of knowledge through research."

An Unparalleled Resource

As an academic medical center, VUMC's hospital is different from others. Along with providing the same patient care services as other types of institutions, it offers many services that are unique to the region. Vanderbilt Hospital and Children's Hospital offer the most comprehensive range of full patient care services of any hospital in the area.

In addition to its teaching role, VUMC has a continued commitment to biomedical research. Research has been at the forefront of the center's mission for more than 70 years. Through its research, VUMC has made medical advancements in the treatment of cancer, diabetes, cardiovascular disease, and many other diseases. Almost $125 million of the medical school's revenues comes from research grants—much of it from the National Institutes of Health

(NIH) as well as other governmental agencies and private sources.

NIH data shows that four basic science departments at VUMC now rank in the top seven nationally in attraction of total dollars of NIH support through an intense national competition. That government investment pays off for everyone, as Robinson explains: "All hospitals, whether private, not-for-profit, or investor owned, benefit from the discovery of new treatments and methods of prevention that emerge from academic research."

A Continued Commitment to Patient Care

The Children's Hospital at Vanderbilt is the only comprehensive provider of children's specialty services in Middle Tennessee. Its outpatient facilities host more than 100,000 patient visits annually, and the VUMC Poison Control Center fields more than 30,000 calls a year—most from anxious parents. The hospital's pediatric trauma team is on call 24 hours a day. It operates specially equipped ambulances—fondly known as Angel III and Cherub—for the regional transport of high-risk newborns to the hospital, which has the area's only Level III neonatal intensive care unit. Children's Hospital not only saves lives, it also improves lives for the children of Middle Tennessee.

VUMC has the region's only Level I trauma center, burn center, voice center, poison control center, and liver transplant program, to cite just a few of its distinctions. Its emergency air transport system, also unique in the area, has carried more than 8,500 patients to Vanderbilt and other hospitals in the past decade. VUMC is the only National Cancer Institute-designated clinical cancer center in the region.

The more than 700 doctors and 90 specialty clinics of the Vanderbilt Medical Group provide more general and specialty care than any other multispecialty practice in the region. VUMC also provides health benefits to more than 50,000 people through its Medicare, TennCare, and commercial HMOs. From the Vanderbilt Addiction Research Center to the Arthritis and Joint Replacement Center, the Vanderbilt Home Health Service to the Center for Molecular Neuroscience, the School of Nursing's nurse-managed primary care clinics to the Vanderbilt-Bill Wilkerson Center for Otolaryngology and Communication Sciences, the soon-to-be Tennessee Lion's Eye Center for Children to well beyond, VUMC and its affiliated institutions offer an unparalleled array of services to Nashville and Middle Tennessee.

All those distinctions contributed to VUMC's repeated impressive showing in the *U.S. News & World Report* ranking of America's Best Hospitals. For example, in 1996, the Medical Center placed among the nation's top 50 health care institutions in six specialties and among the top 20 in four. *U.S. News & World Report* also judged Vanderbilt University Hospital as the top hospital in Tennessee and ranked the Vanderbilt Medical School as number 14 among 125 medical schools nationwide.

An Academic Eye on the Future

More than half of all the doctors in Nashville received at least part of their training at Vanderbilt, which also has one of the largest training programs for advanced nurse practitioners in the country.

Today's academic enterprise at Vanderbilt is designed to produce a health care provider whose mission is not just to heal and offer comfort from human suffering, but to understand the economic and social value of preventive medicine: a provider who can adapt to technological changes and who embraces clinical pathways and teamwork to help control costs and improve results.

An Engine for Growth

ith so many exciting and beneficial things happening at VUMC, one could almost overlook the fact that it is also Nashville's largest private employer, with more than 8,500 people on its payroll. Or the fact that it provides more than $40 million a year in uncompensated and charity care to patients. Or that it generates more than $1.2 billion annually in local economic activity.

With its international reputation, Vanderbilt University Medical Center is geographically, economically, and medically at the heart of Nashville and Middle Tennessee—always there to meet the medical needs of the region.

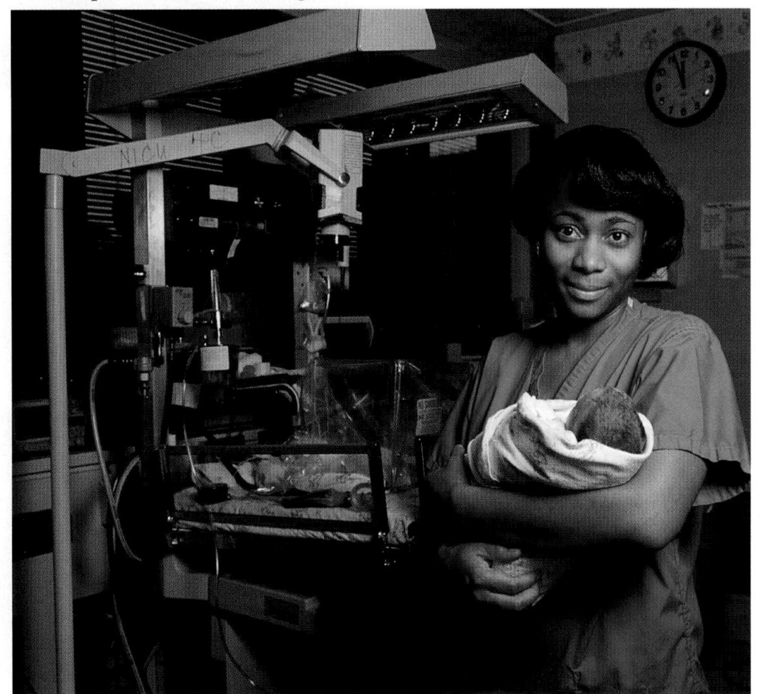

A nurse in VUMC's Level III neonatal intensive care unit holds a baby born three months prematurely.

BellSouth

HAT'S THE DISTANCE FROM THE DISTINCTIVE TWIN spires of BellSouth's downtown Nashville headquarters tower to the corner of Union Street and Seventh Avenue North? About 120 years. ★ On September 1, 1877, a group of visiting scientists placed Nashville's first telephone call using a device invented the prior year by Alexander Graham Bell. The call was made near Union and Seventh from the home of A.G. Adams to his neighbor Mrs. James K. Polk, widow of the former president.

As the *Nashville Republican Banner* reported, one of the scientists sat at the piano and played Strauss' "Blue Danube Waltz" through the line. Pronouncing the new device "perfectly grand," Mrs. Polk insisted: "Play some more. We cannot get enough."

The 1877 news report predicted "wonderful possibilities in the not too distant future" for the newfangled device. One can only wonder what Mrs. Polk would say if she could log on to the Internet through BellSouth's high-speed access, channel-surf BellSouth's entertainment services, or conduct her shopping and banking electronically through BellSouth's state-of-the-art interface.

Destiny Calls

ellSouth traces its local roots to 1879 when the first telephone exchange was established in Nashville. By 1890, the telephone had become a part of everyday life for many Nashvillians, as advertisements featuring two-, three-, and four-digit phone numbers began to appear in newspapers. Soon the ads began to mention the early telephone exchanges, with numbers like Hemlock 317 and Main 119.

Cumberland Telephone and Telegraph Co., established in the 1880s, became part of the old Southern Bell in 1926. In 1968, parts of the Southern Bell system, including Tennessee, became South Central Bell, one of the 22 Bell System operating companies owned by American Telephone & Telegraph Co. In 1984, the Bell System split into seven regional companies. Consequently, South Central Bell and Southern Bell became sister companies owned by the newly created BellSouth Corporation.

South Central Bell and Southern Bell merged in 1992 to create BellSouth Telecommunications and in 1995 both adopted the unified brand name of BellSouth. Headquartered in Atlanta, BellSouth provides telecommunications services in nine southeastern states. The company serves more than 21 million local telephone lines, including more than 2.6 million in Tennessee.

While keeping its Tennessee rates the fourth lowest in the nation, BellSouth has developed a network infrastructure that

BELLSOUTH TENNESSEE'S HEADQUARTERS ARE LOCATED IN DOWNTOWN NASHVILLE (LEFT).

CABLE-SPLICING TECHNICIANS PREPARE TO SPLICE THE LARGEST FIBER-OPTIC CABLE IN NASHVILLE (RIGHT).

◀ VANDO ROGERS JR.

◀ VANDO ROGERS JR.

FROM TC
FRANK H
DELIVER
1924 AS
NESS VE
BUILDIN
A DELIVE

RECOGN
BUSINES
CASSETT
BRICK AN

"WE CON
COAL BU
TIFIED A
WE SERV
CASSETT

(NIH) as well as other governmental agencies and private sources.

NIH data shows that four basic science departments at VUMC now rank in the top seven nationally in attraction of total dollars of NIH support through an intense national competition. That government investment pays off for everyone, as Robinson explains: "All hospitals, whether private, not-for-profit, or investor owned, benefit from the discovery of new treatments and methods of prevention that emerge from academic research."

A Continued Commitment to Patient Care

The Children's Hospital at Vanderbilt is the only comprehensive provider of children's specialty services in Middle Tennessee. Its outpatient facilities host more than 100,000 patient visits annually, and the VUMC Poison Control Center fields more than 30,000 calls a year—most from anxious parents. The hospital's pediatric trauma team is on call 24 hours a day. It operates specially equipped ambulances—fondly known as Angel III and Cherub—for the regional transport of high-risk newborns to the hospital, which has the area's only Level III neonatal intensive care unit. Children's Hospital not only saves lives, it also improves lives for the children of Middle Tennessee.

VUMC has the region's only Level I trauma center, burn center, voice center, poison control center, and liver transplant program, to cite just a few of its distinctions. Its emergency air transport system, also unique in the area, has carried more than 8,500 patients to Vanderbilt and other hospitals in the past decade. VUMC is the only National Cancer Institute-designated clinical cancer center in the region.

The more than 700 doctors and 90 specialty clinics of the Vanderbilt Medical Group provide more general and specialty care than any other multispecialty practice in the region. VUMC also provides health benefits to more than 50,000 people through its Medicare, TennCare, and commercial HMOs. From the Vanderbilt Addiction Research Center to the Arthritis and Joint Replacement Center, the Vanderbilt Home Health Service to the Center for Molecular Neuroscience, the School of Nursing's nurse-managed primary care clinics to the Vanderbilt-Bill Wilkerson Center for Otolaryngology and Communication Sciences, the soon-to-be Tennessee Lion's Eye Center for Children to well beyond, VUMC and its affiliated institutions offer an unparalleled array of services to Nashville and Middle Tennessee.

All those distinctions contributed to VUMC's repeated impressive showing in the *U.S. News & World Report* ranking of America's Best Hospitals. For example, in 1996, the Medical Center placed among the nation's top 50 health care institutions in six specialties and among the top 20 in four. *U.S. News & World Report* also judged Vanderbilt University Hospital as the top hospital in Tennessee and ranked the Vanderbilt Medical School as number 14 among 125 medical schools nationwide.

An Academic Eye on the Future

More than half of all the doctors in Nashville received at least part of their training at Vanderbilt, which also has one of the largest training programs for advanced nurse practitioners in the country.

Today's academic enterprise at Vanderbilt is designed to produce a health care provider whose mission is not just to heal and offer comfort from human suffering, but to understand the economic and social value of preventive medicine: a provider who can adapt to technological changes and who embraces clinical pathways and teamwork to help control costs and improve results.

An Engine for Growth

With so many exciting and beneficial things happening at VUMC, one could almost overlook the fact that it is also Nashville's largest private employer, with more than 8,500 people on its payroll. Or the fact that it provides more than $40 million a year in uncompensated and charity care to patients. Or that it generates more than $1.2 billion annually in local economic activity.

With its international reputation, Vanderbilt University Medical Center is geographically, economically, and medically at the heart of Nashville and Middle Tennessee—always there to meet the medical needs of the region.

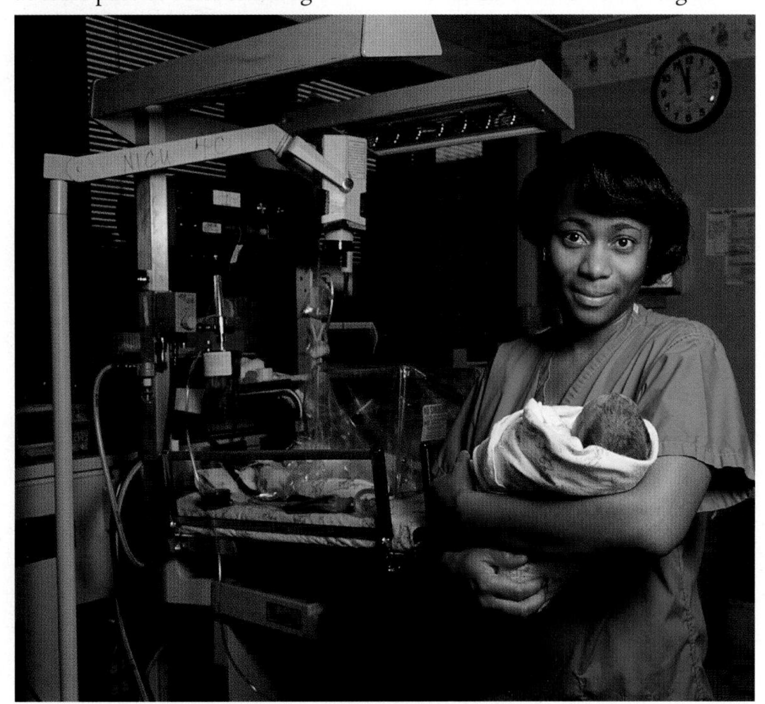

A nurse in VUMC's Level III neonatal intensive care unit holds a baby born three months prematurely.

Alley-Cassetty Coal Company, Inc.

HILE COAL USAGE HAS WAXED AND WANED THROUGH the last century, Alley-Cassetty Coal Company, Inc. has adapted to the fluctuations in fuel consideration by successfully diversifying its products and services. Since its inception in the 1880s, Alley-Cassetty Coal Company has cultivated its small retail coal business into one of the fastest-growing companies according to *Inc.* magazine, and today, it ranks as one of Nashville's largest private 100 companies.

Coal for $3 per Ton

In 1879, when James Cassetty began selling kindling and coal by the bushel, coal was highly regarded as fuel because of its long-burning quality. When Cassetty opened his first coal yard at Nashville's Clinton Street and Jo Johnston—a location still owned by Alley-Cassetty—Nashville homes were heated by coal that sold for as little as $3 to $4 per ton.

Cassetty Coal remained a family business through three generations, from James to his son Fred B. to his grandson Fred J. Fred J. Cassetty died in 1960, just as his son Fred J. Cassetty Jr. graduated from Vanderbilt University with a degree in electrical engineering. In 1964, through the leadership of the younger Cassetty, the company merged with Frank H. Alley Coal Company, another coal firm steeped in Nashville heritage.

Frank Alley's first contact with the coal business came in the early 1900s when he bought coal at wholesale from the yards in Nashville and peddled it from a house in north Nashville. Alley's first retail coal delivery yard was established in 1924 as part of a variety of business ventures, including wagon building, ice manufacturing, and a delivery service. By the 1930s, as electric refrigerators cut into Alley's ice manufacturing operation, he

From top:

Frank H. Alley's first retail coal delivery yard was established in 1924 as part of a variety of business ventures, including wagon building, ice manufacturing, and a delivery service.

Recognizing that the retail coal business was in a decline, Alley-Cassetty began to move into the brick and masonry business in 1972.

"We continue to succeed in the coal business because we have identified a small niche market, which we serve very well," says Fred J. Cassetty Jr.

TO SERVICE ITS TRUCKING FLEET, ALLEY-CASSETTY OPENED CUSTOM TRUCK, A FULL-SERVICE TRUCK DEALERSHIP, IN 1984.

devoted more time to the coal business. His son J.P. "Pete" Alley and son-in-law G.W. West joined the family business within the next decade.

In an effort to combat the growing popularity of electricity and maintain a strong business presence, Alley and West merged their family business with that of Cassetty's, creating a coal powerhouse from two historically successful companies.

"We continue to succeed in the coal business because we have identified a small niche market, which we serve very well," says Fred J. Cassetty Jr. "Because of our long history, we know and understand the coal business. We've managed to stay strong and grow while other small coal companies have gone out of business."

In 1984, the firm opened Owensboro Coal Dock, a new, multimillion-dollar coal loading facility in Owensboro, Kentucky. Today, Alley-Cassetty services the industrial and commercial coal market with customers that include TVA, DuPont, and a number of state buildings and Tennessee state colleges.

DIVERSIFICATION FUELS GROWTH

To diversify the company, Alley-Cassetty entered the brick business by purchasing Capitol Builders Supply in 1971. Alley-Cassetty Coal Company and Capitol Builders Supply consolidated their offices and now operate their corporate headquarters on the banks of the Cumberland River. Jimmy Alley and, a few years later, G.R. West entered the business, which sells masonry products throughout Middle Tennessee, southern Kentucky, and northern Georgia. They have developed a strategic game plan for the future of the building supply business.

As a result of its calculated efforts to grow the building supply division, Alley-Cassetty also opened Gallatin Brick & Block—with its state-of-the-art concrete block facility in Gallatin, Tennessee—in 1980. Expanding its operations beyond Nashville, in 1994, Alley-Cassetty purchased James Brick & Block, a family-owned business servicing Murfreesboro and Columbia, Tennessee. One year later, the company opened Bowling Green Brick in order to expand its building supply presence into southern Kentucky.

"We continue to look for appropriate avenues to expand the building supply business. It is a big focal point for our future," says Cassetty. "Since we ventured into this arena in 1971, we've concentrated on finding really good people. They're the ones who have established the company at the top of the masonry business." Currently, Alley-Cassetty has its sights set on serving the building supply market in Atlanta, opening Atlanta Brick in 1997.

In order to facilitate coal delivery, the company ventured into the trucking industry. In 1980, the firm founded its Alley-Cassetty Trucking division which initially coordinated delivery of Alley-Cassetty coal. Since then, it has flourished into a full-service transportation company, specializing in bulk hazardous and nonhazardous customized hauling for a variety of companies. Alley-Cassetty's impressive trucking fleet, manned by certified and highly trained drivers, has 48-state ICC authority. To service the trucking fleet, Alley-Cassetty opened a full-service truck dealership in 1984—Custom Truck Sales and Service.

By expanding its markets, products, and services, Alley-Cassetty Coal Company has successfully fueled its own growth, as well as significantly contributed to the changing needs of Nashville's burgeoning economy.

IN 1879, WHEN JAMES CASSETTY BEGAN SELLING KINDLING AND COAL BY THE BUSHEL, COAL WAS HIGHLY REGARDED AS FUEL BECAUSE OF ITS LONG-BURNING QUALITY.

BellSouth

WHAT'S THE DISTANCE FROM THE DISTINCTIVE TWIN spires of BellSouth's downtown Nashville headquarters tower to the corner of Union Street and Seventh Avenue North? About 120 years. ★ On September 1, 1877, a group of visiting scientists placed Nashville's first telephone call using a device invented the prior year by Alexander Graham Bell. The call was made near Union and Seventh from the home of A.G. Adams to his neighbor Mrs. James K. Polk, widow of the former president.

As the *Nashville Republican Banner* reported, one of the scientists sat at the piano and played Strauss' "Blue Danube Waltz" through the line. Pronouncing the new device "perfectly grand," Mrs. Polk insisted: "Play some more. We cannot get enough."

The 1877 news report predicted "wonderful possibilities in the not too distant future" for the newfangled device. One can only wonder what Mrs. Polk would say if she could log on to the Internet through BellSouth's high-speed access, channel-surf BellSouth's entertainment services, or conduct her shopping and banking electronically through BellSouth's state-of-the-art interface.

Destiny Calls

BellSouth traces its local roots to 1879 when the first telephone exchange was established in Nashville. By 1890, the telephone had become a part of everyday life for many Nashvillians, as advertisements featuring two-, three-, and four-digit phone numbers began to appear in newspapers. Soon the ads began to mention the early telephone exchanges, with numbers like Hemlock 317 and Main 119.

Cumberland Telephone and Telegraph Co., established in the 1880s, became part of the old Southern Bell in 1926. In 1968, parts of the Southern Bell system, including Tennessee, became South Central Bell, one of the 22 Bell System operating companies owned by American Telephone & Telegraph Co. In 1984, the Bell System split into seven regional companies. Consequently, South Central Bell and Southern Bell became sister companies owned by the newly created BellSouth Corporation.

South Central Bell and Southern Bell merged in 1992 to create BellSouth Telecommunications and in 1995 both adopted the unified brand name of BellSouth. Headquartered in Atlanta, BellSouth provides telecommunications services in nine southeastern states. The company serves more than 21 million local telephone lines, including more than 2.6 million in Tennessee.

While keeping its Tennessee rates the fourth lowest in the nation, BellSouth has developed a network infrastructure that

BellSouth Tennessee's headquarters are located in downtown Nashville (left).

Cable-splicing technicians prepare to splice the largest fiber-optic cable in Nashville (right).

◀ Vando Rogers Jr.

◀ Vando Rogers Jr.

features widespread deployment of fiber-optic facilities and digital switching in every exchange. In Nashville, where more than 13 million calls are made daily, BellSouth has installed more than 50,000 miles of fiber-optic lines. To ensure the reliability and integrity of its services, BellSouth invests about $350 million to grow and modernize its Tennessee infrastructure every year.

But there is more to reliable telecommunications than technology: It takes people, too. Nearly 3,000 people in the Nashville area work for BellSouth. The BellSouth Pioneers—the company's volunteer service organization comprised of both active and retired employees—logged more than 750,000 hours of volunteer time in 1995 on projects in Tennessee communities. Through charitable contributions and participation in community civic activities, BellSouth works to improve the quality of life in areas such as education, economic development, health and human services, and arts and culture.

Making the Connection

The world of communication has traveled a long way from the corner of Union and Seventh. "These days telecommunications technology is being combined with other disciplines to change lives and even occasionally contribute to saving lives," says DeWitt Ezell, president of BellSouth of Tennessee. "That's pretty strong stuff in anybody's book."

A prime example is BellSouth's partnership with the Tennessee Department of Education, connecting the state's elementary, middle, and high schools to the Internet. As part of this program—called ConnecTEN—the schools are using BellSouth's Integrated Services Digital Network (ISDN) for fast and easy connection to the Internet and receiving the benefit of $1.7 million in annual educational discounts. One result: Inner-city schools in Nashville, which often run short of educational resources, offer their students complete access to the World Wide Web. This Internet access has transformed the way teachers teach and children learn.

In the years to come, BellSouth will have even more opportunities to touch the lives of Nashvillians. Changes in state and federal law are opening the way for BellSouth to provide worldwide long-distance services from both standard and cellular telephones, offer home entertainment services, and participate in the research and development of the next generation of telecommunications equipment—all in addition to the broad range of services the company already offers.

"Our aim is to be world class across the board—not just in voice, but in video and data as well," says F. Duane Ackerman, chairman and chief executive officer of parent company BellSouth Corporation in Atlanta. It's not hard to imagine what Mrs. James K. Polk would say if she could see the results of such ambitious plans: "perfectly grand."

MICHAEL HORTON

BellSouth Pioneers—the company's volunteer service organization comprised of both active and retired employees—clown around at their national convention.

VANDO ROGERS JR.

BellSouth's president of Tennessee Operations, DeWitt Ezell (left), and George Yowell, president of Tennessee Tomorrow, address a group at the Tennessee Economic Development Center.

Jamison Bedding, Inc.

Jamison Bedding, Inc., the largest family-owned bedding company in the United States, has been operating in the Nashville area since 1883 with a single objective: to provide a better night's sleep to its customers. ★ Jamison doesn't make a lot of noise with national advertising or franchising, preferring to let its products speak for themselves. Yet, with more than $35 million in annual sales through some 300 individually owned furniture stores and such major corporate clients as Marriott Corp. and the Opryland Hotel, this time-tested company has plenty of reasons to toot its own horn.

From Corn Shucks to Coiled Steel

For more than 20 years, Jamison has supplied every mattress used in Marriott hotels, including the Courtyard by Marriott motels and Fairfield Inns. Jamison's special hotel mattress, designed with input from Marriott, is "the only set of bedding that will stand up for 15 years in hotel use," says Frank Gorrell III, president of Jamison Bedding.

Gorrell represents the fifth generation of Robert D. Jamison's descendants to run the company. In the company's early days, mattresses were made from such materials as cotton, horse hair, corn shucks, and combinations of straw and wood shavings. Jamison was among the first manufacturers to use coiled wire springs within mattresses. This innovation propelled Jamison Bedding to success, and by 1906, the company was mass-producing mattresses at its new plant in east Nashville.

Persevering through the Great Depression years, Jamison again adapted to changing times in the 1930s, offering some of the first sofas and davenports that converted into bedding. Through it all, the company nurtured a stable family of artisans who continued to craft each product with painstaking detail. Their legacy of attention to quality persists to this day; none of the Jamison mattresses in the 3,000-room Opryland Hotel has ever been found to have a quality defect.

Innovations Spur Growth

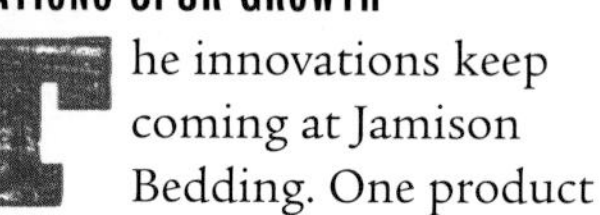

The innovations keep coming at Jamison Bedding. One product improvement is the zero-gravity foam mattress, which Gorrell describes as unlike any other kind that's made. There are five body sections, each offering its own level of support. The coils work in concert with your body contours.

In addition to its Nashville plant, Jamison operates manufacturing facilities in Gallatin, Tennessee, and Albany, Georgia, and maintains executive offices in Franklin, Tennessee. The Nashville facilities, displaced by construction of the city's new NFL stadium after almost 70 years of service, was replaced in October 1996 by a new, 80,000-square-foot facility in the area of Briley Parkway and Brick Church Pike.

In years to come, Jamison plans to stick to the formula that has brought it success for more than 100 years. "We try to provide a better-quality product and a better value to the customer than do the nationally advertised brands," Gorrell explains. For Jamison, part of the equation derives from keeping costs low by avoiding large advertising and marketing expenditures. But the other part—the quality—comes from the people of Jamison, a factor that Gorrell never forgets. "Our mission is to provide the finest product possible to our customers and the finest work environment possible for our employees," he says. "We have a commitment to quality, to our customers, and to our workforce."

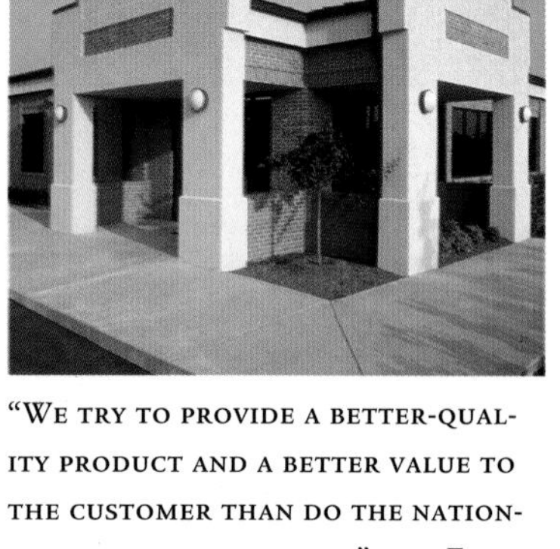

"We try to provide a better-quality product and a better value to the customer than do the nationally advertised brands," says Frank Gorrell III, Jamison Bedding president (top).

In the company's early days, mattresses were made from such materials as cotton, horse hair, corn shucks, and combinations of straw and wood shavings (bottom).

Cooper, Love & Jackson

HEN A COMPANY PLACES ITS CUSTOMERS, RATHER than the president, at the top of the organizational chart, you know it is serious about customer service. Cooper, Love & Jackson, a full-service insurance agency, has been doing just that for more than 100 years.

Cooper, Love & Jackson has built a solid reputation in the Middle Tennessee community since its inception in 1961. However, the heritage of the firm actually dates back to 1885, when William Thomas Love entered the insurance business as a farm agent, soliciting farm insurance throughout the Cumberland Plateau.

Clifford Love, son of the founder, joined him in his Murfreesboro office in 1906, and Clifford Love Jr. took over the business in 1947. In 1952, Love Jr. formed a partnership with Bill Cooper, and later the firm became one of the first tenants in the L&C Tower, then the tallest building in downtown Nashville. Just a few years later, Cooper and Love met Jack Jackson through the Insurors of Nashville and united to form the firm that exists today.

Clay Jackson, son of Jack Jackson, currently serves as president and runs the agency with owner-operators David Sciortino and John Schneider. The trio continues to successfully manage the growth of Cooper, Love & Jackson, which has averaged 10 to 15 percent annual revenue growth for the past five years.

Tailor-Made Policies

Native to Nashville and representing products from major worldwide insurance companies, this independently owned firm has tailored insurance policies as individual as the client.

Cooper, Love & Jackson offers a full spectrum of insurance products ranging from the needs of individuals and small businesses to risk management consulting with publicly held corporations. Personal service, with an independent, objective view of the insurance marketplace, will continue to be of value to the firm's clients, regardless of size.

Retailers, wholesalers, manufacturers, lending institutions, and a vast array of other service providers are served by Cooper, Love & Jackson. The firm also writes medical malpractice policies for physicians and physician groups, professional liability policies for architects and engineers, and many other specialty products such as Directors and Officers Liability Insurance.

To best serve its customers and keep abreast of industry trends and products, Cooper, Love & Jackson values continuous quality improvement, such as continuing education for its sales agents and customer service staff. There is also an ongoing professional development program for all staff members to assure Cooper, Love & Jackson offers and provides the most comprehensive products and services available.

In addition to fulfilling its unique niche in the marketplace, this locally owned and operated firm remains committed to the Nashville and Middle Tennessee community. The firm's employees are active in many local and industry organizations, including the Nashville Area Chamber of Commerce, Insurors of Nashville, Association of Independent Insurance Agents in Tennessee, National Association of Life Underwriters, American Society of Chartered Life Underwriters & Chartered Financial Consultants, Chartered Property and Casualty Underwriters, Risk and Insurance Management Society, and civic and community organizations too numerous to mention.

Focus on the Customer

Cooper, Love & Jackson is committed to aggressive movement into the 21st century. The firm will continue to grow by increasing sales of insurance products and continuing its customer service tradition. However, the main goal of Cooper, Love & Jackson is to never lose sight of the people who really run the company—the customers, whose trust and confidence is earned daily.

Clay T. Jackson serves as president of Cooper, Love & Jackson (left).

Native to Nashville and representing products from major worldwide insurance companies, Cooper, Love & Jackson offers a full spectrum of insurance products ranging from the needs of individuals and small businesses to risk management consulting with publicly held corporations (right).

First Union National Bank of Tennessee

Serving Middle Tennessee for more than a century, the financial institution now known as First Union National Bank of Tennessee has never lost sight of the values upon which it was founded. Since its inception in 1889, the bank has maintained a tradition of trust. ★ In 1889, Herman Justi, a young businessman, felt that Nashville needed a quality company that would manage trusts, wills, and estates. Together with local wholesaler Charles Nelson, prominent physician Walter M. Dake, investor Gales P. Thruston, farmer Joseph Philips, and others, Justi founded the Nashville Trust Company. Nelson became the first chairman of the bank's board.

In July of that same year, the organizers applied for a charter, and one month later the bank was in business. Its letterhead announced, "Boxes to Rent in our new Burglar Proof Vault" and "Loans Negotiated." Surviving the nationwide financial turbulence of the 1890s, the bank grew with the city and entered the new century as a respected pillar of Nashville's economy.

By 1926, Nashville Trust had erected a handsome new headquarters at 315 Union Street, where it held its own in a neighborly but keen competition with the American Trust Company until those two institutions merged in 1930. In the decades that followed, the bank went through several changes of ownership, emerging in the 1970s as Nashville City Bank. After acquiring several banks in the counties surrounding Nashville, Nashville City Bank was acquired by Virginia-based Dominion Bankshares in October 1986.

A Partnership of Strength

In December 1992, First Union Corporation acquired Dominion Bankshares and, with it, the institution once known as the Nashville Trust Company, renaming it First Union National Bank of Tennessee. Today, the bank's customers benefit from the diverse strengths of its parent company. Based in Charlotte, North Carolina, First Union is one of the nation's largest financial institutions, with assets of more than $100 billion and more than 11 million customers from Connecticut to Florida. First Union National Bank of

RICK ALEXANDER & ASSOC.

Since its inception in 1889, today's First Union National Bank of Tennessee has maintained a tradition of trust.

▶ FRED CLARKE

Guiding First Union National Bank of Tennessee today are (from left) Ron Samuels, president of the Metro Region; Beth McCague, chairman, president, and CEO; and Don MacLeod, executive vice president, general banking executive.

Tennessee now has assets of more than $2 billion.

In total, First Union Corporation's full-service banking network has approximately 2,000 offices, making it the nation's largest branch banking system. Long known as a banking innovator, First Union has demonstrated a commitment to investing in the latest technology to better serve its customers. For instance, First Union was one of the first to offer its customers a completely integrated common deposit system within a multistate banking network. The system, known as Emerald, allows the bank to offer new products faster and to achieve merger efficiencies quickly. It links the more than 8 million customers of First Union, enabling them to conduct transactions at any of the bank's branches through the nation's fourth-largest ATM network.

The innovation is still continuing. While the bank will always offer branch service, it is preparing for the banking trends of the future, anticipating that customers will want to conduct more of their financial business through enhanced automated teller machines and interactive video screens, as well as through computers, screen telephones, or televisions located at their homes or work sites. First Union recognizes that its challenge is to provide products and services in the manner most convenient to each individual customer. For that reason, the bank is pioneering alternative delivery methods, ranging from centralized telecommunications centers for one-stop-shopping via toll-free numbers to the development and introduction of card products that use integrated computer chip circuitry, including "smart cards," which have a stored cash value that can replace bills and coins in routine transactions. This management commitment to using proven, cost-effective technology has assured First Union of a place at the forefront of America's banking industry in years to come.

Customer and Community Service

"Our goal is to provide customers with the products they want, when they want them, where they want them, and in the way they want them," says Beth McCague, First Union's chief executive officer. Hand in hand with that commitment to customer service is the bank's commitment to maintain its positive role as a corporate citizen of Nashville. It has extensive programs that offer credit to low- and moderate-income individuals, as well as small and minority-owned businesses. In 1995, First Union was selected by *Working Mother* magazine as one of the 100 Best Companies for working mothers in the nation. And early in 1996, the company received the Corporate Award for the Advancement of Women from the National Council of Women.

The bank has also made a long-term commitment to support education, pledging millions of dollars in corporate resources and employee talent to improve preschool, elementary, and secondary education. A First Union policy allows each employee four hours a month for involvement in educational activities.

As the 20th century ends, First Union National Bank in Nashville continues to build on the strengths it manifested when the century began: innovation in customer service, combined with a deep commitment to the local community.

Baptist Sunday School Board

An internationally known Nashville institution, founded more than a century ago with no funds to support it, is today a significant landmark on the city's skyline. The Baptist Sunday School Board is a vital citizen not only of Nashville, but also of the world, communicating a timeless message through ever changing methods.

Now one of the largest worldwide providers of religious materials, the board was voted into existence by the Southern Baptist convention in 1891 with one assignment—to publish Sunday school literature. J.M. Frost, a Virginia pastor, was named the first leader of the new agency.

Moving to the publishing center of Nashville, Frost began work in a borrowed office. A loan of $5,000 from his wife enabled him to publish the first literature for Sunday schools. From the start, the convention expected the board to be self-supporting, and to this day the agency has never received funds from the denomination. In fact, the board has given millions of dollars and staff support through the years to the local, national, and worldwide work of the Southern Baptist Convention.

The Nashville Baptist Book Store carries religious materials, many of which are produced by the Sunday School Board.

An International Leader in Resources and Ministry

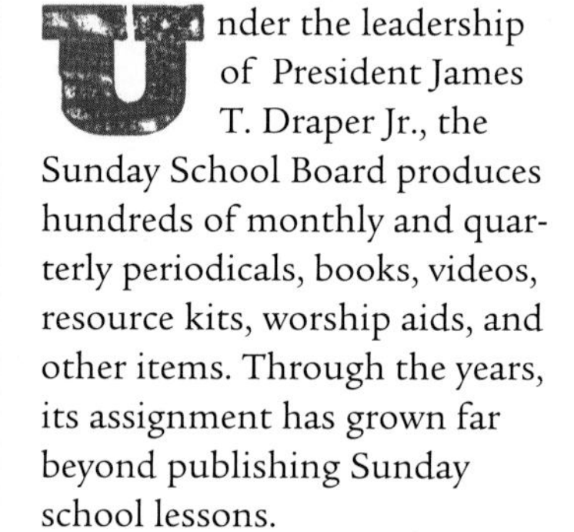

Under the leadership of President James T. Draper Jr., the Sunday School Board produces hundreds of monthly and quarterly periodicals, books, videos, resource kits, worship aids, and other items. Through the years, its assignment has grown far beyond publishing Sunday school lessons.

The board employs more than 1,600 people in its 1 million-square-foot Nashville headquarters; throughout a national chain of more than 60 retail stores; and at its more than 4,500 acres of national conference center property in Ridgecrest, North Carolina, and Glorieta, New Mexico.

While millions of pounds of literature are shipped around the world each year, the board offers more than products, providing an added dimension of ministry.

For example, at the death of a newborn child, a bereaved family contacted the Nashville Baptist Book Store searching for a specific Bible to use at the funeral home. Two employees arranged for the Bible to be delivered to a convenient location, including a sympathy card and a note indicating the Bible was a gift.

An editor, responding to a request from a prison inmate, provided materials for two cell mates who wished to enhance their in-depth Bible study.

A customer service representative who lost more than 100 pounds using First Place, a Christ-centered health program, offers encouragement to customers from her experience, along with facts about the program.

"Leading people to accept Christ as their Savior and grow in their faith is the reason we do what we do," says Draper. "We want to know about the people our products and services are designed to help: the millions who have never heard the good news of Jesus Christ; church members eager to gain a better understanding of the Bible and grow in their faith; choirs practicing over and over to get not only the notes but the message of their music just right; couples struggling in unhappy marriages and those recovering from divorce; individuals plagued by addictions, stress, financial problems, or grief over the loss of a loved one; and college students confronted with a spiritual relativism that weakens their faith. When we keep the people we serve in sight, it makes our work more meaningful. We succeed only as we help churches and individual believers succeed."

A Worldwide Vision

From humble beginnings, the Sunday School Board has emerged as a leader in evangelical publishing and enrichment ministries. In working to meet an ever growing variety of individual and

The Baptist Sunday School Board complex is located in downtown Nashville.

Board President James T. Draper Jr. (center) meets with church staff members during conferences conducted across the United States.

church ministry needs, the board's vision is "to assist local churches and believers to evangelize the world to Christ, develop believers, and grow churches by being the best worldwide provider of relevant, high-quality, high-value Christian products and services."

The board's resources include Bible teaching, discipleship, family needs, church recreation activities, architectural services, media resources, stewardship education, church history education, capital fund-raising, men's and women's enrichment ministries, Christian school and home school ministries, student ministry materials, music literature, and pastor-staff and administration aids. It publishes books specifically for Southern Baptist needs, as well as a range of books and Bibles for the larger evangelical world.

In addition to the international distribution of resources, the board maintains contact with individuals and churches from many parts of the world through its World Wide Web site on the Internet: http://www.bssb.com.

Tours Provide a Firsthand Experience

Thousands of persons each year include a visit to the Sunday School Board as a part of experiencing Nashville's rich heritage. Special features of the Nashville complex include the office in which Frost borrowed space to begin the board's work, the Van Ness Auditorium with its stained-glass parable windows, the E.C. Dargan Research Library, and the World Bridge, where visitors may view both historic memorabilia and contemporary products. A brief video and samples of print products provide an idea of the Sunday School Board's wealth of Christian products and services.

Nashville Speedway USA

HILE THE VISION AT NASHVILLE SPEEDWAY USA IS pointed toward the future, the real story begins with its heritage. The area now occupied by the speedway first opened as a venue for horse track harness races on October 20, 1891. As times changed, so did the track—to accommodate the industrial age's brightest star, it became a one-mile dirt track for auto racing on June 14, 1904.

By the 1940s and 1950s, stock cars, sprint cars, and motorcycles were tearing for the finish on the track, which was still doing double duty as a horse track. By the late 1950s, track operators finished a lighted quarter-mile track for weekly Saturday night racing and a half-mile banked asphalt track to handle special events. At this same time, the first NASCAR National Sweepstakes (forerunner to today's Winston Cup) took place on the brand-new half-mile oval.

After the 1969 racing season, the half-mile oval was reconstructed into a five-eighths-mile "super short track." Boasting 35-degree banked turns, the track became the fastest five-eighths-mile track in the world. It is reported that the banking was so steep and the radius of the turns so short, many local race cars had holes cut into the roofs so drivers could see ahead in the turns. In May 1973, the track again was reconstructed to the present-day 18-degree banked track for the Music City 420.

Through the 1970s and 1980s, the track went through many legal, political, and social changes. By 1985, NASCAR decided no more Winston Cup races would be run in Nashville. While this looked like the kiss of death for the track, there were two things that kept the Nashville racing tradition alive: the fans and their beloved heroes—the drivers.

MIKE HORTON

COURTESY OF METRO ARCHIVES

The starting field for the 1996 BellSouth Mobility/Opryland 320 Busch Series Race moves past a jam-packed grandstand at Nashville Speedway USA (top).

The pace car leads a field of modified specials at the old Fairgrounds Speedway half-mile track on September 4, 1961 (bottom).

Breathing New Life into an Old Friend

In 1994, racing industry veteran Bob Harmon took over the helm of what many thought was a ship adrift. As racing blossomed in popularity across the country, Nashville's racing hopes were pinned on one man.

Harmon and his management crew, of whom he speaks with admiration and respect, recognized that the fans, the drivers, and the corporate sponsors could all come together to make Nashville Speed-

RICKY HAYNES

DARRELL WALTRIP (SECOND FROM RIGHT) POSES WITH CREWMEMBERS IN VICTORY LANE AFTER ONE OF HIS 67 WINS AT NASHVILLE SPEEDWAY.

way USA the best and brightest hope for racing in Tennessee.

Initiating computer programs, special events, major corporate sponsorships, personal seat licenses, and a genuine appeal to families who love racing, Harmon and his staff revved up the engines on what was to be the next step for the storied track. In addition to Harmon, Velma Jones, vice president/general manager; Dave Kohler, director of public relations; and a full-time staff of eight collectively brought to the starting line more than 200 years of racing experience.

Today, the Nashville track is the premier short track in the nation. It averages 10,000 fans each weekend at the Fairgrounds, receives extensive local and regional media coverage, and has become the gateway for the up-and-coming NASCAR superstars of tomorrow.

THE DRIVERS AND THE FANS

The winningest driver of all time at Nashville Speedway USA is favorite son Darrell Waltrip with 67 total wins. Other famous drivers who have captured the checkered flag at Nashville Speedway USA include Richard Petty, Curtis Turner, Bobbie and Donnie Allison, Cale Yarborough, Dale Earnhardt, Rusty Wallace, Harry Gant, and Clifton "Coo-Coo" Marlin.

Today, a new breed of American heroes has gone on to be NASCAR superstars. The stellar list includes Sterling Marlin (two-time Daytona 500 winner); Bobby Hamilton; David, Jeff, and Mark Green; and Jeremy Mayfield. "We produce more NASCAR superstars than any other racetrack in the country," says Harmon. "This is the Home of the Champions."

Its commitment to the drivers is another reason for the track's popularity with the racing teams. In 1995, the approximate per-week purse was $16,500; that number grew to $18,700 per week in 1996, and has been increased to $25,230 in 1997.

The track is proud to sponsor the Mark Collie Celebrity Race for Diabetes every year, raising more than $1 million in the last three years to help find a cure for diabetes. The track cosponsors the Brooks and Dunn Summer Legends Shootout Series, where celebrities drive for charitable donations. Harmon contends that the racing community is the most generous of any sport. It is not uncommon for drivers and pit crews to collect money for racing families in need, and for the Nashville fans to give with overwhelming kindness.

The fans also are recognized as brand and driver loyal, arriving at the track in their NASCAR-patched clothing and sporting the colors of their favorite driver.

THE EVENTS

side from the roar of the crowd and the rumble of the engines heard on Saturday nights mid-March through October, there are three special events that attract record crowds every year to the speedway. Held in April, the BellSouth Mobility/Opryland 320 roars through Nashville, challenging 40 of the best and the brightest stars in NASCAR's Busch Grand National Series. Traditionally held in August, the Federated Auto Parts 250 NASCAR Craftsman Truck Series is offered as the premier summertime racing event in the Mid-South. And continuing to draw record crowds is the Mannheim Auctions All American 400, traditionally held in mid-October.

With a rich and colorful tradition that stretches from horses to horsepower, Nashville Speedway USA has ridden successfully into the winner's circle as the True Home of the Champions.

H.G. Hill Realty Co.

NE DAY IN APRIL 1995, NASHVILLE'S QUIETEST REAL ESTATE company made a lot of noise. With the opening of the Hill Place residential development, H.G. Hill Realty Co. created a sensation. Buyers lined up to purchase lots on the historic Hill farm, often bidding well in excess of the asking price. Half the lots sold by sunset.

It was a rare moment in the spotlight for H.G. Hill Realty. The firm has maintained a relatively low profile over the years—even as it grew into one of Nashville's most prominent commercial landlords, one of its largest sources of property tax revenue, and one of its most generous corporate citizens.

ROBT AMES COOK

H.G. Hill Realty has broadened its horizons to encompass national, as well as local, tenants.

H.G. Hill Realty traces its origins to the same street corner as companion company H.G. Hill Stores: 18th Avenue North and State Street, where H.G. Hill Sr. opened his first grocery store in 1895. Today, on the ledgers of H.G. Hill Realty, this parcel is identified simply as lot #1.

Partner to a Growing City

Many of the numerous commercial properties owned by the company in Metro Nashville started out long ago as store sites. Scores of local independent merchants are now Hill tenants, many operating in neighborhood shopping centers anchored by H.G. Hill Stores. The company is also a landlord to businesses in surrounding communities such as Brentwood, Clarksville, Columbia, Hendersonville, and Murfreesboro.

Hill Realty's first residential development took place before World War II on land that H.G. Hill Sr. purchased early in the century. A portion of the tract had once belonged to Daniel Dunham, one of Nashville's original settlers. As the area was developed, it came to be known as Hillwood.

"A great deal of care was taken in how it was laid out," recalls John B. Hardcastle, president of Hill Realty. "There aren't any straight roads in Hillwood. It's all contours. It was designed to be parklike in its layout." Home building in Hillwood accelerated in the late 1940s and 1950s, its large, tree-shaded lots setting the standard for high-quality suburban living in postwar Nashville.

In the Hillwood area and elsewhere in Nashville, H.G. Hill Realty has donated land numerous times for public and philanthropic purposes—including two police facilities, two public schools, a church, a country club, and three YMCA facilities. The company is also among the top corporate taxpayers on Nashville's property assessment rolls.

Breaking New Ground

H.G. Hill Realty has broadened its horizons to encompass national, as well as local, tenants in its commercial properties—building new facilities for Walgreen and Eckerd drugstores, Blockbuster Video, and Ruby Tuesday Restaurants on Hill properties since 1995.

As the first families move into Hill Place, the company is once again helping to shape the way Nashville lives. The 99 parcels on the 141-acre property are virtually sold out—both the larger, luxury home lots and the quarter-acre lots of the Caldwell Close planned unit development within Hill Place. Soon, the former pasture of the Hill family's farm will be a community unto itself.

With the opening of the Hill Place residential development, H.G. Hill Realty Co. created a sensation.

ROBT AMES COOK

H.G. Hill Stores, Inc.

A BROWSE THROUGH THE ARCHIVES OF THE MORE THAN 100-year-old Hill grocery chain shows how it has remained imbued, from the chain's beginnings to this day, with the values of founder H.G. Hill Sr. and his way of doing business. ★ A 1904 newspaper advertisement for Hill's downtown store makes clear that then, as now, the company was an innovator. The ad spells out a cash-and-carry policy that revolutionized grocery shopping in the Southeast.

A 1915 price list for "flour, meat, lard, fruits, etc." bears the trademark Hill guarantee of customer satisfaction, a policy unchanged since its founding in 1895.

A 1934 photo of a storefront shows a sign with the motto generations of Nashville-area shoppers know by heart: "You always do better at Hill's."

Grocer to Generations

Traditions are the hallmark of Hill's—among them a tradition of trailblazing. As the company enters its second century, it combines the bedrock values of local family ownership with a new spirit, expressed in such recent developments as Sunday opening, prepared foods, and many other new features.

In its first 98 years, H.G. Hill Stores had two chairmen. Horace G. Hill Jr. took over upon his father's death in 1942 and actively took part in operations until two days before he died in 1993, at the age of 92.

Taking over at the dawn of the supermarket era, H.G. Hill Jr. engineered fundamental strategic changes in the company. Before World War II, the local Hill franchise had included more than 100 small grocery stores. H.G. Hill Jr. concentrated that capacity in fewer, larger outlets and decided to shed the company's holdings in other areas of the Southeast.

The civic and philanthropic deeds of both the father and the son stir warm memories for many Nashvillians. During the Great Depression, H.G. Hill Sr. opened his wallet to rescue a local bank from collapse and also helped both daily newspapers stay afloat. He and his son were long known as major benefactors to many charitable causes, such as Peabody College and the YMCA.

▶ ROBT AMES COOK

One of the earliest H.G. Hill grocers, located downtown on the corner of 2nd Avenue at the Public Square, gave birth to today's modern chain.

Old Values, New Faces

Today the great-grandchildren of customers who traded with H.G. Hill Sr. on Nashville's old Public Square shop at 14 Hill supermarkets in and around the city. One dollar of every 10 spent on groceries in Nashville is spent at Hill's. In recent years, amid an ongoing campaign to remodel, revamp, and enlarge the stores, even more shoppers have chosen Hill's: Its share of the local market has grown 2 percent since 1994.

Wentworth Caldwell Jr., nephew of H.G. Hill Jr. and now chairman of H.G. Hill Stores, represents the third generation involved with the company. (Daughter Ashley Caldwell, well known for her appearances in Hill's television ads; Hill Granbery; and Jimmy Granbery represent the fourth generation.)

"I started out sweeping the parking lot at 29th and West End when I was 16," Wentworth Caldwell remembers fondly. Still, among the extended family of Hill's employees, quite a few have been on the payroll since before Caldwell got that first job in the 1950s. In a city that has changed dramatically over the years, their familiar faces and friendly service offer a welcome continuity to Nashville shoppers.

▶ ROBT AMES COOK

Visiting the old H.G. Hill Food Store #68 in Hillsboro Village was always a treat. The fresh produce available at today's Hill stores speaks to the ongoing quality of products sold there.

CASTNER KNOTT CO.

ROLLEY CARS ONCE CARRIED LADIES DRESSED IN THEIR BEST to downtown Nashville where fine shopping was to be had. Whether being fitted for new gloves or purchasing an outfit for a child, a morning of browsing at Castner Knott was an event. ★ For almost 100 years Castner Knott Co. has clothed the families of Nashville and its surrounding areas and brought stylish furnishings into their homes. It has remained true to its vision to be a highly profitable, leading department store through its customer service, value, fashion, and visual presentation.

Founded by Charles Castner and William Knott in 1898, the first Castner Knott department store was located in the historic residence of Nashville's prominent DeMoville family on Summer Street (now 5th Avenue) downtown. Following rapid growth, the store moved a few blocks in 1906 to 7th Avenue and Church Street, where it remained until February 1996.

In 1914, Castner Knott was purchased by Mercantile Stores Company, Inc. of New York City. Today, Mercantile is headquartered in Fairfield, Ohio, operating 106 stores in five divisions with 14 names across 17 states. The company is among the top organizations in its industry in per-square-foot sales. As an affiliate, Castner Knott has enjoyed major expansions and record sales.

Since its inception, 14 Castner Knott stores have opened in Middle Tennessee, southern Kentucky, and northern Alabama, as well as a freestanding Hair & Nail Salon in the Hermitage/Old Hickory, Tennessee, area. While the store has been an anchor in the Green Hills-area shopping scene since 1955, Nashville's outlying suburbs are the lucky recipients of the company's recent expansion. Bellevue Center in Bellevue, CoolSprings Galleria in Franklin, and Stones River Mall in Murfreesboro have all opened Castner Knott locations in the 1990s.

MODERATELY PRICED AND DESIGNER MERCHANDISE

astner Knott no longer sells groceries as it did at its downtown location in the early 1900s, but for the most part, the product mix has not changed for this hometown department store. Today, a selection of moderately priced and designer merchandise is presented in a specialty shop atmosphere. Marble and brass appointments, comfort lighting, and modern

CLOCKWISE FROM RIGHT:
CASTNER KNOTT CARRIES DESIGNER SPORTSWEAR AND SEPARATES FROM SUCH DESIGNERS AS ELLEN TRACY, DKNY, DANA BUCHMAN, GUESS, LIZ CLAIBORNE, AND CHRISTIAN DIOR.

FOR THE BUSINESSMAN AND -WOMAN, CASTNER KNOTT OFFERS MANY LINES OF DESIGNER SUITS AND ACCESSORIES.

CASTNER KNOTT CATERS TO ITS YOUNGEST CUSTOMERS THROUGH THE INFANT BOUTIQUE, WHICH OFFERS A WIDE VARIETY OF GIFTS, TOYS, AND CLOTHES FOR INFANTS AND TODDLERS.

fixtures help showcase the clothing, cosmetics, and home furnishing offerings.

Merchandising and buying teams working from the local area with Mercantile's corporate staff are able to quickly react to customers' needs. These professionals monitor trends and buy some of the finest brand names, including Ellen Tracy, DKNY, Dana Buchman, Guess, Estée Lauder, Chanel, Clinique, Liz Claiborne, Lancome, Christian Dior, Hart Schaffner & Marx, Tommy Hilfiger, Ralph Lauren, Waterford, Calphalon, and Lenox. The store also presents private labels, including Kate Landry, Club Classics, Sutter & Grant, and 955 Originals. Alteration services are available at each store to assist with a perfect fit.

Customer Service and Satisfaction

s time is a precious commodity for many shoppers these days, Castner Knott proudly offers a free personal and corporate shopping service. Trained service professionals work to alleviate demands on shoppers' time and do everything from selecting a new seasonal wardrobe for a busy executive to selecting and wrapping gifts for special occasions such as Secretary's Day.

Customer satisfaction is the company's primary goal, and a number of services have been developed based on customer needs and wants. These include a toll-free phone order service, convenient credit options, and state-of-the-art hair and nail salons. Additionally, a popular bridal gift registry and china club have helped many newlyweds furnish their homes; a baby registry, a grandparents club, and a hosiery and intimate apparel club provide added value for shoppers; and over the holidays, gift cards and gift wrap services enjoy a flurry of activity.

While Castner Knott stores carry a high level of merchandise and serve many economic and social levels, the company takes great pride in being the department store "where there are no strangers" and "where the customer comes first." Sales and customer service staffs are trained in both people and product skills to ensure a friendly attitude and a keen sense of how best to satisfy the customer. The company is voraciously committed to customer satisfaction and backs every sale with this statement: "Our guarantee is the only thing we won't take back."

Community Contributions

ith an interest in community service, the company often participates in fund-raisers to benefit charitable and civic organizations. One of the ways this is done is by staging and wardrobing fashion shows. Past shows have included the Castner Knott Designer Show to benefit the Nashville Symphony; the Ladies' Auxiliary of the National Kidney Foundation of Middle Tennessee Fashion Show; the Music City Fashion Show to benefit the T.J. Martell Foundation; and the FrivoliTIES Fashion Show and Fundraiser benefiting Nashville Family and Children's Services. Castner Knott is also one of the top three local contributors and corporate sponsors of the March of Dimes' Walk America. As a corporate sponsor of the Nashville Ballet Premiere Season, the company has received the Corporate Service Award for its financial and creative commitment to the performing arts. The company also supports the Tennessee Botanical Gardens of Cheekwood and the Tennessee Performing Arts Center by underwriting various events.

A New Century of Service

uture growth is based on past performance, and Castner Knott anticipates the 21st century with the same energy that propelled it through the 20th century. A global mix of merchandise, trends, and lifestyles has created a strong need for the stores to bring a variety of new ideas, brand names, and innovative concepts into the marketplace. The company's local and corporate buyers and merchandisers work in worldwide markets to meet this challenge.

A Return to Home

ecognizing today's focus on the family and a trend toward customers spending more time in the home, Castner Knott has aggressively explored the merchandise mix and lifestyle and created the company's first freestanding market center in CoolSprings Galleria. It is a seamless home store where customers can enjoy a shopping environment that includes everything from the latest culinary art to a full range of home furnishings. It also includes an upscale coffeeshop as well as a Ralph Lauren for the Home shop, the largest in Mercantile's 106-store network. The futuristic store will operate under the signature of Castner Knott for the Home.

Striving for progress; succeeding in service excellence. That's the credo for Castner Knott's past, present, and future.

Castner Knott's extensive selection of menswear and boys wear ensures that father and son are dressed impeccably (top).

Castner Knott's new home concept is a seamless home store where customers can enjoy a shopping environment that includes everything from the latest culinary art to a full range of home furnishings (bottom).

NationsBank

NATIONAL COMPANY WITH AN ACTIVE COMMUNITY SPIRIT, NationsBank of Tennessee is committed to meeting the needs of every customer—both consumer and commercial—with the same consistent quality of service. NationsBank has a retail banking franchise in 16 states and the District of Columbia. It has more than 5,000 locations in the Southeast, Southwest, Mid-Atlantic, and Midwest. With financial assets totaling more than $239 billion in 1996, NationsBank became the fourth-largest bank in the United States. NationsBank has the product breadth and geographic scope to help its customers operate in an increasingly global economy.

A Nashville Heritage

ationsBank dates back to Nashville's German American Bank, founded in 1916. In 1923, the name changed to Commerce Union Bank, a name familiar to most Middle Tennesseans. For more than six decades, Commerce Union served residents and businesses of the burgeoning Middle Tennessee area and eventually expanded to communities across the state.

During the late 1980s and early 1990s, the banking industry experienced rapid consolidation. Commerce Union merged with Sovran Financial, whose history dates back to the 1860s in Virginia. Sovran Financial later merged with the Citizen and Southern Corporation of Georgia in 1990. In 1991, C & S/Sovran merged with North Carolina-based NCNB to form NationsBank. In 1996, NationsBank substantially expanded its franchise with the purchase of Boatmen's Bancshares, Inc., which added seven more states to its delivery system.

A Diverse Financial Services Company

ationsBank serves three broad customer groups—the General Bank, Global Finance, and nonbank companies or Financial Services.

The General Bank serves individuals and small- to medium-sized businesses. It provides customers with traditional banking services, along with products such as credit cards from the eighth-largest bank card issuer, mortgages from one of the top five mortgage servicing companies, and indirect auto financing. Commercial customers turn to NationsBank for financing, investment services, asset management, and many other needs. The NationsBank Private Client Group has customized resources for high-income and/or high-net-worth individuals, including portfolio management and estate and personal trusts, a leading fiduciary manager of oil and gas properties, and a leading manager of bank proprietary mutual funds.

Global Finance serves larger corporate customers, government agencies, and institutions. Operating in 34 states and 10 foreign countries, the Global Finance unit is a leading provider of credit,

▼ VANDO ROGERS

Located in the heart of the financial district in downtown Nashville, the unique NationsBank Building is on the corner of Fourth and Union.

VANDO ROGERS

NationsBank Bank at Work Group has developed partnerships with companies in Tennessee to offer a comprehensive array of financial products and services as an added feature to employee benefit programs. NationsBank has on-site, full-service banking centers at several company headquarters in Middle Tennessee, including the Ingram Banking Resource Center shown here.

investment banking, loan syndications, interest rate protection, debt underwritings, and mergers and acquisitions advice. With its diverse range of financial resources, NationsBank has the expertise, experience, and economic power to meet the fast changing needs of corporate America.

The fastest growing area of NationsBank is its Financial Services division. Financial Services is a group of nonbank companies, doing business as NationsCredit. NationsCredit Consumer provides secured and unsecured personal loans, home equity, and mortgage loans to consumers who do not meet the traditional bank customer profile. NationsCredit Commercial focuses on small- to medium-market companies with specialized capital or financial needs.

Community-Minded

NationsBank has a long tradition of supporting the arts, education, and health and human services, as well as other civic programs. In addition to encouraging its employees to volunteer their time and energies, NationsBank of Tennessee makes significant financial contributions to a myriad of causes and programs.

Tens of thousands of Nashvillians attend the annual Iroquois Steeplechase, for which NationsBank is the Patron of the Day. Proceeds from this popular horse race benefit the Vanderbilt University Children's Hospital. The bank's support of the Nashville Symphony goes back more than 30 years. It is also an active supporter of the NationsBank Pop Concert Series.

Through the company's support of such organizations as Humanities Outreach of Tennessee, the Nashville Shakespeare Festival, and the Cumberland Chamber Orchestra, schoolchildren of Middle Tennessee are exposed to these performances. NationsBank has been a long time Adopt-a-School partner. The bank is currently supporting the Caldwell Early Childhood Center with funds, employee volunteers, and use of facilities.

NationsBank of Tennessee has received high accolades and awards for its community involvement, including the Corporate Award from both the YWCA Academy for Women of Achievement and the National Conference of Christians and Jews, as well as the Points of Excellence Award from the PENCIL Foundation.

Financial Center of the Future

NationsBank remains committed to meeting the constantly changing needs of its customers by identifying and serving customers according to their needs and preference. NationsBank is expanding the delivery channels and building the systems to give its customers 24-hour access, seven days a week. The bank is also expanding its access in non-traditional locations such as supermarkets, convenience stores, and gas stations. NationsBank of Tennessee now has nearly 400 ATMs throughout the state. For those looking for an even more convenient banking solution, NationsBank offers PC banking as well as information on the Internet.

Growing leaps and bounds, NationsBank currently serves more than 14 million households and businesses in the United States and select international markets through its broad retail and global banking network. Grounded in social responsibility and fueled by an open culture that encourages diverse opinions, rewards individual achievement, and fosters teamwork, NationsBank is poised for continued success.

VANDO ROGERS

The Small Business Resource Center—sponsored by NationsBank, U.S. Small Business Administration, and U.S. Department of Commerce Minority Business Development Agency—provides business owners with information intended to enhance their knowledge and capabilities to increase the chances of their business' survival and prosperity.

DuPont Old Hickory

oodrow Wilson was president when DuPont's Old Hickory plant was first conceived. World War I was still being fought, and Delaware-based DuPont—one of the oldest continuously operating industrial enterprises in the world—built a gunpowder factory in accordance with a government request, located in the rural environs east of Nashville.

Though the armistice came before the plant could contribute to the war effort, the Old Hickory facility was destined to become a part of history on the home front.

Old Hickory is the worldwide headquarters for two of DuPont's businesses—PET Resins & Chemicals and Sontara® Technologies.

In 1929, it began manufacturing rayon, a cellulose-based synthetic fabric that—when used to make clothing and other products—changed the American way of life.

In the 1950s, DuPont Old Hickory was recognized as the world's safest industrial plant. Many of the parent corporation's top leaders, including current Chief Executive Officer Jack Krol and former CEO (now DuPont Chairman) Edgar S. Woolard Jr., worked at Old Hickory earlier in their careers.

Weaving the Fabric of a Community

s the years went by, the DuPont Old Hickory plant anchored the suburban development of the area. Today, it has grown to encompass a more than 500-acre industrial campus, whose deep roots in the community are exemplified in institutions like the DuPont Hadley Middle School and DuPont Elementary School, schools currently "adopted" by the Old Hickory plant.

The Old Hickory facility is the worldwide headquarters for two of DuPont's businesses—PET Resins & Chemicals and Sontara® Technologies. PET Resins & Chemicals offers a variety of versatile, polyester-based products for a broad range of end users that include films, fibers, engineering resins, and specialty products, and also offers opportunities through key technology to recycle polyester-based products for reuse. The plant also produces materials for superior quality videotape as part of an American-Japanese joint venture, Teijin-DuPont Film, Inc. Sontara Technologies offers a family of products made from spunlaced fabric in a process that uses high-pressure water jets to needle the fibers into a strong sheet structure.

Discovery, Inc.

hat these products have in common is DuPont's legacy—in Krol's words—as "a discovery company."

"Building on a long record of innovation, DuPont is committed to using science and technology to improve everyday life," Krol says. "As we move into the 21st century, our goals are clear. We intend to compete globally, to sharpen our business focus, and to increase productivity.

"At the same time, we are committed to safety, health, and environmental excellence; to empowering people; and to extending our significant scientific and technological achievements even further."

In 1996, for the ninth year in a row, *Working Mother* magazine tabbed DuPont as one of the most family friendly companies in America—citing its work-life programs and flextime, job-sharing, and telecommuting arrangements. Simply put, DuPont makes a serious investment in its most important resource: its workforce.

The quality of its people has always set DuPont apart—people committed to making life easier and better for everybody, proud to be a part of an enterprise making "better things for better living."

That mission was true when the first rayon rolled from Old Hickory's mills in 1929. And it is just as true today.

Tennessee Orthopaedic Alliance, P.A.

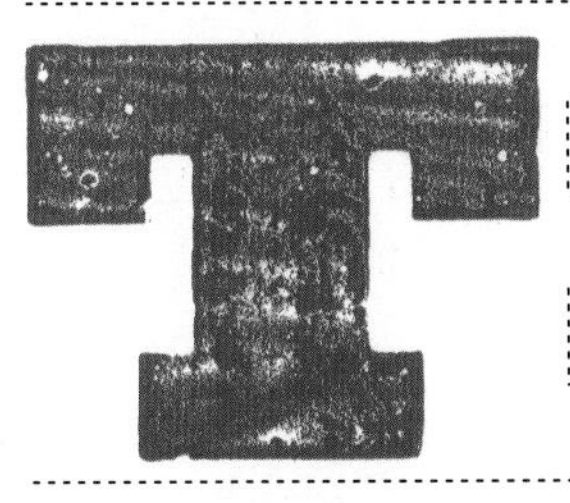

ennessee Orthopaedic Alliance, P.A. (TOA), a premier provider of orthopaedic care, is one of Middle Tennessee's most established medical practices, dating back to 1926. As the largest orthopaedic practice in Middle Tennessee, the group is able to offer comprehensive and cost-effective care for musculoskeletal diseases and disorders.

Tradition of Excellence

hen Dr. George Carpenter Sr. began one of Nashville's first practices of orthopaedic surgery in 1926, he established two fundamental goals: to provide the highest-quality patient care and to be responsive to patients' needs. That practice, the Nashville Orthopaedic Associates, grew successfully and eventually merged in 1994 with Orthopaedic Surgical Associates, a group launched by another founding father of orthopaedics in Nashville, Dr. Eugene Regen Sr.

Although the practice changed its name to Tennessee Orthopaedic Associates in 1994, the tenets set forth by Carpenter remain true today. "Our practice is committed to delivering the highest level of care for the treatment of any kind of bone or joint disorder," says Barrett Rosen, M.D., president of TOA. "We offer complete care that includes diagnosis, education, treatment, and rehabilitation. These services are provided in the most convenient and economic manner possible."

TOA's group consists of 33 of the region's most highly respected orthopaedists. Many have served as past presidents of professional societies including the Nashville Academy of Medicine, Nashville Orthopaedic Society, Tennessee Medical Association, American Academy of Orthopaedics, and American Hand Society.

In the pursuit of the highest level of care for patients, TOA has focused on subspecialization into the many areas of orthopaedics that now benefit from additional training beyond residency. TOA physicians have received fellowship training in spine surgery, total joint replacement, joint revision, hand surgery, laser surgery, sports medicine and arthroscopy, physiatry, foot and ankle surgery, and pediatric orthopaedics and scoliosis.

While serving patients is its foremost commitment, TOA is also dedicated to meeting the needs of employers, insurance company managers, and attorneys. The size and scope of TOA is integral to fulfilling these commitments through the management of its four central offices. TOA maintains offices adjacent to Baptist Hospital, in Nashville's Centennial Medical Center, at Saint Thomas Hospital, and in nearby Murfreesboro.

Future of Orthopaedic Care

OA's response is forward looking and innovative when dealing with the changes under way in today's managed care medical delivery system. "We are a results-oriented practice, continually monitoring our services and efficiency. The pursuit of cost-effective medicine, attention to research, and quality assurance methods has helped us maintain high standards," says Mark Christofersen, M.D.

TOA's surgeons and the highly specialized nature of their work is further testament to Nashville's growing reputation as a leading center of the health care industry. Their personal care for patients is a time-honored practice that finds its roots in its founders and its hope in the future.

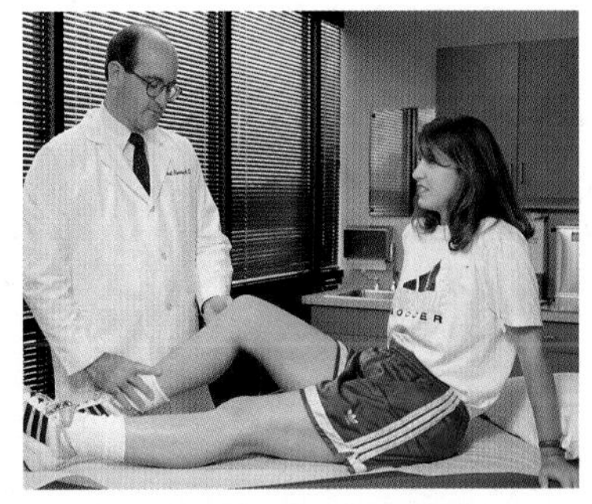

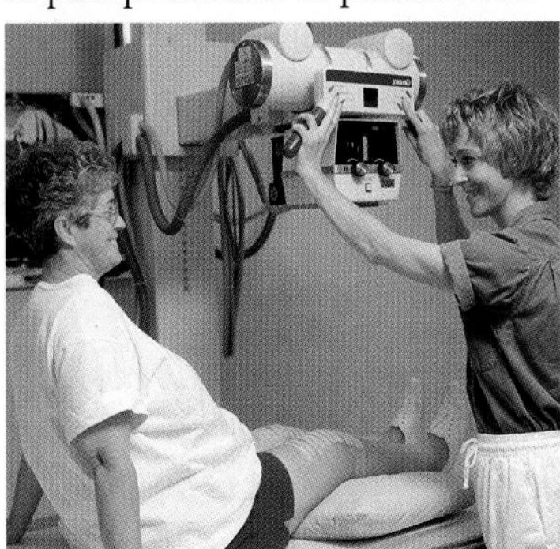

Dr. Stewart Stowers examines a student from Hendersonville High School, as part of Tennessee Orthopaedic Alliance's contribution to the Nashville-area community (top).

Dr. Jeffrey Herring discusses a treatment plan with a pediatric patient (bottom right).

Becky Kreitner, RRT, prepares to x-ray the knees of a bilateral total joint recipient (bottom left).

Francis & Lusky Co., Inc.

HEN HIS BUSINESS PARTNER DISAPPEARED WITH THE company till in 1919, J.C. "Julius Caesar" Lusky's printing enterprise came to a sudden halt. But in that same year, he quickly assembled his new team, enlisting the help of a young pressman, Virgil W. Francis. The name of the new company was easy—Francis & Lusky.

This partnership between the Francis family and the Lusky family has endured for more than 75 years and is still going strong. Today the fourth generations of the two families manage one of the oldest full-service printing and sales promotion companies in Nashville.

With such pearls of wisdom as "treat your customers in a way that when you see them next time, you're greeted with a smile instead of a frown" passed through each generation, it's no wonder the company has flourished. The strong work ethic of the two families and their commonsense approach to customer service has contributed significantly to Francis & Lusky's success. The company now posts annual revenues of approximately $14 million and has received countless industry awards.

In addition to providing calendar manufacturing and commercial printing services, Francis & Lusky imprints promotional products with corporate logos and seals.

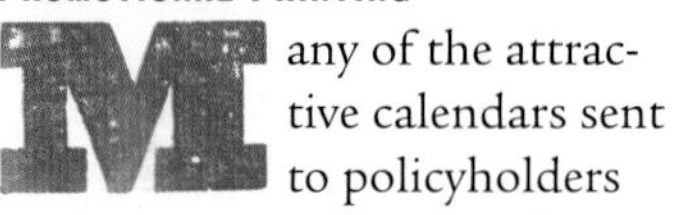

Promotional Printing

Many of the attractive calendars sent to policyholders by insurance agents are printed by Francis & Lusky. In fact, the company is now the fifth-largest calendar company in the country and the largest calendar co-op company. And while the calendar business has a short, three-month production span, the sheer volume makes this area the company's core profit maker.

Unique to the printing industry is Francis & Lusky's prepress program, which allows many of its customers the ability to transmit all prepress information electronically and to customize each calendar. This is particularly important to insurance companies who want to customize calendars with the names of each agent. Several pieces of equipment in the facility have been specially designed for Francis & Lusky as a result of the company's search for cost-effective solutions to the myriad calendars being produced. Another unique feature is the fact that the entire process—prepress, printing, binding, sales, and shipping—is completed under one roof.

The seasonality of the calendar business affords Francis & Lusky the ability to expand upon its existing resources and move into the traditional commercial printing business—printing product catalogs, brochures, and presentation folders. "We're in a unique position to be a low-cost provider of quality promotional printing," says Richard Francis, president and chief executive officer. "The sheer volume of our calendar business creates our profit. Any promotional printing we do outside our calendar business creates a win-win situation. We're able to cover our year-round overhead while providing our customers with prices that are significantly below market rates. Promotional printing is an area that we plan to grow in the future."

Advertising Specialty Distributors

In addition to its printing ventures, Francis & Lusky provides the beautifully stylized lead crystal awards presented to the winning artists at the annual Country Music Awards for 28 years. While most Americans are watching the nationally televised program from the comfort of their living rooms, Chairman of the Board Larry Lusky enjoys a unique backstage perspective of the Grand Old Opry as he hands the awards to the presenters.

If that doesn't captivate every country music fan and capture the essence of Nashville, consider this: All the exquisite bronze plaques at the Country Music Hall of Fame, featuring names like Roy Acuff, Loretta Lynn, and Johnny Cash, are also supplied by Francis & Lusky.

Those are perhaps two of the most visible examples of another facet of the company's business—advertising specialty distribution. Out of 12,000 promotional products companies in the United States, Francis & Lusky's sales and distribution put the firm in the top 1 percent.

The final facet of the business, launched in 1997, is the production of motivational books.

With a soup-to-nuts approach, the company manages the creating, writing, printing, publishing, and sales of these popular gift books.

A Spirit of Service

ll areas of Francis & Lusky's business are serviced by its 100-plus employees, who maintain a customer-oriented approach. Chairman of the Board, Emeritus Monnie Lusky proudly notes that all the family members were raised in the business to do the right thing. "We have a passion for making it easy for people to do business with us," he adds. Larry echoes his father's sentiments: "The customer is far and away the most important part of our business." The underlying corporate credo is "if you're not serving the customer directly, you'd better be serving someone who is."

As a caring commercial resident of Nashville for almost 80 years, Francis & Lusky does its best to serve the community. The company contributes financially to the United Way and to many of the area's colleges and universities, as well as participating in Nashville's Adopt-a-School program. Many employees represent the company in organizations like the Lion's and Kiwanis clubs.

The company's policy of not taking anyone or anything for granted is evident in the way it treats its customers and in the way it respects employees. Francis & Lusky's commitment to its employees, its product, and its customers is a testament to the company's lasting success and to the unusual duration of the partnership between the two families. Perhaps that commitment is also why Francis & Lusky's first customer in 1919 is still a customer today.

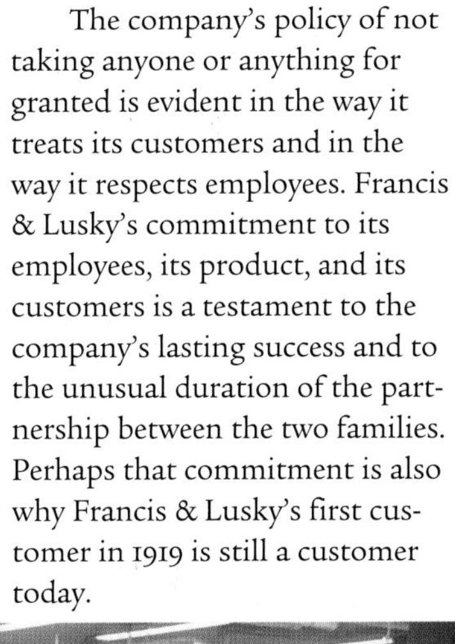

Clockwise from top left:
Francis & Lusky recently acquired two additional four-color printing presses, which have increased the company's capacity and improved its promotional printing capabilities.

Francis & Lusky provides full publishing and bindery capabilities with a complete selection of customized and stock designs.

Francis & Lusky's customer service representatives work closely with customers from the moment orders are placed until the items are delivered.

With more than 60,000 square feet of warehouse, manufacturing, and office space in one location, Francis & Lusky representatives can ensure that products are taken care of every step of the way.

J.C. Bradford & Co.

ROM ITS BEGINNINGS IN NASHVILLE 70 YEARS AGO, J.C. Bradford & Co. has grown to be a regional investment powerhouse, with 96 offices throughout the Southeast. As one of the few securities firms in the country to survive the 1929 stock market crash and Great Depression, J.C. Bradford & Co. has a long history of offering customers in the Southeast the best in personalized service and Sun Belt financial market expertise.

Surviving Hard Times

In 1927, J.C. Bradford Sr. was looking for a new business challenge. Previously, he had turned around the performance of Piggly Wiggly grocery stores, served as vice president of American National Bank of Nashville, and run his own insurance company. That year, Bradford purchased a small securities business, the Joe B. Palmer Company, for $10,000. He set up shop in the Nashville Trust Building, and J.C. Bradford & Co. was born.

On January 1, 1929, Nashville executive Walter Robinson entered into a partnership with Bradford that was dissolved 11 months later after the stock market crash. This left J.C. Bradford alone to guide his remaining clients through a treacherous postcrash stock market.

But it was the flexibility of the one-man shop that allowed J.C. Bradford & Co. to survive when other firms were failing.

"I think as everyone else left, my father sat there and kept fighting," says James Bradford Jr., now senior partner at J.C. Bradford & Co.

"At one time, things got so bad he told his bookkeeper to send checks to all the clients for the credit balances in their accounts. Then one day, a customer walked into his office, pulled out a check for $98,000 and asked him why it had been sent.

"My father told him with banks failing, he did not want his customers to be dragged down

In 1927, J.C. Bradford Sr. was looking for a new business challenge and purchased a small securities business, the Joe B. Palmer Company. He set up shop in the Nashville Trust Building, and J.C. Bradford & Co. was born.

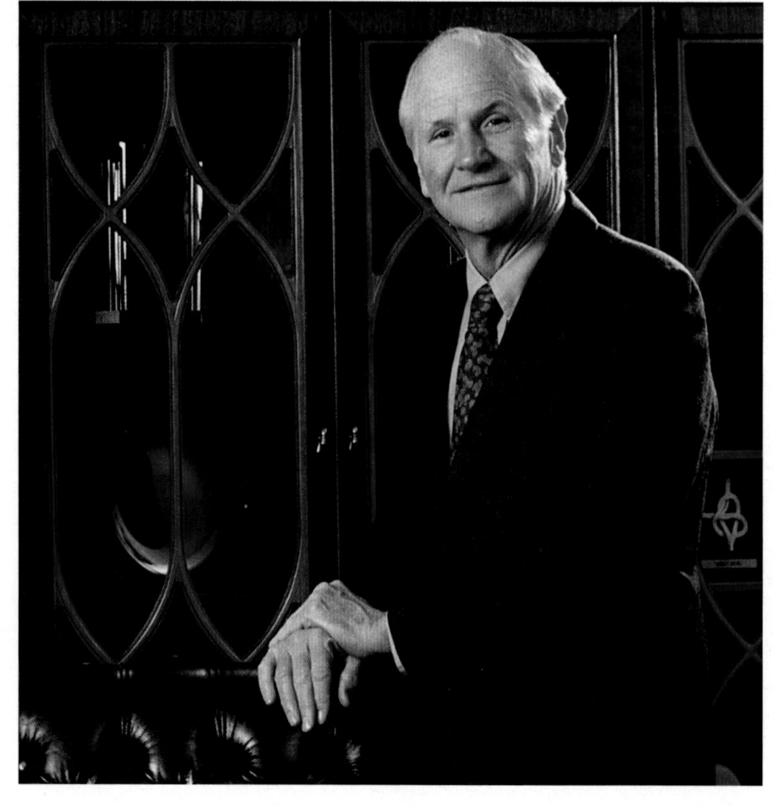

In 1959, J.C. Bradford Jr. joined the company and set to work developing new investment banking capabilities, which helped establish the company not only as a brokerage house for individual investors, but also as a provider of financial services for businesses.

with him if something happened. The customer said he trusted him more than the banks, put the check back in his pocket, walked out and never cashed it. In retrospect, it was this kind of trust with his customers that helped pull the company through."

THE TIDE TURNS

As the economy gradually improved, so did the growth of the company. In 1930, J.C. Bradford & Co. was the first Tennessee firm to buy a seat on the New York Stock Exchange. In 1934, Bradford was appointed by the Tennessee Commissioner of Insurance as the chairman of the voting trust that would take over the management of the Nashville-based Life & Casualty Insurance Company.

Another stock market crash in 1937 dealt a heavy blow to the young company, but again, Bradford responded by keeping his focus on the customer. He put all his "customers' men" on salary and gave them a list of customers to call on personally—an approach virtually unheard of in the commission-driven brokerage houses of the time. When the market turned up, the company had record-breaking business, providing the momentum it needed to evolve into its present form.

By 1943, J.C. Bradford & Co. had opened an office in Knoxville. Then, in 1959, J.C. Bradford Jr. joined the company and set to work developing new investment banking capabilities, which helped establish the company not only as a brokerage house for individual investors, but also as a provider of financial services for businesses. J.C. Bradford & Co. became well known for taking companies public by raising millions for companies such as Comdata, Shoney's, and Endata during their initial public offerings.

TODAY'S COMPANY

In 1975, J.C. Bradford Jr. took over as managing partner of the firm, becoming senior partner after his father's death in 1982. During the 1980s, the company experienced a remarkable period of growth, dramatically increasing the number of brokers, building a larger research department, participating in $1.5 billion worth of equity offerings, and making a primary market in 120 stocks.

Today, from its downtown Nashville offices, the firm oversees the activities and growth of more than 900 brokers at 96 offices in 16 states. And as the firm makes its presence felt in the Southeast and beyond, senior partner J.C. Bradford Jr. says the firm's success goes back to one thing. "While we're growing larger all the time, our business is really based on something very small—that one-on-one relationship between the broker and the client, " says Bradford. "For us, that's the real bottom line."

From its downtown Nashville offices, the firm oversees the activities and growth of more than 900 brokers at 96 offices in 16 states.

In 1930, J.C. Bradford & Co. was the first Tennessee firm to buy a seat on the New York Stock Exchange.

SunTrust

THE ODDS AGAINST A BANK OPENING ITS DOORS A FEW YEARS prior to the Great Depression and thriving into the next century seem overwhelming. But while the odds did not prevail, Third National Bank did. When Frank Farris and Walter J. Diehl opened the institution on July 18, 1927, the bank achieved a record $1 million in deposits on its first day. Third National Bank is still serving Nashville today under its new name, SunTrust.

Remarkably, those visionary founders recognized the need for a new bank even though there were already 13 existing in the city. Their hard work laid the foundation, and Sam Fleming's continuing leadership as president and chief executive officer propelled Third National Bank from being a "new" bank to being one of the top three in the city.

Third National Bank boasted a long list of local firsts: The first drive-up window, the first nationally recognized bank credit card (Bank Americard), and the first automated voice computer to answer customers' questions about checking account balances—all debuted at Third National Bank in Nashville.

Even without the benefit of mergers and acquisitions, Third National Bank remained one of the largest banks in Nashville up until 1986 when it became a subsidiary of Atlanta-based SunTrust, one of the largest financial institutions in the Southeast and the 17th-largest in the United States. SunTrust Banks, Inc. operates more than 700 full-service banking offices in Tennessee, Florida, Georgia, and Alabama under the SunTrust identity. Today, approximately 1,700 people are employed by SunTrust in the Nashville area alone.

SunTrust Bank, Nashville, takes great pride in knowing its customers and being their partner. Focusing on the local market and having the ability to make decisions on the local level are of utmost importance.

Relationship Banking

Not until 1995 did Third National Bank change its name to SunTrust to reflect the name of its holding company. The magnitude and strength of a large super-regional bank are very beneficial, but its decentralized philosophy is perhaps most critical to what SunTrust represents—relationship banking. Because the bank takes great pride in knowing its customers and being their partners, focusing on the local market and having the ability to make decisions on the local level are of utmost importance.

"This bank got to be where it is today by believing in people and building strong relationships," says John W. Clay Jr., chairman and chief executive officer, SunTrust Bank, Nashville. "We are not simply a transactional bank, but a relationship bank involved in multiple ways with our customers as partners. We make every effort to remove any barriers that exist to fully developed relationships. Understanding our customers' situations and having them feel comfortable talking about everything from estate planning to

their checking accounts is what we're about."

Reinforcing the relationship banking philosophy remains in the plans for SunTrust. "We will build our bank based on how our customers grow," Clay says. "Our goal is to accommodate the changing lifestyles of today's consumer and to provide banking access 24 hours a day, seven days a week."

SunTrust continues to refine its delivery system to include access to accounts in a variety of ways, including via telephone, personal computers, the Internet, automated teller machines, and other non-traditional sites such as grocery and convenience stores. In addition to these alternative modes of delivery, SunTrust has recently continued to expand the products and services within its 42 branch offices in Middle Tennessee, offering banking, investments, trusts, and mortgage products.

SunTrust's current and future strategy is to serve both business and individual customers with a broad array of products. One of its core strengths is the trust and investment business. "We are aggressively expanding that business, particularly on the investment side," says Clay. "We are a financial services company as opposed to just a bank. We offer 18 proprietary mutual fund products that range from regional to international in scope."

SunTrust's traditional strengths lie in maintaining and transferring wealth through estate planning and trusts. An additional strength is in business banking, from the largest to the smallest organizations. SunTrust's private banking functions are an additional commitment to those sectors. The company has developed a specialty in health care lending, beginning with the first loan to Hospital Corporation of America (HCA) in the 1960s. In fact, SunTrust serves the health care community with a special office located in the heart of Nashville's medical community.

Similarly, a specialty office exists on Music Row to serve the music and entertainment community. SunTrust also operates a private banking unit that offers personalized service to the professional and executive community.

As one of the largest loan originators in the city, SunTrust has also made its mortgage banking services an area of priority. Conducting home-purchasing classes in the community for first-time buyers is one of the bank's priorities for building this area of business.

Investment in Community

With a firm commitment to reinvesting in the community, SunTrust donates nearly $1 million per year to charitable and civic organizations ranging from the United Way and affordable housing to education and the arts.

"We are fortunate to be in Nashville at this time. There is so much going on in entertainment, sports, health care, insurance, finance, publishing, printing, and manufacturing," concludes Clay. "SunTrust is proud to be a part of the growth of Nashville. We're obviously not a 'here today, gone tomorrow' type of business. We continue to draw upon our roots and strengths, and we constantly reaffirm our commitment to quality, integrity, and performance in all that we do."

From top:

SunTrust continues to refine its delivery system to include access to accounts in a variety of ways, including via telephone, personal computer, and the Internet, and has recently continued to expand the products and services within its 42 branch offices in Middle Tennessee, offering banking, investments, trusts, and mortgage products.

"This bank got to be where it is today by believing in people and building strong relationships," says John W. Clay Jr., chairman and chief ececutive officer, SunTrust Bank, Nashville.

Opening day—July 18, 1927: The hard work of Frank Farris and Walker J. Diehl laid the foundation, while Sam Fleming's continuing leadership as president and chief executive officer propelled Third National Bank from being a new bank to being one of the top three in the city.

Southern Baptist Convention

Since its organization in 1845 in Augusta, Georgia, the Southern Baptist Convention (SBC) has grown to 15.8 million members who worship in more than 40,000 churches in the United States. Southern Baptists sponsor about 5,000 home missionaries serving the United States, Canada, Guam, and the Caribbean, as well as sponsoring more than 4,100 foreign missionaries in 126 nations of the world.

The term Southern Baptist Convention denotes both the denomination and its annual meeting. Working through 1,221 local associations and 39 state conventions and fellowships, Southern Baptists share a common bond of basic biblical beliefs and a commitment to proclaim the gospel of Jesus Christ to the entire world.

The Convention's purpose, as stated in Article II of its constitution, is "to provide a general organization for Baptists in the United States and its territories for the promotion of Christian missions at home and abroad, and any other objects such as Christian education, benevolent enterprises, and social services, which it may deem properly advisable for the furtherance of the Kingdom of God."

The annual Convention meeting consists of representatives, or "messengers" as they are called, from cooperating churches, who gather to confer and determine the programs, policies, and budget of the Convention. Each church may be represented by up to 10 messengers, ensuring equal accessibility for small and large congregations alike.

The Southern Baptist Convention manages its worldwide efforts through 12 boards and agencies that are organized for various ministry endeavors. Support for its work comes from contributions through the Cooperative Program, a plan of giving that enables individual churches to share in these extensive national and international ministries. In 1996, Southern Baptist churches gave more than $274 million through the Cooperative Program and special foreign and home missions offerings.

The Executive Committee

The Executive Committee was formed in 1917 and established its offices in Nashville in 1927. At that time, the Southern Baptist Convention enlarged the committee's scope of duties to include acting on behalf of the Convention between annual sessions. Currently, the Executive Committee is comprised of 81 representatives chosen from qualified state conventions.

Although the Executive Committee does not control or direct the activities of Convention agencies, it reviews their financial statements and recommends the Convention annual operating budget. In addition, it receives and distributes the moneys Southern Baptists give in support of denominational ministries, acts as the recipient and trust agency for all Convention properties, and provides public relations and news services. It also performs other tasks assigned by the SBC and promotes the general work of Southern Baptists. To carry out these duties, the committee employs an executive and professional staff in its Nashville offices.

Baptists represent more than a third of church members in the United States. More than 40 percent of all Baptist churches are affiliated with the Southern Baptist Convention. Local churches aligned with the Southern Baptist Convention are committed to the goal "that every person in the world shall have the opportunity to hear the gospel of Christ by the year 2000."

Dr. Morris H. Chapman, president and chief executive officer, Executive Committee, Southern Baptist Convention (top).

The Southern Baptist Convention building is home to the offices and staff of the Executive Committee (bottom).

NASHVILLE ELECTRIC SERVICE

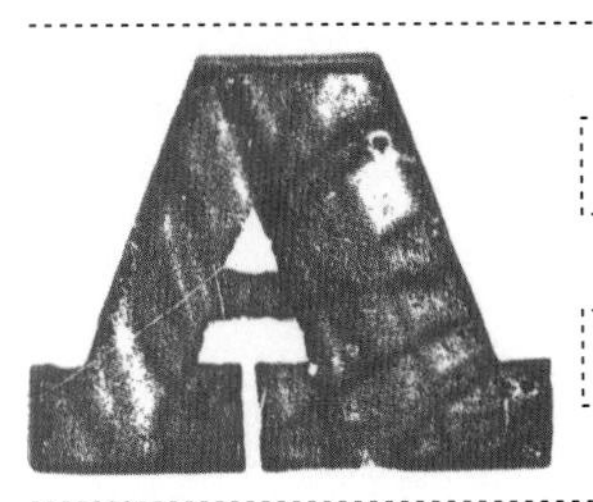

S ONE OF THE 10 LARGEST PUBLIC UTILITIES IN THE NATION, the Nashville Electric Service (NES) supplies approximately 300,000 residential, commercial, and industrial customers over a 700-square-mile area encompassing Davidson County and parts of surrounding counties. NES boasts rates that are lower than any other major city in Tennessee and competitive with the rest of the nation. The utility has not increased rates since 1989—actually decreasing rates in 1990. The low rates and the bustling economy in middle Tennessee have contributed to the successful growth of NES.

Established in 1939, NES has a rich history and a deep commitment to Nashville. Throughout the years, the public utility has contributed significant financial and human resources to the community. For example, NES remains the largest taxpayer in metropolitan Nashville. Its ongoing safety and education programs have expanded to include preschoolers and senior citizens in addition to elementary and high school students. Through the Adopt-a-School program, NES employees give time as well as financial assistance to needy schools and children, and, most recently, employees have pitched in to build their third home for Habitat for Humanity.

PLANNING FOR THE FUTURE

Anticipating changes in the industry, NES is taking steps to prepare itself for an increasingly competitive environment. While stability was imperative for success in the past, a need for flexibility and diversity is its rallying cry for the future.

Customer satisfaction is the largest single focus for NES, both now and in the future. Based on responses in consumer surveys, NES implemented a number of improvements, which have dramatically increased service reliability and responsiveness. A new, state-of-the-art answering service can handle 20,000 calls per hour, thereby improving service during major outages and emergencies. More customer service representatives have been trained and are available 24 hours a day, seven days a week. In an effort to be more efficient, flexible, and accountable, NES reorganized its management team to eliminate redundant management layers.

From an operational standpoint, working smarter is also a necessity for the future. Training and education are taking on increased importance at all levels. All NES representatives now receive continuous, customer-based training. NES is making better use of resources, especially human resources, by dividing crews into smaller, more flexible work groups, allowing for quicker response time.

Another key to future success for NES in today's competitive environment is to create innovative uses for new technology. NES is installing a new radio system to facilitate communication and coordination of work crews, and is participating in a pilot project to offer new services to customers, including home and business automation services, remote meter reading, remote service connection and disconnection, and real-time pricing. NES is also developing a distribution management system that can be used for faster service restoration, facilities management, automated mapping, computer-aided design, and automated vehicle locating capability.

With a well-developed strategic plan for continued commitment to employee training, controlling costs, and innovative use of technology, NES is focused on servicing the needs and wants of the Nashville community—for now and for the future.

CLOCKWISE FROM TOP:

CUSTOMER SATISFACTION IS THE LARGEST SINGLE FOCUS FOR NES, BOTH NOW AND IN THE FUTURE.

NES IS INSTALLING A NEW RADIO SYSTEM TO FACILITATE COMMUNICATION AND COORDINATION OF WORK CREWS.

AS ONE OF THE 10 LARGEST PUBLIC UTILITIES IN THE NATION, THE NASHVILLE ELECTRIC SERVICE (NES) SUPPLIES APPROXIMATELY 300,000 RESIDENTIAL, COMMERCIAL, AND INDUSTRIAL CUSTOMERS OVER A 700-SQUAREMILE AREA ENCOMPASSING DAVIDSON COUNTY AND PARTS OF SURROUNDING COUNTIES.

▲ BOB SCHATZ

◀▲ BOB SCHATZ

Equitable Securities Corporation

Nashville may be a long way from Wall Street, but the Music City's own Equitable Securities Corporation stands toe-to-toe with the investment industry's giants in the categories that count: investment performance and service to clients. ★ Founded in 1930 on Union Street—which came to be known as the Wall Street of the South—Equitable Securities soon established a national reputation as a dealer in municipal bonds and corporate securities. Actively investing for its own account, as well as dealing in securities for its clients, the firm emerged in 1950 as the largest single stockholder of the American Express Company. By the 1960s, Equitable Securities had the second-largest net worth of any investment banking firm in the nation. In 1968, Equitable Securities merged into American Express.

In 1972, a group of Equitable Securities' Nashville-based executives led by William H. Cammack, now the firm's chairman, reacquired Equitable Securities from American Express, and the company once again became an independent investment bank and a member of the New York Stock Exchange, Inc.

In the past decade, the firm has experienced steady and substantial growth under the leadership of Cammack, Chief Executive Officer William P. Johnston, and President Katie H. Gambill. In 1988, Equitable Securities had 42 employees; at the end of 1996, it had more than 180, with additional offices in Atlanta and Houston.

A Trusted Adviser

Equitable Securities seeks to be a leading force in its five business specialties: investment banking, institutional equity, institutional fixed income, private investment services, and investment advisory and trust services.

The firm has built a highly effective investment banking business in recent years, regularly taking leading roles in underwriting syndicates that include the biggest names on Wall Street. Clients come from many of Nashville's and the region's most prominent sectors—health care, business and information services, restaurants and entertainment, privatization, and specialty finance. It is typical that companies taken public by Equitable Securities continue to rely on the firm for assistance in financing their future growth, merger and acquisition advice, or other investment banking services, attesting to Equitable Securities' performance and client satisfaction.

Research is the heart of the firm's business, providing accurate insight into the appropriate valua-

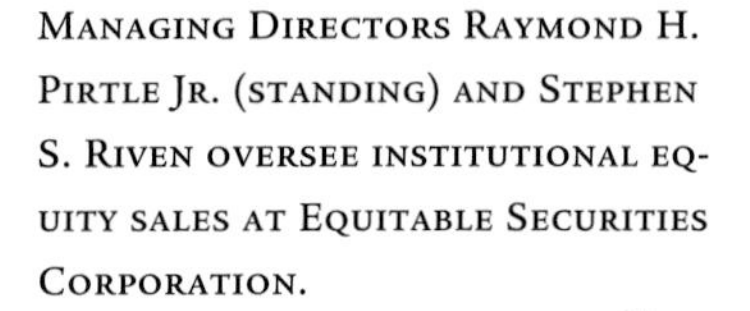

Managing Directors Raymond H. Pirtle Jr. (standing) and Stephen S. Riven oversee institutional equity sales at Equitable Securities Corporation.

William P. Johnston, CEO (left), Katie H. Gambill, president, and William H. Cammack, chairman, are committed to the firm's mission of providing superior investment services and opportunities.

tion of a company and positioning a securities offering for the best possible reception by institutional and other experienced investors. The firm specializes in generating new investment ideas for clients through original research of both small- and mid-capitalization, high-growth companies, and special situations where the firm has significant industry knowledge and there appears to be an extraordinary investment opportunity for Equitable Securities' clients. The firm's institutional equity sales and trading team effectively presents these ideas to professional money managers throughout the United States, Europe, the United Kingdom, and Canada.

Public finance and the sales and trading of municipal bonds have always occupied a place of prominence at Equitable Securities. Just as government services are fundamental to the public, financing these services is fundamental to the firm. For more than six decades, Equitable Securities has helped public entities provide the schools, roads, hospitals, utilities, corrections facilities, and industrial development that are expected by a modern society.

Equitable Securities' Private Client group offers individual investor services ranging from traditional securities brokerage to access to equity and debt private placements, specialized unaffiliated money managers, and firm-sponsored initial public offerings. Emphasis is placed on the client's long-term objectives and implementation of a diversified program designed to meet those objectives. These comprehensive services are critical to investors with commitments to preserving and significantly enhancing wealth through disciplined investing.

Equitable Trust Company, organized in 1991 as a subsidiary, is dedicated exclusively to providing investment management and trust services to families, endowments, foundations, and retirement plan sponsors. Equitable Securities provides investment consulting services, manages private investment partnership funds, and serves as adviser to the ESC Strategic Funds, a family of mutual funds available to the investing public both through Equitable Securities and through other firms. Equitable Asset Management, also a subsidiary, specializes in managing equity securities portfolios with a goal of significant appreciation through both growth and value approaches. In early 1997, aggregate funds under administration and management with the Investment Advisory group and Equitable Trust combined exceeded $1.5 billion.

"In each of the five core specialties of Equitable Securities, the firm's mission," says Johnston, "is to be a trusted adviser and provide superior investment services and opportunities. The key measurement of our accomplishment is the satisfaction and loyalty of our clients and customers."

Tom R. Steele (center) leads the Private Client group at Equitable Securities.

Metropolitan Nashville Airport Authority

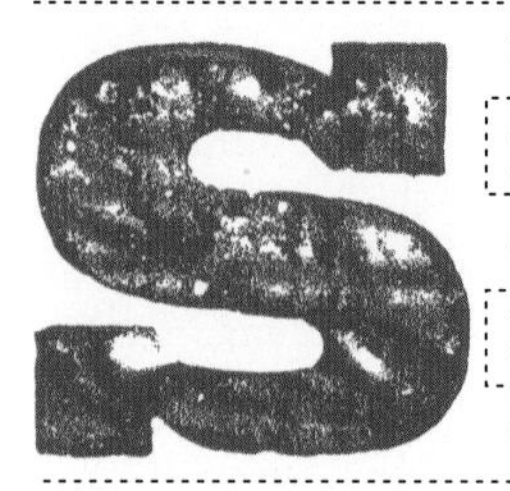

Sixty years ago, Nashvillians rejoiced as 337 acres of pasture were transformed into the city's first commercial airport. At the dawn of the 21st century, the Metropolitan Nashville Airport Authority carries forth the legacies of those early efforts—the world-class Nashville International Airport and John C. Tune Airport, named after the late Nashville attorney and aviation enthusiast.

Berry Field, built with the help of the Works Progress Administration, was dedicated with gala festivities on the weekend of June 12 and 13, 1937.

Taking Flight

Modern commercial aviation in Nashville got off the ground after the city, with the help of the Great Depression-era Works Progress Administration (WPA), purchased land along the famed Dixie Highway. There the city built Berry Field—named for Colonel Harry S. Berry, Tennessee administrator for the WPA. The project's cost was $1.18 million. The airport was dedicated on the weekend of June 12 and 13, 1937, with gala festivities that included aerial acrobatics, a mock bombing of Nashville, and the departure of Eastern and American Airlines flights to Chicago, Miami, and Washington, D.C.

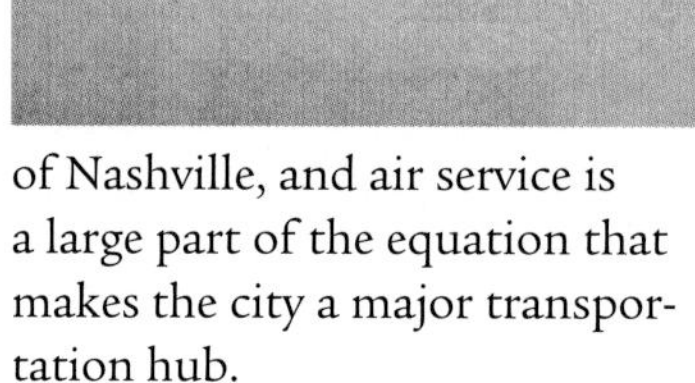

Nashville had reason to celebrate, as airline connections had become vital to the economic life of many cities. But they became an especially important component of Nashville's appeal as a business center both centrally located and in proximity to other American cities. Today, half the nation's population lives within 600 miles of Nashville, and air service is a large part of the equation that makes the city a major transportation hub.

Understanding the need to make the most of Nashville's aviation assets, the city created the Metropolitan Nashville Airport Authority (MNAA) in 1970. A self-supporting, self-financing public agency, the Airport Authority operates without the benefit of local tax dollars. Numerous U.S. cities, as well as the governments of Bermuda and Canada, have studied Nashville's Airport Authority as a model airport governance organization.

The mission of the Airport Authority is twofold. One element is the planning, construction, operation, and management of the city's commercial air facilities. The other element is the promotion and development of commerce and industry through air transportation. Since 1984, MNAA has functioned under the leadership of William G. Moore, a retired four-star air force general, and a 10-member volunteer board of commissioners, headed by Robert C.H. Mathews, reappointed as chairman for a third term in 1995.

Important figures in Nashville's airport system are (from left) the late John C. Tune, the first chairman of MNAA; Gen. William G. Moore Jr., president of MNAA; and Robert C.H. Mathews, chairman of MNAA.

A Strategy for Growth

Since the inception of the Airport Authority, Nashvillians have enjoyed dramatic improvements in the air services available to them. By 1977, the airport site had grown to 3,300 acres and contained three runways, and the total number of passengers served had reached 1.9 million people

annually. By 1980, that number had increased to 2.3 million.

Nine major airlines and four commuter carriers were then serving the Nashville market. This increase in air traffic was possible because MNAA had the foresight to carry out a $30 million terminal renovation and expansion in 1977. In 1984, the design for a new terminal was unveiled and the Airport Authority issued $128.5 million in airport revenue bonds to finance it. The present terminal opened in September 1987, 10 months ahead of schedule and under budget.

Much of this progress came about through the leadership of the late John C. Tune, a Nashville attorney and longtime aviation enthusiast. Tune was among the Airport Authority members who recognized the need for a general aviation airport in Nashville that would better serve smaller aircraft and aid the expansion of jet service at Berry Field. Fittingly, the facility that opened in West Nashville's Cockrill Bend in July 1986, was christened John C. Tune Airport.

Serving the needs of regional corporate and private aircraft, Tune Airport is vital to the economic health and progress of Middle Tennessee. It allows Nashville International's scheduled air carrier traffic to flow with fewer constraints and congestion, and it meets important smaller aircraft aviation needs. In addition, Tune Airport provides an excellent pilot training environment, with modern facilities for the transient and corporate operator well away from the busy airspace around Nashville International Airport.

Tune Airport is financially self-supporting, although some improvements are made with state and federal assistance. A modern terminal building opened in October 1995, and parking facilities have been upgraded as well.

Nashville International Airport, one of the central pieces of the city's infrastructure, encompasses more than 4,400 acres.

An Economic Stalwart

Nashville International Airport has become one of the central pieces of the city's infrastructure. It now encompasses more than 4,400 acres. The terminal complex covers some 820,000 square feet, with 46 air carrier gates and 38 commuter aircraft parking positions. Berry's airfield, which started out with a single, 4,000-foot runway, now boasts four runways of up to 11,000 feet, including parallel strips for simultaneous landings and takeoffs. From 1985 to 1996, passenger traffic increased 153.6 percent to 7.1 million passengers. Nearly 60,000 tons of cargo move through the airport annually, and that number grows every year. More than 20 international forwarders and customs brokers serve the Middle Tennessee shipping community. The airport is served by 12 all-cargo carriers. It has two freight terminals, which offer more than 130,000 square feet of space and 259,000 square feet of ramp area.

The bottom-line significance of all these numbers is that Nashville International Airport contributes thousands of jobs and more than $1 billion annually to the economy of the Nashville region.

Nashville doesn't stand still, and neither will its airport in years to come. In 1993, the Airport Authority developed a master plan, based upon traffic projections by independent sources, to anticipate Nashville's air service needs through the year 2023. It is a community plan, with input from a broad cross section of interested citizens. The plan recommends, among other enhancements, building a fifth runway after 2013. Whatever the future may hold, the Metropolitan Nashville Airport Authority's role is to ensure that good things are in the air for Nashville.

▶ Gary Layda

Nashville International's interior provides a warm, enticing welcome to the city's urban economy and lifestyle (left).

▶ Gary Layda

The new terminal at John C. Tune Airport is the focal point of the full-service general aviation facility.

The Mathews Company/R.C. Mathews Contractor

Building on a history of integrity, The Mathews Company has been adding value to real estate for three generations. From the construction of one of Nashville's first office buildings to the resurgence of Nashville's downtown, The Mathews Company has played a significant hand in guiding Nashville's silhouette as one of the Southeast's most dynamic and progressive cities.

"We've been successful because we've watched the city grow for a long time," says Chairman R.C.H. "Bob" Mathews Jr. "And we've been able to manage and anticipate a lot of the changes Nashville has experienced. The best way to determine the highest and best use for a piece of property is to know something about the land and its history. Our mainstay has really always been in knowing this area."

Building on a Solid Foundation

When R.C. Mathews Sr. started his construction company back in 1938, he drew from his experience in building railroad bridges between New York City and Philadelphia. His solid engineering skills, entrepreneurial spirit, and strong values served him well in the postwar economy of Nashville. Among his first projects was the headquarters for Third National Bank at the corner of the financial center for downtown Nashville. Soon Mathews was constructing facilities for Genesco, National Life, and other leading businesses of the community.

In 1951, Mathews' son Bob joined the firm and began expanding the scope of The Mathews Company—first with the development of Metropolitan Industrial Park, followed by the development of MetroCenter, Elm Hill Industrial Park, and First Union Tower.

By the 1980s, when Bob's sons Bert and Walker joined the firm, The Mathews Company was positioned to lead Nashville into its most prolific growth period. During this time, the company built or developed major projects from one side of Nashville to the other—such projects as a new headquarters for J.C. Bradford, Commerce Street Parking Garage, Grassmere Business Park, The Village of Vanderbilt, Grassmere Wildlife Park, National Baptist World Center, and more.

Among the many projects The Mathews Company has developed is the First Union Tower (top).

When a group of investors wanted to provide a quality office park, The Mathews Company rolled out the topographic maps and determined that the Grassmere land was best suited for the project (bottom).

Offering Clients the Services They Need

Beginning with site acquisition, The Mathews Company today focuses on adding value to real estate by lending their expertise to any type of project.

Simply put, The Mathews Company locates and advises,

constructs and renovates, purchases and develops, sells and leases, manages and maintains—providing some or all of these services, depending on the client's needs.

When the Gaylord Entertainment Corporation decided to join the booming entertainment excitement of downtown, it depended on R.C. Mathews Contractor for the complete renovation of one of the most historic buildings in Nashville—The Ryman Auditorium.

A few years later, Planet Hollywood needed a construction company that had its finger on the pulse of the local industry and could deliver its innovative renovation on time and on budget. Again, Mathews was the chosen team.

"Our approach to construction is that it's a service business. You start with an idea and you orchestrate all of the design professionals, trade subcontractors, and suppliers to fulfill your client's needs. It's very satisfying to have that sense of completion—to walk by a building and know that I had something to do with giving that client a building that does what they need it to do," says Walker Mathews.

The role Mathews has played in construction projects is growing year by year: Opryland Theme Park, Nashville House in MetroCenter, the renovation of Ensworth School, Primus Automotive Headquarters, the Nashville Arena and the campus around it, Credit Information Center, and Baptist Williamson County Medical Center.

When a group of investors wanted to provide a quality office park, The Mathews Company took on the role as developer, rolled out the topographic maps, and determined that the Grassmere land was best suited for the project. The investors then chose Mathews to oversee the purchase and zoning, develop the infrastructure, construct the buildings, lease the spaces, and manage and maintain the entire project. A similar process occurred with One Nashville Place and The Village at Vanderbilt, Nashville's first true urban mixed-use development.

Guiding The Mathews Company today are (from left) Walker C. Mathews, Robert C. H. Mathews Jr., and Robert C.H. Mathews III.

A Vision for the Future

These are just a few of the success stories associated with The Mathews Company. Day to day, this team of dedicated professionals is a part of a community that has enjoyed steady growth when many larger cities have been at the mercy of feast or famine cycles. Being able to maintain a straight, clear pattern of gradual success comes from experience; it comes from having a confident grasp of the past and a careful eye to the future.

"We pride ourselves on being problem solvers," explains Bert Mathews. "We see our role within the community growing to encompass city planning as we did with development of the Ryman Center, which includes the area around the BellSouth Building; and the Gateway Project, which includes the area around the new Nashville Arena. Yet our answer for today's demanding real estate market is the same as it always has been—exceptional service for our tenants, careful attention to expenses, and understanding our clients' needs."

Sage advice comes from the voice of experience: "In real estate, timing is everything," states Bob Mathews. "So we try to be at the right place and the right time—with the right land. In order to have the right land, you have to know about its history. We like working in Nashville because we know the history. You can learn a lot about the future of land by looking at its past."

When the Gaylord Entertainment Corporation decided to join the booming entertainment excitement of downtown, it turned to R.C. Mathews Contractor for the complete renovation of one of the most historic buildings in Nashville—The Ryman Auditorium.

FLIGHT OF STARES

★

1944
Hermitage Lighting Gallery

1946
Lankford Hardware & Supply Co., Inc.

1955
The Mall at Green Hills

1956
Murray, Inc.

1958
Kraft Bros., Esstman, Patton & Harrell, PLLC

1961
Earl Swensson Associates, Inc.

1961
Fox Ridge Homes Inc.

1966
Charles Hampton A-1 Signs

1967
Fleetguard, Inc.

1968
Columbia/HCA

1969
Comdata Corporation

1969
Thomas Nelson, Inc.

1974
Baker, Donelson, Bearman & Caldwell

1974
Olsten Staffing Services

1976
Film House

1978
Barnes Real Estate Services, Inc.

1979
Tractor Supply Company

1980
Davis-Kidd Booksellers, Inc.

1980
Gould Turner Group, P.C.

1980
Nissan Motor Manufacturing Corporation U.S.A.

Hermitage Lighting Gallery

WHETHER REFURBISHING AN EXISTING HOME OR BUILDing a new one, Hermitage Lighting Gallery offers an abundance of decorative solutions for every room in the house. Lighting fixtures, home accessories, antique furniture, kitchen cabinets, appliances, and Jacuzzis fill every nook and cranny in the showroom, located near downtown Nashville.

While the showroom offers far more than the name implies, light fixtures are the main focus. Whether searching for a $400 imported Italian lamp or a $40,000 antique crystal chandelier, Hermitage Lighting Gallery is the place to look. And the gallery's Certified Lighting Consultants, who have been professionally trained by the American Lighting Association, are available for consultations and can work within any budget.

Customers who visit one of the company's lighting labs can quickly see how the layering effect of light completely changes the ambience and appearance of any room. Dining room, kitchen, bathroom, and exterior landscape lighting labs allow customers to test the real-life applications of the products they are considering.

Industry-Certified Training

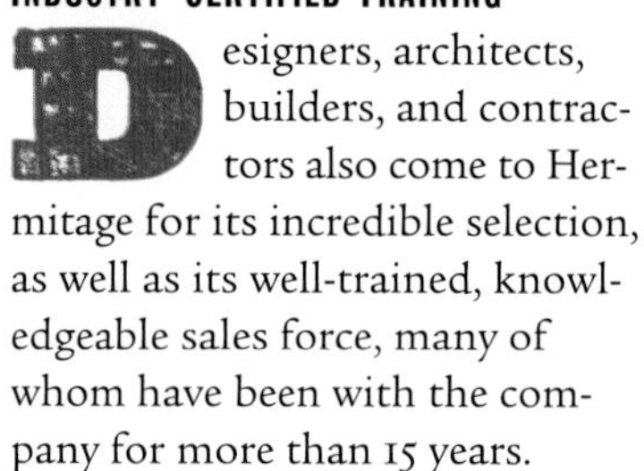

Designers, architects, builders, and contractors also come to Hermitage for its incredible selection, as well as its well-trained, knowledgeable sales force, many of whom have been with the company for more than 15 years.

"We go to great lengths to train our consultants on an ongoing basis in an effort to offer our customers the maximum benefit for their dollar," says Jerry Fleischer, chairman of the board. "Our sales staff does not cross over into other departments. They are focused on their product group. Needless to say, their ability to help customers is exceptional."

A Sampling of the Global Marketplace

Because of Hermitage Lighting Gallery's aggressive product selection process, the company is able to offer competitive pricing. The selection is unparalleled, with products not typically seen in a showroom. Jack Fleischer, president, travels frequently and imports an array of products from Italy, China, Spain, Mexico, Canada, and other countries. The showroom's heavy volume and constant showcasing of new products allows Hermitage to change 400 to 600 items every month.

The state-of-the-art kitchen cabinets, appliances, and hardware on display are works of art to any home cook. Hermitage Lighting Gallery boasts a staff of Certified Kitchen Designers who can help customers design the kitchen of their dreams with products from companies like Gaggenau, Kitchen Aid, Dacor, Viking, and Whirlpool. Hermitage designers manage the design project from the initial renderings on paper through the final installation.

With a heritage dating back to 1944, the family business was established by the late Jack Tenzel. Today, his daughter Doris serves as secretary/treasurer and her husband, Gerald "Jerry" Fleischer, is chairman of the board. Their son, Jack Fleischer, is president of the firm. Hermitage Lighting Gallery services customers in Middle Tennessee and throughout the Southeast. Its commercial division sells to all 50 states.

"Our longevity sends a positive message to our customers. We are stable, reliable, and we try to do the right thing," says Jack Fleischer. "We have a very strong referral business with many loyal, repeat customers. Lighting a home is an art that is subjective," he continues. "Whether a homeowner is into Classical, Renaissance, or Impressionistic styles, Hermitage Lighting Gallery can deliver the look and the ambience selected by its clients. Staying on top of cutting-edge trends, monitoring the global marketplace, and providing top-notch service are the illuminating ingredients of Hermitage Lighting Gallery's long-term success."

Clockwise from top:

With a heritage dating back to 1944, Hermitage Lighting Gallery services customers in Middle Tennessee and throughout the Southeast.

Whether searching for a $400 imported lamp or a $40,000 antique crystal chandelier, Hermitage Lighting Gallery is the place to look.

Dining room, kitchen, bathroom, and exterior landscape lighting labs allow customers to test the real-life applications of the products they are considering.

Lankford Hardware & Supply Co., Inc.

From hammers to hand-painted basins, Lankford Hardware & Supply Company offers a full range of builder's hardware for commercial and custom residential use. The firm stakes its 50-year reputation on consistently carrying the highest-quality, most reliable products. Commercial and custom residential builders and architects have come to rely on the expertise offered by Lankford's knowledgeable staff.

Founded in 1946 by Samuel L. Lankford during the building boom following World War II, Lankford's originally sold commercial contract hardware. Throughout the years, the business focus has shifted in response to local needs, government regulations, and economic changes. But one thing has remained constant: the Lankford family. Following Sam Lankford's retirement in 1969, his son Bill served as president until 1994. Since that time, Bill's wife, Betty, has taken over the helm and added her special touch to the business. Another constant is the company's policy of "listening to customers, for they will tell you what they want."

Strong, secure doors from Lankford's grace commercial and residential properties throughout the region.

Custom Residential Wares Second to None

Lankford's has one of the largest custom retail bath and door hardware showrooms in the South. High quality and good value are the criteria used to select the unique products represented by Lankford Hardware. Customers find fully operational showers, whirlpools, and therapeutic bathtubs on display to assist them with their selection.

Leading the Industry in Commercial Service

The level of expertise of its commercial hardware staff has always been a trademark of Lankford Hardware and a major force in the company's success. Through specialized, ongoing training, the staff stays abreast of county, state, and federal commercial building codes. This technical expertise is invaluable to commercial customers who have come to depend on Lankford's for help.

The Contract Hardware Division specializes in builder's hardware, commercial bath accessories, and hollow metal and wooden doors. A full line of high-security products for special applications serves the unique needs of commercial customers.

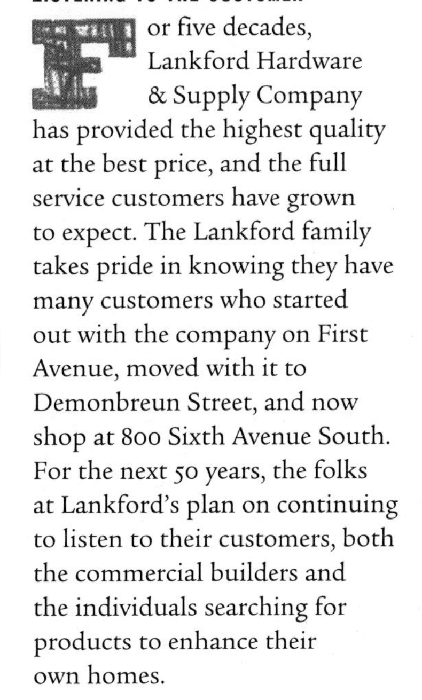

Community Support

Management believes that, as a locally owned business, Lankford's has an obligation to support community activities. Since 1986, the company has been a corporate sponsor of the Decorators' Showhouse to support the work of the local design community and charities supported by the Junior League of Nashville.

Listening to the Customer

For five decades, Lankford Hardware & Supply Company has provided the highest quality at the best price, and the full service customers have grown to expect. The Lankford family takes pride in knowing they have many customers who started out with the company on First Avenue, moved with it to Demonbreun Street, and now shop at 800 Sixth Avenue South. For the next 50 years, the folks at Lankford's plan on continuing to listen to their customers, both the commercial builders and the individuals searching for products to enhance their own homes.

With one of the largest bath and door hardware showrooms in the South, Lankford's provides unique, high-quality products for custom residential baths.

The Mall at Green Hills

Nostalgia is strong for Nashvillians who grew up shopping at the quaint strip center in Green Hills. Opened in 1955 when its anchor store, Castner Knott, opened, today's Mall at Green Hills reflects the winds of change, dynamically renovated into an enclosed 24.1-acre mall housing a diverse array of upscale merchants.

Through the years the mall has served residents in some of Nashville's most affluent and wealthiest neighborhoods—including Green Hills, Belle Meade, Forest Hill, and Oak Hill, to name a few—with top quality merchandise and has become a fashion destination for all of middle Tennessee. Residents have continuously rated the mall the best place to shop in surveys conducted by local newspapers.

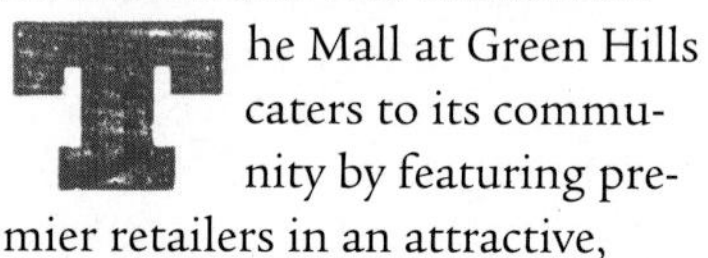

Distinctive Shopping Environment

The Mall at Green Hills caters to its community by featuring premier retailers in an attractive, pleasant shopping environment. "The mall has remained true to a particular niche, showcasing more one-of-a-kind and exclusive stores than other shopping destinations in the area," notes General Manager Dave Twomey.

Three highly regarded department stores—Dillard's, Castner Knott, and Gus Mayer—anchor the mall complex. Other prominent names in retail represented at The Mall at Green Hills include Brooks Brothers, Laura Ashley, Ann Taylor, Eddie Bauer, Banana Republic, The Disney Store, The Museum Company, Gymboree, The Nature Company, Benetton, Jos. A. Bank, Crabtree & Evelyn, and Williams-Sonoma. The mall also houses such regional stores as Harold's, featuring the best in traditional apparel, and the intriguing fashion shop Accenté. Sporting goods retailers and music stores are also included among the diverse mix of merchants.

Additionally, customers can feed their souls with a quiet respite at Tiba de Nuhad Khoury, which offers a unique menu of European-style spa treatments, or feed their stomachs in one of the many specialty food shops.

With a continuous focus on customer satisfaction, the mall's Customer Service Center assists shoppers by offering gift wrap, coat/package check, overnight shipping, gift certificates, strollers, wheelchairs, taxi and limousine services, and tourism information.

Design-Winning Renovations

In the early 1980s, renovations provided for a fully enclosed mall, and in 1992, a $40 million renovation was completed, adding three major parking decks and a second level to the mall, which provided room for 50 new stores and an expansion of Dillard's. These renovations, coupled with the mall's impressive list of retailers, afford the Mall at Green Hills the highest sales per square foot in the Nashville retail area.

A recipient of a major design award from the International Council of Shopping Centers, the mall is comprised of a series of pyramidal glass skylights that illuminate two grand atrium courts containing two-level arcades. The marble and brass appointments, flowering plants, and bright, open space contribute to the pleasant shopping ambience.

The Mall at Green Hills participates extensively in local charitable endeavors, sponsoring such events as The Iroquois Steeple Chase and the Antiques & Garden Show, to name a few. It even offers fun and exciting community events like Kid's Club, a weekly program designed to entertain and educate young children.

Providing the finest retailers in the area, The Mall at Green Hills has indeed established itself as Nashville's Grand Tradition—a part of the fabric of Nashville life and an upscale shopping experience second to none.

A recipient of a major design award from the International Council of Shopping Centers, the mall is comprised of a series of pyramidal glass skylights that illuminate two grand atrium courts containing two-level arcades (left).

Whether in search of the latest fashions, a unique gift, or a distinctive collectable, The Mall at Green Hills is the place to shop (right).

Fox Ridge Homes, Inc.

AS ONE OF THE LARGEST SINGLE-FAMILY HOME BUILDERS AND developers in Middle Tennessee, Fox Ridge Homes, Inc. has been providing gracious living and lasting value to residents since 1961. The company boasts 60 innovative floor plans with a diverse array of sizes and price ranges, now offered in more than 20 superior locations throughout Middle Tennessee.

Because Fox Ridge's focus and home base is Middle Tennessee, the company understands the market, the popular home styles, and the best construction methods for this terrain. Additionally, Fox Ridge's strong relationships with local financial institutions enable the company to secure the most competitive interest rates for customers and keep rates fixed while the home is being built.

Growth Through Leadership

The driving force behind Fox Ridge is Chief Executive Officer Al Davis, who has been with the company since 1970, and has worked in virtually all areas from sales and marketing to operations. For years, Fox Ridge catered to the first-time buyer. But because Davis has helped expand the company's market in the last decade, Fox Ridge has introduced new floor plans designed for an executive audience as well.

Through extensive market research, the company keeps close tabs on the needs of home buyers and is able to design floor plans accordingly. Years of analyzing market trends have consistently paid off. Fox Ridge's superior designs have been recognized by the Middle Tennessee Sales and Marketing Council, the Parade of Homes, and the Southern Showcase of Homes. In 1996, a Fox Ridge home received Best of Show during the Middle Tennessee Parade of Homes.

Location, Location, Location

Prime locations are a given when buying a Fox Ridge home. Convenience to interstates and shopping, excellent school systems, and natural beauty are an integral part of the Fox Ridge communities. And with more than 20 communities in a myriad of suburban locations, there is a perfect location for every buyer.

As a home is often the largest single purchase an individual will ever make, ensuring quality craftsmanship is equally critical for prospective and current homeowners. Fox Ridge backs its work with an extensive warranty program, providing each new home with a two-year major systems warranty and a 10-year structural warranty. Additionally, a full-time warranty team is on call to service each new home for the first year.

Providing lasting value to homeowners is the foundation of Fox Ridge's success. With a 36-year track record and a profound knowledge of the industry and of Middle Tennessee, the company is able to use the most efficient construction methods and materials available, adding credence to its slogan, "Where Quality Is a Tradition." Offering buyers support from sales through construction, Fox Ridge Homes is dedicated to satisfying and fulfilling its clients' expectations. After all, there's no place like home.

From left:
Fox Ridge's superior designs have been recognized by the Middle Tennessee Sales and Marketing Council, the Parade of Homes, and the Southern Showcase of Homes.

Fox Ridge Homes, Inc. has been providing gracious living and lasting value to residents since 1961.

The company boasts 60 innovative floor plans with a diverse array of sizes and price ranges, now offered in more than 20 superior locations throughout Middle Tennessee.

Murray, Inc.

NE OF THE GREAT RITES OF PASSAGE FOR ANY CHILD IS GETTING that first bicycle. Having manufactured more than 65 million bikes, Murray, Inc. has no doubt outfitted many a child with that first two-wheeler and inspired generations of dreams. ★ While Murray, Inc. is renowned for galvanizing spirited bike races down suburban America's streets, the company also has provided a worldwide market with its fine automotive equipment, outdoor power equipment, and toys. In the decades since its 1919 inception, Murray, Inc.'s production has echoed the changing times, and the company has defined itself through innovative engineering and value-driven product design.

Signs of the Times

Murray Ohio Manufacturing Company was founded in Cleveland, Ohio, at the end of World War I. Initially, the firm found rapid success in supplying fenders, gas tanks, and running boards for America's burgeoning automotive industry.

In 1923, Murray achieved more prosperity when it decreased the scale of these parts and began producing a line of toy cars for children. Steelcraft Wheel Goods soon became an American icon—one that endured for more than 50 years. It was in 1936, in the midst of the Great Depression, that Murray began manufacturing its other enduring icon—the Mercury bicycle, its first line of bikes. Murray had to dramatically increase production of the Mercury to keep up with demand of these well-crafted two-wheel machines.

In a stark reflection of the times, Murray lent a hand to the wartime effort in 1941 and shifted its production capabilities, building rocket housings and magazines for antiaircraft guns.

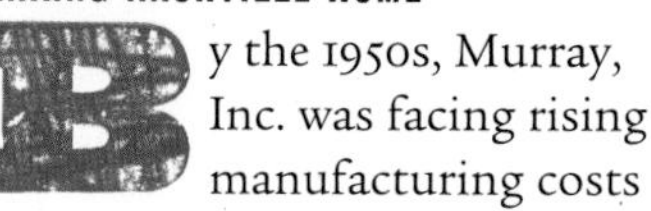

Making Nashville Home

By the 1950s, Murray, Inc. was facing rising manufacturing costs and an outdated facility at its Cleveland base. Following an exhaustive search for a new site, company officials moved its operations to Lawrenceburg, Tennessee, in 1956, simultaneously moving its corporate headquarters to Nashville. Attracted to the area, the people, and the sound work ethic, about 100 families relocated to Lawrenceburg, 75 miles southeast of Nashville,

Murray, Inc. relocated its corporate headquarters to the Greater Nashville area in 1956.

where a new manufacturing plant was built. This began a period of unprecedented growth for the company, as demand from baby boomers for Murray bikes and toys was seemingly insatiable.

As years passed and Americans moved to the suburbs in droves, Murray once again capitalized on opportunity and began production of its first lawn mowers in 1967. Since then, Murray's growth in the lawn care industry has catapulted to enormous heights. As one of the world's largest manufacturers of outdoor power equipment, the company boasts more than 4 million square feet of manufacturing space in its three final-assembly plants located in the United States.

The facilities produce a complete line of outdoor power equipment including walk-behind mowers, garden tractors, edgers, tillers, and chipper/shredders. Murray is also the leading manufacturer of snow throwers in North America.

Cutting Edge of Value

he Cutting Edge of Value" is an appropriate tag line for a company that worked to manufacture the first mass-market lawn tractor equipped with hydrostatic automatic drive. This premium feature, previously found on much more expensive tractors, allows the operator to control forward and reverse speeds without shifting or clutching. In 1997, Murray again came through with premium features for a mass-market tractor. Revolutionizing the industry, Murray used RailFrame technology, building its Wide-Body tractors with two solid steel beams as a foundation, to create the first line of consumer-engineered lawn tractors that offer premium features at a value price.

Since it began manufacturing lawn care products 30 years ago, Murray has put more than 19 million walk-behind mowers and 4 million riding mowers to work for its vast consuming public. And while the famed Mercury bike is no longer in production, Murray did have foresight into the emerging mountain bike craze, introducing the first BMX bike series to stores nationwide in 1975.

Through its remarkable history, Murray has fulfilled many dreams for young and old alike. Well-engineered products and value pricing—the keys to its success in the past—will serve the company well for many years to come.

War Memorial Plaza

Kraft Bros., Esstman, Patton & Harrell, PLLC

THE LARGEST INDEPENDENT CPA FIRM BASED IN NASHVILLE, Kraft Bros., Esstman, Patton & Harrell, PLLC (KraftCPAs), describes itself as the family firm for family businesses. Founded in 1958 by Joe Kraft, who died in 1993, and his brother Cyril, KraftCPAs has grown to employ more than 90 people and today has 14 member/owners and two offices in Middle Tennessee.

Despite tremendous growth, the firm hasn't outgrown the traditions of its founders—integrity, hard work, and commitment to the community. Lee Kraft, Joe's son, is now the only Kraft practicing with the firm, but the influence of family is still felt strongly, both within the firm and in the clients the firm serves.

"KraftCPAs has given three generations of Cohens the highest-quality corporate and personal advice. The firm's succession planning and tax planning advice has been invaluable to our family," says Larry S. Cohen.

Shirley Zeitlin agrees: "My family and I have trusted KraftCPAs with our business and personal finances for three generations. I have confidence in their professional ability and their commitment to first-class service."

The Kraft niche has always been family-owned and closely held businesses. "Because we started as a family business ourselves, we have experienced firsthand many of the complex issues and concerns of other family businesses," says Lee Kraft. This experience and the changing needs of their closely held clients prompted KraftCPAs to develop several unique specialties and affiliated companies.

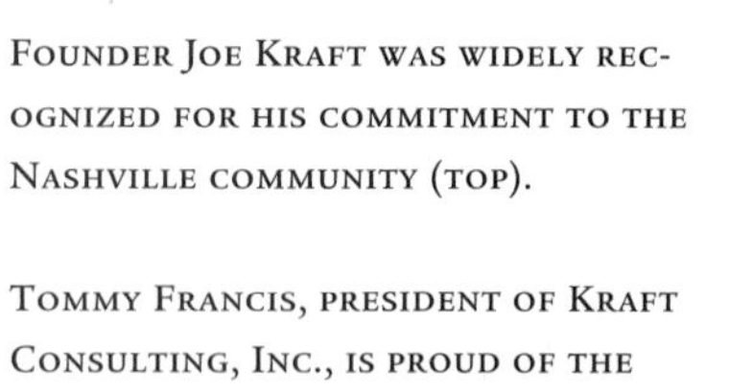

FOUNDER JOE KRAFT WAS WIDELY RECOGNIZED FOR HIS COMMITMENT TO THE NASHVILLE COMMUNITY (TOP).

TOMMY FRANCIS, PRESIDENT OF KRAFT CONSULTING, INC., IS PROUD OF THE COMPANY'S NOVELL- AND MICROSOFT-CERTIFIED STAFF (BOTTOM).

◄ DANA THOMAS

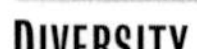

Diversity

In the early days, KraftCPAs focused primarily on tax, accounting, and auditing. But today, clients need and expect more from their CPA," according to Vic Alexander, the firm's chief manager. "We've always been the trusted adviser, but now our advice and expertise cover a wider range of issues—areas like computer technology, human resources, personal financial planning, financing, and profit enhancement strategies."

As pioneers in the field of personal financial planning, the firm created LINC (Licensed Independent Network of CPA Financial Planners) in 1984. Today, this organization of fee-only CPA financial planners has more than 260 members throughout the United States. The HR Group, LLC, formed in 1990, helps companies cope with the increasingly complex realm of personnel management by providing human resources consulting and executive search. Kraft Consulting, Inc., founded in 1993, provides consulting, products, and services in the vital area of technology management. Created in 1994, 2nd Generation Capital Corp. handles the financing issues that accompany corporate succession plans within a family-owned or closely held business. Most recently, Centennial Valuation Group, PLLC was started in 1996 to perform the valuations of businesses and intellectual property necessary for succession and estate planning, mergers and acquisitions, and a variety of other cases such as legal proceedings and disputes. The firm is also the exclusive provider in Middle Tennessee of The 100 Ways Profit Enhancement Process—a unique process designed to help organizations achieve their profit potential.

Although many of the firm's specialized services focus on the needs of closely held companies, KraftCPAs has cultivated a widely diversified client base, including substantial concentrations in health care—the fastest-growing industry group for KraftCPAs in terms of related revenue—as well as manufacturing, banking, service, distribution, music and entertainment, real estate, and not-for-profit and governmental entities.

Wynne E. Baker, member in charge of KraftCPAs' Banking Industry Group, serves as chair of the AICPA Banking and Savings Institutions Committee and president of the Tennessee Society of CPAs.

The diversity of the firm evolved in support of its mission. "The business mission of the firm is not just to provide compliance services or to react to situations as they arise, but to be proactive in helping our clients achieve success," Alexander emphasizes. Furthering that mission is KraftCPAs' membership in BKR International, an independent association that links select, locally owned CPA firms with resources beyond their immediate markets. The BKR affiliation allows KraftCPAs to provide resources and expertise nationally and internationally for clients whose interests extend beyond Middle Tennessee.

Commitment to Community and Family

Community involvement is a tradition that's still vibrant at KraftCPAs. The firm is a founding sponsor of the Center for Family Business at Belmont University, where it shares its expertise and experience with entrepreneurs and students. Members of the firm serve on numerous boards of civic, professional, and not-for-profit organizations, and all staff are encouraged to seek similar opportunities to serve the community.

A family-friendly firm, KraftCPAs received the first Academy for Women of Achievement award from the Nashville YWCA in recognition of the firm's efforts to create a business environment conducive to the advancement of women in the workplace. "We believe in creating a balance between work, family, and community involvement, which helps us attract and retain top professionals," explains Alexander.

DANA THOMAS

Karen Saul, president of the HR Group, LLC, was named to *Business Nashville*'s Top 40 under 40 list in 1996.

The Future

Alexander predicts that the future of KraftCPAs will look a lot like the recent past. The firm's goals are to remain diversified, to stay focused on closely held businesses, and to continue developing new products and services to meet clients' changing needs. "It's not important to us to be the biggest firm in town," says Alexander. "We're just working hard to be the best."

DANA THOMAS

The members and principals of KraftCPAs are (seated from left) Laroy Wolff, Nina Sivek, Phil Duncan, Lynn Edwards, Tommy Francis, (standing from left) Tom Boles, Vic Alexander, Mike Collins, Beverly Horner, Stephen High, Kent Harrell, Lee Kraft, Becky Harrell, Larry Carter, and Mike Ingram. Not pictured: Wynne E. Baker.

Earl Swensson Associates, Inc.

look in any direction around Nashville reveals the work of Earl Swensson Associates (ESa), one of the Southeast's premier architectural firms. Since 1961, ESa has left an imprint on the city that is unparalleled in the history of Nashville architecture. ★ ESa has designed more than 3,000 projects throughout the United States and has earned a national reputation in the health care and hospitality industries. The innovations and originality the firm has brought to projects in 34 states can be seen locally in the Opryland Hotel and Convention Center; Centennial and Summit medical centers; the landmark BellSouth Tennessee Headquarters building, affectionately nicknamed the "Batman" building because of its distinctive spires; Wildhorse Saloon; and Willis Corroon Plaza.

In years past, ESa brought to life such structures as the Tennessee State University Downtown Campus; WTVF-Channel 5 studios; Southern Baptist Convention Headquarters; and Loews Vanderbilt Plaza, a hotel/office complex where ESa offices are located. Each of these projects bears the creative signature that marks all of ESa's work—a unique marriage of form and function.

For the People

rue architecture is for people," says native Nashvillian Earl S. Swensson, FAIA, chairman and CEO of the firm. "It solves human problems and provides an environment for living with which people are comfortable," he adds. Based on that guiding principle, the firm has grown from a two-person operation to employing more than 130 people, including 36 registered architects.

The Opryland Hotel Convention Center embodies ESa's architectural approach. The glass-enclosed, climate-controlled environments of the Conservatory, the Cascades, and most recently, the four-acre Delta, provide a natural, outdoor experience, complete with waterfalls, boat rides on the quarter-mile river, and lush gardens, no matter what the weather outside. The phenomenal success of the Opryland Hotel is testament to the response ESa designs strike with their users.

Health Care Specialists

ealth care projects such as Centennial Medical Center emphasize a healing environment; convenience for families, patients, and staff; and cost-effective construction and floor plans. ESa is on the leading edge of health care facility design and enjoys a national reputation for redefining the hospital experience for millions of patients by designing patient-friendly facilities. Likewise, the twin spires of BellSouth in downtown Nashville, the state's tallest office building, could symbolize the firm's constant striving to break new architectural ground by combining dramatic design with function and cost efficiency. With its long history of both innovation and functionality, ESa is positioned to continue shaping Nashville's skyline into the next century.

The innovations and originality the firm has brought to projects in 34 states can be seen locally in (clockwise from bottom right) Centennial Medical Center; the Opryland Hotel Convention Center; and the landmark Bell-South Tennessee Headquarters building, affectionately nicknamed the "Batman" building because of its distinctive twin spires.

◀ Jon Miller, Hedrich-Blessing

◀ Jonathan Hillyer

◀ Norman McGrath

Charles Hampton A-1 Signs

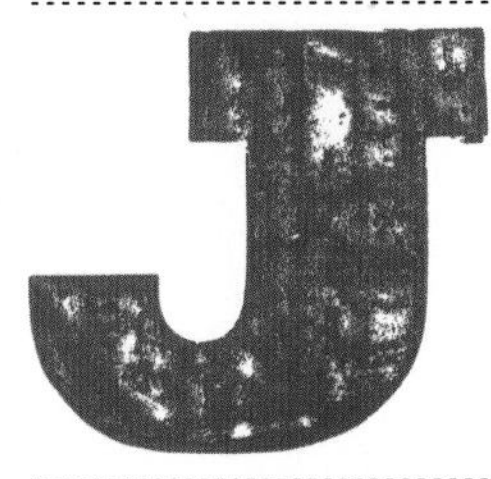

JUST 35 MILES WEST OF NASHVILLE IS A COMPANY THAT TAKES pride in teaching a trade through an old-fashioned apprenticeship program. Since its inception in 1966, Charles Hampton's A-1 Signs has been honing its craft of custom sign construction for both small businesses and large corporations.

While the training is appropriately hands-on, old-world style, the 30,000-square-foot A-1 facility is anything but old fashioned. Located on approximately eight acres in Dickson County, the fully computerized manufacturing operation is equipped to construct all signs—from raw materials to finished product—on-site. A-1 specializes in the heavy manufacture of custom signs in neon and plastic, as well as any other type of lighted sign.

"Since most of our customers are from out of town, we've purchased our own aircraft to transport our staff and crew to customer sites," says Charles Hampton, founder. "That makes us a bit unique in the industry." Hampton cites Nashville's ideal location—within 600 miles of 70 percent of the U.S. population—as well as its favorable business climate and lifestyle, as key factors in A-1's growth and success.

The Customer Comes First

Fully self-contained, A-1 loads and delivers the signs with its own crew and truck fleet, and installs the finished products with the help of the local companies. Even after installation, A-1 continues to handle maintenance. "Customer service is the most important thing in our business," notes Hampton. "Being involved in installation anywhere in the country is in keeping with our company philosophy. We sell value and service, not price, because that's what keeps us in business."

As another value-added service, the company scouts potential building sites for interested parties. Prior to the purchase of the property, A-1 will ascertain codes, survey and video the site, and present an analysis of what type of sign will be most beneficial in making that business location successful.

Changing with the Times

Charles Hampton initially set up shop as a sign painter, lettering windows, trucks, and similar surfaces. As Interstate 40 was being completed from Dickson to Nashville, he capitalized on the area's progress by building and leasing billboards. When legislation was passed in 1974 to restrict billboards to commercial property, Hampton launched A-1's heavy manufacturing business.

A-1's eye-catching neon signs draw customers into motels and restaurants, including O'Charley's, Logan's Roadhouse, Rafferty's, Cracker Barrel, Rio Bravo, Drury Inn, and Clubhouse Inn. The signs welcoming individuals into American General Insurance offices nationwide are also A-1's well-crafted products.

"We have grown and will continue to grow by following the needs of our customers. We've been fortunate because our success has followed the success of our customers," adds Hampton.

Although the company is growing rapidly, Hampton remains committed to the small-business approach, maintaining, "The good thing about small business is that every customer is part of our quality control. We have the ability to be more creative and incorporate everyone's input for the best final outcome." That formula has worked for A-1 Signs since 1966 and will continue to bring success to the company for many years to come.

A-1'S EYE-CATCHING NEON SIGNS DRAW CUSTOMERS INTO A VARIETY OF FACILITIES, INCLUDING RIO BRAVO, CUMBERLAND SCIENCE MUSEUM, LOGAN'S ROADHOUSE, CLUB HOUSE INN, AND COOLSPRINGS GALLERIA.

Fleetguard, Inc.

A WALL-SIZE MAP OF THE WORLD INDICATING OFFICES IN SHANGhai, Quimper, Mexico City, São Paulo, Melbourne, and Nashville—to mention just a few—greets visitors at the corporate headquarters of Fleetguard, Inc., one of the largest manufacturers of heavy-duty filtration products in the world.

With approximately 75 employees in its Nashville headquarters and another 2,400 employees spanning the globe, Fleetguard manufactures and distributes filtration products to original equipment manufacturers, distributor/dealer networks, and end users around the world. The company operates production and distribution facilities in North America, South America, Europe, Australia, and Asia, and most recently opened a state-of-the-art manufacturing plant in Shanghai, and a new distribution center in South Africa.

"Fleetguard stands for the principles of quality, innovation, and integrity," says M. David Jones, president. "These principles are the core of Fleetguard's remarkable growth and success."

Fleetguard began as an in-house manufacturer of filters for Cummins diesel engines in 1958. To serve the overwhelming number of applications requiring filtration products, Fleetguard began producing several different products for heavy-duty equipment under its own Fleetguard brand and opened the first Fleetguard filter manufacturing plant in Cookeville, Tennessee, in 1967. Executives chose the plant site to take advantage of Tennessee's technological opportunities.

In 1970, the company became a full subsidiary of Cummins Engine Company, the world's largest manufacturer of heavy-duty diesel engines. Cummins, a Fortune 500 company traded as NYSE:CUM, reports $5.2 billion in annual sales. In 1995, Fleetguard became a Cummins' strategic business unit. Cummins' other strategic business units are Automotive, Power Generation, and Industrial. Each business unit includes worldwide marketing, engineering, and manufacturing capabilities.

Innovative Filtration Leader

Fleetguard attracts top business school graduates and engineers as part of its diverse, global workforce. Using the most advanced technology tools, Fleetguard engineers are on the cutting edge of filtration technology, as evidenced by the design of products like the patented LF3000 combination stacked disk/bypass lube filter and the state-of-the-art DCA4™ cooling system chemistry, and by the development of high-efficiency synthetic filtration media like new StrataPore multilayered media, which recently won the prestigious American Filtration & Separations Society Award for

Fleetguard manufactures and distributes filtration products to original equipment manufacturers, distributor/dealer networks, and end users around the world.

innovation in filtration media technology.

Fleetguard's comprehensive line of filtration products includes air, fuel, lube, hydraulic, and coolant filters. Additionally, a full range of cold-weather products, service tools, cooling system products, and fluid analysis programs comprise the product line.

Fleetguard also has three subsidiary businesses in North America: Kuss Corporation, a specialty filter manufacturer; Lubricant Consultants, Inc., which consists of fluid analysis laboratories; and Separation Technologies, which manufactures filters for military/aerospace markets.

Customer-Driven Quality Philosophy

With total commitment to quality, Fleetguard thoroughly tests both its raw materials and finished product. This includes extensive multi-pass, flat-sheet, pressure, on-line, and field tests, as well as computer-monitored lab tests.

Evidence of Fleetguard's commitment to a strong quality system has been validated by numerous external audits by customers and third-party registrars. Fleetguard has an extensive list of customer certifications worldwide, including John Deere, Navistar International, JI Case, Ford, RVI, Scania, and DAF. Six locations around the world have ISO 9000 certification. While this list is impressive today, Fleetguard recognizes that it must continue to improve. The company achieved QS-9000 registration in January 1997. Improvement will continue beyond QS-9000 by using the Malcolm Baldrige National Quality Award/Tennessee Quality Award criteria to improve the total business process.

Jones stresses this quality philosophy with employees. "Quality means excellence in everything we do—in our products, services, communications, plants, distribution centers, and offices. Our quality commitment reaches beyond just product and includes how telephones are answered, how customer tours are conducted, and the housekeeping in our places of work."

"Fleetguard stands for the principles of quality, innovation, and integrity," says M. David Jones, president. "These principles are the core of Fleetguard's remarkable growth and success."

Customer Satisfaction and Service

While the company operates in an innovative and high-tech world, its commitment to customers is its top priority. Jones says, "The most important product is our people. Innovation in services and customer support is just as important as innovation in product technology."

Fleetguard offers customers a complete value package of products, services, and information. These services include solving maintenance problems beyond traditional filtration concerns, use of the Internet to communicate with customers, and a 24-hour multilanguage Customer Assistance Center. Additionally, Fleetguard offers distributor and end user training that presents customers with detailed product information and preventive maintenance measures.

Building on Integrity

With steady, consistent global growth as its hallmark, Fleetguard continues to stretch its operations to serve the worldwide market. Part of the company's strategy is also to improve the communities in which it does business. Locally, the company is proud of its Tennessee home and actively participates in providing scholarships and grants for students in Putnam and Davidson counties. Fleetguard recently formed a four-year partnership with Tennessee State University in Nashville to reward achievement and academic excellence for economically disadvantaged African-American youth. The program includes summer employment, internships, scholarships, and research project funding. In addition, a foundation benefiting area charities administered by Cummins Engine Company recently provided a $20,000 grant to build an innovative, new community playground in Cookeville.

COLUMBIA/HCA

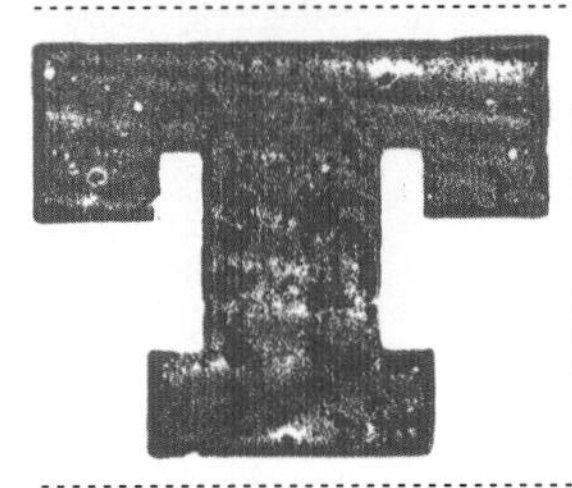

THROUGH A SERIES OF JOINT VENTURES, STRATEGIC MERGERS, and partnership agreements, Columbia/HCA Healthcare Corporation has grown to become one of the nation's largest providers of health care services, with 133 surgery centers, 560 home health locations, and 347 hospitals in the United States, England, and Switzerland.

Columbia/HCA serves the Nashville area with nine hospitals, which have a combined total of more than 1,700 beds. Providing more than $318 in uncompensated and charity care last year, these facilities offer a vast array of primary care, emergency care, and specialty services, including the midstate's largest full-service psychiatric facility, the area's most comprehensive cancer program, and one of the region's leading women's health centers, as well as having one of only eight training sites in the world for minimally invasive heart surgery.

Columbia/HCA was formed from the merger of two hospital companies. The original company, Columbia Hospital Corporation, was founded in 1987 by Richard Scott in Dallas. Columbia merged with Hospital Corporation of America (HCA) in 1994 and adopted the name Columbia/HCA Healthcare Corporation. Recently, the corporation commemorated the 35th anniversary of the opening of the former Park Vista Convalescent Hospital and Nursing Home in Nashville—the founding HCA facility.

A NEW STANDARD IN HEALTH CARE

With its grand opening on December 20, 1961, Park Vista was touted in local newspapers as "the first of its kind in the city" and "the largest facility of its kind in the South." The $1.2 million facility, designed to serve as a nursing home and hospital, was eventually converted to acute care, and the name was changed to Park View Hospital.

In 1968, Park View was sold to a group of physicians and businessmen, who formed HCA. Composed of Dr. Thomas F. Frist Sr., one of the original owners of Park View; his son, Dr. Thomas F. Frist Jr.; and local businessman Jack Massey, the group believed that a network of hospitals, if operated properly, could provide high-caliber medical care at competitive costs and still be self-supporting and financially successful. The corporation acquired 11 hospitals

CLOCKWISE FROM TOP: COLUMBIA NASHVILLE MEMORIAL HOSPITAL, A FULL-SERVICE, 315-BED MEDICAL CENTER SERVING ALL OF MIDDLE TENNESSEE AND SOUTHERN KENTUCKY, IS KNOWN PARTICULARLY FOR ONCOLOGY, NEUROLOGY, EMERGENCY SERVICES, ORTHOPAEDICS, OUTPATIENT CARE, AND NEUROSURGERY.

RECENTLY NAMED ONE OF THE TOP 100 HOSPITALS IN THE NATION BY HCIA, COLUMBIA HENDERSONVILLE HOSPITAL HAS SERVED THE RESIDENTS OF SUMNER COUNTY AND SURROUNDING AREAS SINCE 1979.

ONE OF THE NATION'S TOP-PERFORMING HOSPITALS, COLUMBIA HORIZON MEDICAL CENTER IS A FULL-SERVICE, 176-BED FACILITY LOCATED 35 MILES WEST OF NASHVILLE.

COLUMBIA SOUTHERN HILLS MEDICAL CENTER HAS BUILT A REPUTATION FOR OUTSTANDING EMERGENCY SERVICES, AS WELL AS OBSTETRIC, NEUROSURGERY, CARDIOLOGY, AND ORTHOPAEDIC SERVICES.

A FIRST-RATE MEDICAL AND SURGICAL FACILITY, COLUMBIA SUMMIT MEDICAL CENTER IS KNOWN FOR EMERGENCY CARE, COMPREHENSIVE DIABETES MANAGEMENT, AND OBSTETRIC SERVICES.

within its first year and became publicly owned in April 1969.

Now known as Columbia Centennial Medical Center, the former Park View has grown into one of the largest Columbia facilities, encompassing a 32-acre campus. It is one of eight Columbia facilities located in and around Nashville, and is also home to Columbia's corporate offices.

A 685-bed facility located in the heart of Nashville, Columbia Centennial Medical Center offers a full array of primary care, emergency, cardiac, neurologic, orthopaedic, obstetrics, psychiatric, and other specialty services. Columbia Centennial is composed of four main facilities: The Women's Hospital, Parthenon Pavilion, The Sarah Cannon Cancer Center, and Centennial Tower, which houses the region's most advanced tertiary care treatment capabilities and links all four campus facilities.

Providing Health Care to Middle Tennessee

Recently named one of the Top 100 Hospitals in the nation by HCIA, a Baltimore-based health care information company, Columbia Hendersonville Hospital has served the residents of Sumner County and surrounding areas since 1979. The 120-bed hospital offers state-of-the-art medical/surgical care, obstetrics/gynecology, critical care and skilled nursing services, 24-hour emergency services, MRI, cardiac catheterization lab, home health, and outpatient services.

One of the nation's top-performing hospitals, Columbia Horizon Medical Center is a full-service, 176-bed facility located 35 miles west of Nashville. The hospital encompasses nuclear medicine, MRI, and a 24-hour physician staffed emergency room, as well as complete labor, delivery, and nursing services. Columbia Cheatham Medical Center in Ashland City has an additional 29 beds. Both facilities are supported by the Jackson Clinic, a 56-member physician group covering 20 medical specialties. A foundation has also been established for the Dickson County community to finance various charitable, educational, and cultural endeavors.

Columbia Nashville Memorial Hospital, a full-service, 315-bed medical center serving all of Middle Tennessee and southern Kentucky, is known particularly for oncology, neurology, emergency services, orthopaedics, outpatient care, and neurosurgery. The hospital offers a skilled care unit, rehabilitation, home health services, and a fitness center open to the general public.

A Columbia affiliate and nonprofit facility, NorthCrest Medical Center recently moved to a brand-new, 164,000-square-foot medical complex located on 43 acres in Springfield, 45 miles north of Nashville.

A first-rate medical and surgical facility, Columbia Summit Medical Center is known for emergency care, comprehensive diabetes management, and obstetric services. The 214-bed facility, completed in 1995, also provides progressive laparoscopic and other same-day surgery, psychiatric care, home health care, neurosurgery, and orthopaedic and pediatric services.

Serving patients in the fast-growing communities of south Davidson, Rutherford, and Williamson counties, Columbia Southern Hills Medical Center has long been known as a strong source of quality primary care physicians. The 180-bed, award-winning facility has also built a reputation for outstanding emergency services, as well as obstetric, neurosurgery, cardiology, and orthopaedic services.

Additionally, seven Columbia Care Medical Centers, which focus primarily on occupational medicine and urgent care, serve the Nashville area.

The Columbia Healthcare Network (CHN) also provides consulting, contracting, medical management, data management, and claims administrative services for physician groups and hospital facilities across Tennessee and into surrounding states.

With the broad range of health care services offered at the hospitals of Columbia's Nashville Division, Columbia/HCA has taken to heart the words of Dr. Thomas F. Frist Sr.: "A quality hospital does not mean bricks and mortar. It stems from quality care." With Columbia's commitment to lowering the costs of health care while simultaneously improving quality, outcomes, and patient satisfaction, this philosophy has led to a positive result. According to Gallup surveys, 94 percent of former Columbia patients in Tennessee hospitals are "satisfied to very satisfied" with the care they received at a Columbia facility. No doubt Columbia is committed to taking care of Nashvillians for many years to come.

Centennial Tower houses the region's most advanced tertiary care treatment capabilities and links all four Centennial campus facilities.

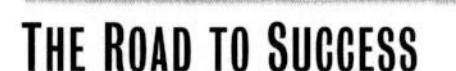

Comdata Corporation

omdata Corporation moves money and makes the complex business of moving it a safe bet for its customers in the transportation and gaming industries. From its headquarters in Brentwood, Comdata's proprietary telecommunications and computer network annually handles more than 60 million transactions, fields more than 118 million telephone calls, processes more than $10 billion in cash transfers, and employs more than 2,100 people in 14 locations.

With operations in the United States and Canada, Comdata is a wholly owned subsidiary of Ceridian Corporation, a $1.5 billion information services and defense electronics company based in Minneapolis.

"Comdata's mission is to continue to be the largest and best provider of information, financial, and decision support to the ground fleet transportation industry of North America and to the gaming industry worldwide," says Chairman George L. McTavish.

The Road to Success

omdata was founded in 1969 to address the over-the-road needs of the long-haul trucking industry. This is now a multibillion-dollar indus-try in the United States. Before, Comdata motor carriers had no simple way to provide secure fund-ing for drivers on the road or to obtain detailed tracking information on those funds.

Today, Comdata is a leading provider of these services to the transportation industry, in addition to serving more than 8,000 merchant locations with transaction processing systems and data services. The majority of America's long-haul trucking companies, representing hundreds of thousands of truck drivers, use the multipurpose Comdata Comchek card to receive cash advances, access personal as well as company-provided funds at ATMs, and pay for fuel, phone calls, and meals while on the road. Payroll and trip settlements also are deposited on this Comchek card, from which the drivers can draw funds throughout North America. It's like a traveling bank account.

Comdata serves the back-office needs of trucking companies at the same time that it makes drivers' lives easier on the road. Comdata provides reports to the fleets as to what funds were used, as well as when and where purchases were made.

Comdata's permitting service facilitates compliance with shipping regulations, its auditing program corrects the drivers' logs for DOT revisions, its safety and training services ensure that trips are made safely, a professional counseling service helps the drivers and their families cope with personal problems, and Comdata's SuperDriver™ audio magazine entertains and instructs the driver along the way.

Comdata's fuel tax reporting service makes use of breakthrough technologies, including optical character recognition (OCR) and image character recognition (ICR). The innovative application of these technologies helps carriers improve efficiency and accuracy by automating the data entry process associated with processing their fuel tax forms. The service also allows carriers to maintain their own vehicle database while exchanging data with Comdata via diskette or a direct computer-to-computer link. This interactive data linkage significantly reduces processing and data entry requirements, resulting in benefits for carriers and a major competitive edge for Comdata.

An additional service using these same technologies allows a carrier to bill its customers through Comdata within 24 hours of delivery of goods, and Comdata also

Comdata is proud to sponsor two of Nashville's NASCAR race cars (top).

Providing debit and credit card advances, as well as other types of cash advance opportunities, Comdata is the leader in electronic financial transaction services for America's growing gaming industry (bottom).

From its headquarters in Brentwood, Comdata's proprietary telecommunications and computer network annually handles more than 60 million transactions, fields more than 118 million telephone calls, processes more than $10 billion in cash transfers annually, and employs more than 2,100 people in 14 locations.

will fund its accounts receivable immediately, thus radically improving the carrier's critical cash flow.

Gaming Services

Providing debit and credit card advances, as well as other types of cash advance opportunities, Comdata is the leader in electronic financial transaction (EFT) services for America's growing gaming industry. The gaming includes casinos, racetracks, cruise ships, and pari-mutuel establishments, and is currently a multibillion-dollar international industry.

With more than 15 years of experience in the gaming services industry, Comdata has a presence in virtually all gaming locations in the United States and a growing presence in locations in the Caribbean and abroad. In the past, gaming patrons were limited to cash advances as dictated by bank-operated ATMs, with limited funding capabilities, or to in-house credit extended by each individual gaming location. Using Comdata's services, patrons have unlimited access to their own funds in the form of personal cash advances. In addition, Comdata provides gaming properties with a simple workstation system that lets customers process all types of financial transactions and simultaneously allows the gaming properties to capture valuable customer data.

The security of funds provided by Comdata, coupled with the company's wide array of services—including ATMs, inside money machines, "in-the-pit" services, Western Union wire transfers, debit card services, and a growing database of industry information—makes Comdata the supplier of choice in funds transfer among gaming locations.

Data As a Service

A total, companywide commitment to providing superior customer service is the hallmark of Comdata and the driving force of our business," McTavish says. Comdata maintains its exacting service standards by combining leading-edge technology with expert, friendly people to provide the optimum in customer satisfaction. Comdata's systems are innovative enough to meet ever changing needs, yet reliable enough to get the job done when an excited player needs cash in Reno or an overworked trucking executive needs fuel and trip data in Dallas.

As a technology-based company with 27 years of experience, Comdata has a solid reputation for providing outstanding service. Both the transportation and gaming industries have unique needs, but in each case, the common denominators are the three core areas in which Comdata offers unparalleled expertise: transaction processing, information services, and financial controls.

Comdata maintains its exacting service standards by combining leading-edge technology with expert, friendly people to provide the optimum in customer satisfaction.

Thomas Nelson, Inc.

ROM ITS HUMBLE BEGINNINGS AS AN APPRENTICE BOOKSELLER in Scotland to its position as the world's largest Christian publisher, Thomas Nelson, Inc., which produces Christian and inspirational books, Bibles, and gifts, is committed to sharing an inspirational message with the mainstream population. Its new product introductions, expansion of existing lines, and new market channels have propelled Thomas Nelson, Inc. into a success story measured not only in message but also in revenues approaching $250 million.

Building a Publishing Empire

The company roots reach deep into late 18th-century Scotland where an apprentice bookseller named Thomas Nelson had a dream of producing books for the masses, not just the wealthy elite. In 1798, his dream became a reality when he began to publish excerpts from classics such as *The Pilgrim's Progress.*

In 1854, Nelson's son opened a New York branch—Thomas Nelson & Sons—making Nelson the first British publisher to open an office in the United States. The year 1901 proved to be a milestone year for the company as it published the American Standard Version of the Bible.

Sam Moore is president and CEO of Thomas Nelson, Inc. (top).

Thomas Nelson Gifts is the fourth-largest manufacturer and marketer of gift and stationery items in the world. Its products include photo albums and social books, baby and wedding memory books, decorative boxes, stationery, gift wrap, and bags (bottom).

Decades later, Thomas Nelson & Sons caught the eye of a young Lebanese immigrant, Sam Moore, who eventually purchased the company. Moore had paid his way through college at the University of South Carolina and at Columbia Bible College and Seminary by selling books door-to-door. He drew upon his sales experience in college and founded the National Book Company, a door-to-door book distribution company, in 1958. In 1961, Moore merged his company with Royal Publishers, Inc., a leading Bible publisher.

Under Moore's direction, Royal Publishers, Inc. purchased the U.S. division of Thomas Nelson & Sons in 1969 for $2.6 million and moved the corporate headquarters to Nashville in 1972. The deal garnered Moore increased distribution channels and a respected name in the world of religious book publishing.

Moore is credited with changing the face of the company by broadening and building upon its core Bible business. "Good people and a sound strategy of focusing on market niches that the company can serve well is really all it takes," says Moore.

A Recession-Proof Business

The heart of Thomas Nelson's business is Bibles. With nine of the leading Bible translations on its backlist—King James, American Standard, Revised Standard, New Revised Standard, New King James, Today's English, Living Bible, New American, and Contemporary English Version—the division reports annual Bible revenues of approximately $45 million. As the world's largest Bible publisher, the company produces more than 1,300 editions and formats of the Bible and biblical reference products in the various translations for a worldwide market.

Byron Williamson is president of NelsonWord Publishing Group (left).

Joseph Moore is president of Thomas Nelson Gifts (right).

With its 1992 acquisition of Word, Incorporated, a Dallas-based Christian book publisher, Thomas Nelson has broadened its customer base significantly. In addition, the company's Book Division publishes more than 200 Christian and inspirational books per year. With publishing authors like Billy Graham, Charles Swindoll, Charles Stanley, Frank Peretti, Barbara Johnson, and Bodie and Brock Thoene, Thomas Nelson and Word titles consistently dominate the Christian best-seller list in hardcover and paperback. New authors appealing to a secular audience include Evander Holyfield as well as H. Jackson Brown Jr., who penned *Life's Little Instruction Book*.

Thomas Nelson has also tapped into new distribution channels through mass merchandisers like Wal-Mart, Sam's Wholesale Club, and Target. This marketing tool has generated additional revenue for the company as well as introduced the Thomas Nelson name to the general-interest audience.

Thomas Nelson's gift division more than doubled its size in 1996 through the acquisition of the prestigious C.R. Gibson Company. The acquisition brought together four major brands: C.R. Gibson, Markings, Pretty Paper, and Creative Papers, creating Thomas Nelson Gifts, the fourth-largest manufacturer and marketer of gift and stationery items in the world. The company's product offering now includes more than 6,000 items marketed under the trademarks of the four brands and boasts a custom sales force of more than 100 representatives.

Products include photo albums and social books, baby and wedding memory books, ceramics, decorative boxes, stationery, gift wrap and bags, and paper tableware. The design-driven, award-winning product line features such best-sellers as the Beatrix Potter Baby collection and groupings by such high-profile designers as Carol Endres, Warren Kimble, Williamsburg, Waverly, and Lillian August, as well as partnerships with such companies as Disney, Warner Brothers, and Looney Tunes.

In keeping with the spirit at Thomas Nelson, Inc., its 700-person workforce in Nashville continually reaches out into the community, participating in American Red Cross Blood Drives and the Juvenile Diabetes Walk for a Cause. The company as a whole contributes to many charitable endeavors, including Nashville Union Mission, Second Harvest Food Bank, Junior Achievement, Earning by Learning, Nashville Reads, Nashville Symphony, and Fisk University. With some 1,200 employees nationwide, Thomas Nelson, Inc.—now traded on the New York Stock Exchange (TNM)—has achieved great milestones since its 18th-century founding. With double-digit earnings and sales gains and a broadening customer base, the world's largest Christian product provider remains true to its mission statement: to honor God, serve humanity, and enhance shareholder value.

Thomas Nelson's Book Division publishes more than 200 Christian and inspirational books per year, and its titles consistently dominate the Christian best-seller list in hardcover and paperback.

Baker, Donelson, Bearman & Caldwell

Building on a rich tradition of legal practice that spans the Southeast, Baker, Donelson, Bearman & Caldwell has become the state's largest law firm, numbering more than 230 attorneys, and one of the few southeastern firms in the *National Law Journal*'s ranking of the top 150 firms in the United States.

The present firm is a result of steady growth and a number of combinations since its founding in 1911. The most recent name change occurred in 1994 with the combination of Heiskell, Donelson, Bearman, Adams, Williams & Caldwell with Baker, Worthington, Crossley & Stansberry. The latter firm was founded in 1888 by the grandfather of former Senate Majority Leader and White House Chief of Staff Howard Baker. Baker and former Secretary of State Lawrence Eagleburger now lead the firm's Public Policy and International groups, respectively, while John A. Gupton III is currently the managing director of the firm's Nashville office.

In addition to its Nashville office, Baker, Donelson maintains offices in Memphis, Chattanooga, Knoxville, Tri-Cities TN/VA, and Huntsville, Tennessee; Jackson, Mississippi; and Washington, D.C. Although the firm's practice is concentrated in Tennessee and the Southeast, its clients' business activities span the nation and the world.

Investment in Experience

No other law firm in the region has the level of experience across so many practice areas, from management of corporate matters and transactions, complex litigation, alternative dispute resolution, and international transactions to industry-specific, multidisciplinary teams. As the firm has grown, it has aggressively broadened and deepened its practice areas by combining with others known for their experience in various fields. In addition, Baker, Donelson actively recruits and trains the best new attorneys. The firm is committed to enhanced client service by maintaining industry teams comprised of attorneys, advisers, paralegals, and support staff, and by exploring issues and industry trends that will impact its clients in the future.

Diversity in Expertise

Employing more than 500 people, including paralegals and support staff, the firm focuses on 18 areas of practice. These include bankruptcy and creditors' rights, commercial lending, communications, corporate, environmental, ERISA and employee benefits, estate planning and probate, health law, intellectual property, international, labor and employment, litigation, mergers and acquisitions, public policy, real estate, securities, tax, and transportation.

With more than 230 attorneys and eight offices, the firm has a considerable pool of resources available to handle any matter, regardless of size, as well as the critical experience and leading technology to manage and communicate effectively between offices. This capability allows the attorneys to tap into a large base of industry and legal experience to better serve their clients. Each matter is aggressively managed to ensure efficiency and to maintain control of costs.

The following attorneys are certified as Civil Trial Specialists by the Tennessee Commission on Continuing Legal Education and Specialization: Thomas O. Helton (Chattanooga), and Jill

Before beginning construction on the world's largest super battery plant, one of the firm's clients needed environmental permits. To meet the client's deadlines, Baker, Donelson, Bearman & Caldwell coordinated a fast-track process so that all permits were filed and in place within 60 days (top).

After retention as statewide counsel, 17,000 pending product liability asbestos cases were resolved in three months (bottom).

Baker, Donelson, Bearman & Caldwell's experience with securities includes a multitiered financing deal for a manufacturing concern resulting in an initial public offering of stock ranked as the third-largest in the Southeast.

M. Steinberg (Memphis). John C. Speer is chair of the Litigation Department, which encompasses the areas of Employment, Environmental, Commercial Litigation, Tort, and Bankruptcy and Creditors' Rights. Charles T. Tuggle Jr. is chair of the Corporate Department, which encompasses the areas of Intellectual Property, General Corporate/Mergers and Acquisitions, International, Public Policy, and Securities. Richard G. Cowart is chair of the Health Law Department. Thomas L. Howard is chair of the Tax Department. Robert C. Liddon is chair of the Commercial Lending and Real Estate Department. These department chairmen are not currently certified in any areas of specialization.

Clients and Industries Served

Baker, Donelson represents a wide variety of public and private companies at the local, regional, national, and international levels. Industries served include securities, technology, engineering, construction, telecommunications, manufacturing, restaurant chains, insurance, banking, transportation, energy, defense, aerospace, financial institutions, investment banking, health care, pharmaceuticals, real estate development, and real estate investment trusts.

The firm represents clients in significant transactions, including representing a specialty health care company and its simultaneous acquisition of the assets of 54 medical practices in 10 states—one of the largest physician combinations in history. In the international arena, a multibillion-dollar U.S. company engaged in the international telecommunications business had its cellular service abruptly halted in an Asian country. Through Baker, Donelson's negotiation efforts in the United States and abroad, the company's communications system was restored.

The size and scope of the firm places at the disposal of its clients an abundance of resources to handle any matter regardless of size—from a simple real estate transaction to complex class-action litigation involving thousands of plaintiffs. The firm has both the experience and leading-edge technology necessary to communicate and coordinate the efforts of its eight offices. Attorneys aggressively manage each matter to ensure efficiency and cost control.

Focusing on Client Service

Baker, Donelson provides exceptional service and results to its clients on a cost-effective basis. To maintain excellence in client service, the firm has incorporated into its strategic plan tactics for continuously monitoring and evaluating client satisfaction—a form of total quality management brought to the legal profession.

The firm's outstanding record of performance stems from vigilance in strategic planning and responsiveness to the newest professional resources available to enhance client service. Baker, Donelson's sophisticated communications network sets the firm apart from competitors, allowing for instant communication among attorneys and paralegals in all of the firm's offices. The system provides Internet access, electronic mail, voice mail, electronic database research, access to research materials on CD-ROM, document sharing, and direct networking with clients.

These competitive advantages have brought about improved customer service and satisfaction. Baker, Donelson has continued to increase revenues and expand its client base following the 1994 merger—no small challenge for an organization undergoing a major transition.

Commitment to Community Service

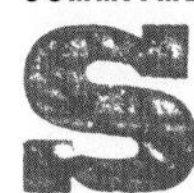Service of another sort is also central to the core values of Baker, Donelson. In addition to the public service and pro bono work of its members, each associate attorney donates 100 hours a year of service and pro bono work to activities benefiting the Nashville community. The firm is involved with the Nashville Bar Association, Tennessee Bar Association, Nashville Area Chamber of Commerce, Iroquois Steeplechase, Downtown Nashville Partnership, The Hermitage, Nashville Symphony, area museums, and other local civic and charitable organizations. Attorneys frequently speak at schools and introduce young people to the field of law. The tenets of exceptional service to its clients and to the community are part of the more than 100-year history of Baker, Donelson, Bearman & Caldwell.

Certification as a specialist in the following areas of practice by the Tennessee Commission on Continuing Legal Education and Specialization is not currently available: Environmental Law; Estate Planning and Probate; Health Care Law; Labor & Employment Law; Patent, Trademark & Copyright Law; Securities Law; and Taxation Law. Certification as a specialist in the following areas of practice by the Tennessee Commission on Continuing Legal Education and Specialization is currently available: Civil Trial, Business Bankruptcy, Consumer Bankruptcy, and Creditors' Rights.

OLSTEN STAFFING SERVICES

Y FILLING POSITIONS RANGING FROM A CHIEF FINANCIAL officer to a cleaning crew, Olsten Staffing Services helps Middle Tennessee businesses maintain smooth operations by providing qualified temporary and full-time employees. "We're in the human resource field, and we're in the business to find qualified applicants. Doing our job well allows our clients to focus on their business," says Mike Conyer, general manager. "We're not just going to send them anyone. We'll send someone who can do the job."

MAKING A PERFECT MATCH

Olsten provides staffing solutions in the full range of skill categories, including production, warehousing, and comprehensive office services. Its professional services division places qualified candidates in areas including accounting, legal support, computers, banking, and engineering. Through its Olsten Healthcare subsidiary, the company's 600 health care offices provide caregivers for home health care and institutions, as well as management services to hospital-based home health agencies. In addition to traditional staffing needs, Olsten establishes partnerships with companies who source out all their human resource functions.

"Employees—salary and benefits—are a company's largest expense," says Conyer. "We can help with staffing during peak periods and allow businesses to run more efficiently to improve their bottom line."

Olsten's enhances its expertise through a state-of-the-art software testing and training system called Precise®, which allows Olsten to test applicants using a skill-based system that evaluates the candidate's work on accuracy, efficiency, and timeliness. Working for Olsten gives assignment employees an opportunity to increase their skills though hands-on training. "Perhaps more important is that we treat employees as part of the team, and not just a number. We are very committed to the best interests of our employees and our clients," says Conyer.

To meet the needs of major corporations, the Olsten Partnership Program® provides a managed services approach to staffing that includes on- or off-site dedicated managers and master vendor arrangements. Under this program, Olsten recruits, trains, and manages large groups of assignment employees and provides Customized Added-Value SM services that maximize the client's staffing investment.

AN INTERNATIONAL NETWORK

Olsten's nine offices in Middle Tennessee and southern Kentucky are part of a network of more than 1,400 offices on three continents. Considered the father of temporary staffing companies, William Olsten founded the company that bears his name in 1950. In 1974, the company opened its first Nashville office. By 1988, there was an Olsten office in every state.

Today, Olsten Staffing Services is one of the largest human resources providers in North America—with more than 650,000 employees providing services to more than 575,000 client/patient accounts. The company reported 1996 systemwide sales of more than $4.1 billion and revenues exceeding $3.5 billion. Olsten has established more than 350 strategic partnerships nationwide with a myriad of companies that are household names.

Bolstered by the support of its national network, the Nashville office services many of those strategic partnerships locally. "While we have a strong national base, we maintain total autonomy and flexibility on a local level," adds Conyer. Olsten handles its purchasing locally, and supports many local charities and events.

A well-trained, qualified workforce is key to Nashville's continued growth and economic development. As part of Olsten's long-term commitment to Nashville, it will aggressively pursue training to improve assignment employees' skills—in part with plans to open a freestanding training center for this purpose and to expand into Middle Tennessee through branch offices as needed.

The natural environment of Nashville Zoo features more than 600 exotic animals.

TOWERY PUBLISHING

Film House

hen Film House was founded in 1976, there were only a handful of hungry filmmakers in Nashville. Since its earliest days, the company has taken a leadership role in efforts to grow the local film and video community—helping to develop Nashville from just a music center into one of the world's major producers of multimedia entertainment. And that growth continues today as new companies, exciting new creative coalitions, and dizzying technological advances all combine to make the sky the limit for Nashville's film and video industry.

Almost from the beginning, Film House has been privileged to work with a clientele of world-class names, including Coca-Cola, Whirlpool, Texas Instruments, and Hartmann Luggage. In 1981, Film House made its debut in the business of producing television commercials to promote radio stations, and quickly established itself as the worldwide leader in that highly specialized field, helping to engineer landmark successes for hundreds of radio stations in the United States, Canada, and around the globe. Film House created the revolutionary Birthday Bucks television campaign to promote radio stations, which continues to shatter audience ratings records for stations from Capital Radio in London to WSIX-FM right here in Nashville.

The sweeping interior balconies and open spaces of Film House were designed to promote creative networking. The unique facility has won an award for design and construction excellence.

In 1996, Film House opened The Drive-In, a division launched to promote the unique talents and expertise of Film House's on-staff directors. Their diverse experience and backgrounds are now being unleashed on commercials, industrials, and related projects for clients in all areas of business.

Over the years, Film House has also done its share of pro bono work. A particularly proud moment came when Film House received the most prestigious honor in the nontheatrical film industry, the Golden Eagle Award from the Council of International Non-Theatrical Events (CINE). It was presented to Film House for a seven-minute video the company created for the Tennessee Division of the American Cancer Society. The video, titled "Camp Horizon: My Time to Shine," will now go on to represent the United States in international film festivals.

Film House is Nashville's largest full-service film and video production company under one roof, having moved into its newly constructed, 39,000-square-foot studio and office complex in June 1996. The new building is more than a testament to the success of Film House. It is a dynamic symbol of the continuing growth of Nashville's film and video community, and a breathtaking vision of Nashville's future as a new world center in the film and video arts.

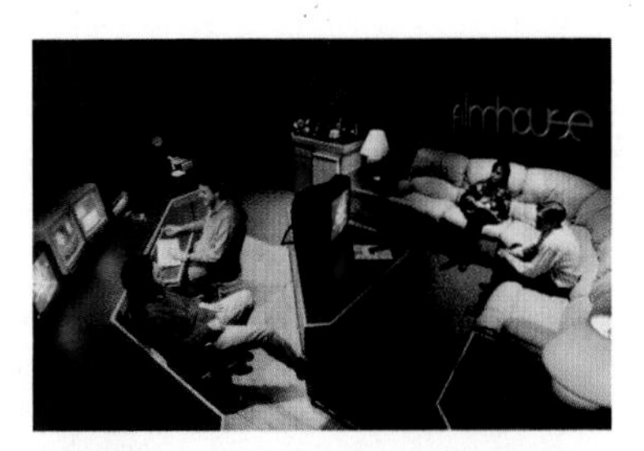

Film House features two identical digital video editing suites, each with characteristic Film House attention to detail in client comfort and convenience.

The Film House studio in Nashville becomes actress Teri Garr's Manhattan apartment for New York City client Viacom International (left).

Barnes Real Estate Services, Inc.

"Selling Greater Nashville," the motto of Barnes Real Estate Services, Inc., is an appropriate message for a city that is bursting beyond its traditional boundaries and a company that helps manage that growth. The company's mission statement reiterates Barnes' commitment to its customers and to Nashville: "In an ever changing economy and industry, we are committed to staying current so that we may better serve our customers, clients, and associates . . . We are committed to grow in the Greater Nashville market through planned expansion based on sound business principles."

Building on a real estate heritage begun by his father, David Barnes is president of Barnes Real Estate Services, Inc. (left).

Dorris D. Barnes began working for a real estate firm following retirement from military service, and in 1978, he founded his own real estate company (right).

Like Father, Like Son

Dorris D. Barnes and his son David have built Barnes Real Estate Services, Inc. into one of the most respected names in real estate in the Nashville area. Following retirement from military service, Dorris began working for a real estate firm. In 1978, he founded his own real estate company, and, under his leadership, the staff grew from five agents to more than 150 in fewer than 10 years.

His son David Barnes followed a similar path, completing military service in 1978. Eventually, he entered real estate sales and took over management of Barnes' Brentwood office in 1984.

In 1991, four years after Barnes Inc., Realtors had been acquired by a large national real estate firm, David reestablished the Barnes name in local area real estate as Barnes Real Estate Services, Inc. While the company's responsibilities are now David's, he quickly notes, "My father is still extremely active in our company. In real estate sales, he is an incredible salesperson, and he manages our Harding Place office. Undoubtedly, he is a key reason for the company's success."

A residential broker serving Greater Nashville from office locations around the area, including Brentwood, Harding Place, Donelson, and the northeast office in Joelton, Barnes Real Estate Services represents the spectrum of the market—from first-time buyers to executive homes. "Our 150 agents work in Nashville/Davidson and all surrounding counties to service a wide range of buyers," says David Barnes. "Unlike many firms in Nashville, we are not niche brokers. We believe that the $100,000 buyer today becomes the $200,000 buyer tomorrow, moving from one area to another as incomes and employment scenarios change. Our goal is to always be able to service their real estate needs.

"Also unique to our company is that we are locally owned and

Dorris D. Barnes and his son David have built Barnes Real Estate Services, Inc. into one of the most respected names in real estate in the Nashville area.

totally independent from any parent company or franchiser," notes Barnes. "And I think we are one of a handful of real estate companies here in Nashville that is extremely active in watching real estate trends around the country."

High-Caliber Sales Professionals

"I am very proud of the number and the strong caliber of our agents," says Barnes. "We actively recruit agents who we know will help us achieve our mission, which is to provide the public with outstanding real estate services based on trust, integrity, and commitment." These agents bring a wealth of experience to the firm, serving on committees of the National Association of Realtors, the Local Association of Realtors, and the Middle Tennessee Regional Multiple Listing Service.

Both Dorris and David Barnes have served as past president of the Greater Nashville Association of Realtors and as director of the Tennessee Association of Realtors. David has also been president of the Nashville Area Multiple Listing Service and Real Estate This Week.

The firm employs a director of career development, who is responsible for the recruitment and training of the company's sales associates. Customized workshops designed for various levels of experience are offered on an ongoing basis for Barnes' agents, and a protégé program is available to team new agents with an experienced mentor for a hands-on learning experience. Additionally, all sales professionals at Barnes are encouraged to continue developing their skills by achieving a CRB (Certified Real Estate Brokerage Manager), CRS (Certified Residential Specialist), or GRI (Graduate Realtors Institute) designation.

Barnes comments, "Our agents provide valuable experience in helping clients prepare their homes for sale or for purchasing a new home. They are trained to build rapport and to be flexible. It's important to maintain that flexibility and have that rapport with customers and clients in order to best meet the needs of each client."

"We actively recruit agents who we know will help us achieve our mission, which is to provide the public with outstanding real estate services based on trust, integrity, and commitment," says David Barnes (standing, top).

Barnes Real Estate has grown in many directions to serve the ever changing needs of its agents, customers, and clients (bottom).

Special Services

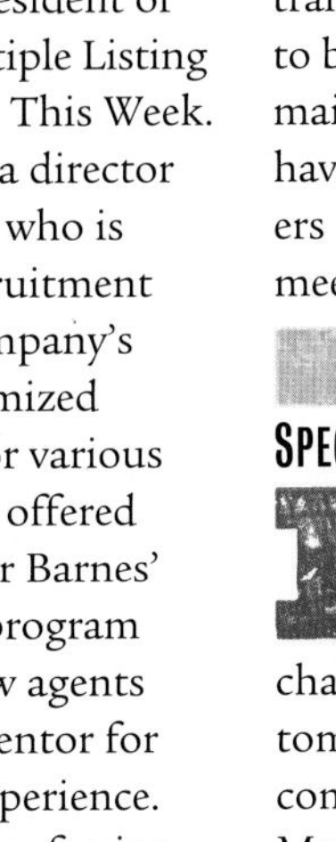

Barnes Real Estate has grown in many directions to serve the ever changing needs of its agents, customers, and clients. In 1994, the company established Arlington Mortgage Corporation, a separately operated, but wholly owned subsidiary of Barnes Real Estate designed to meet the increasing demand for home mortgages. In June 1997, Arlington Mortgage was acquired by Southeastern Mortgage of Tennessee, a local area lender with a full-service line of mortgage products. Southeastern Mortgage works closely with Barnes sales associates, providing finance training and keeping the company apprised of the ever changing mortgage industry.

The company also created a relocation services division, having a relocation director dedicated to actively managing this facet of Barnes Real Estate. The company works with national corporations and relocation companies in relocating transferees into and out of the Greater Nashville area. Barnes is a member of RELO®, the oldest and largest national relocation network of independent brokers. "Our membership in RELO® is an important part of our business, both in the relocation area, and in being involved in a network of brokers from all over the country who deal regularly with similar business issues," notes Barnes.

Finally, in an effort to keep up with the changing times, Barnes Real Estate Services has established an Internet address (www.barnesre.com) in order to keep its agents and customers current with the most recent trends in marketing and technology.

TRACTOR SUPPLY COMPANY

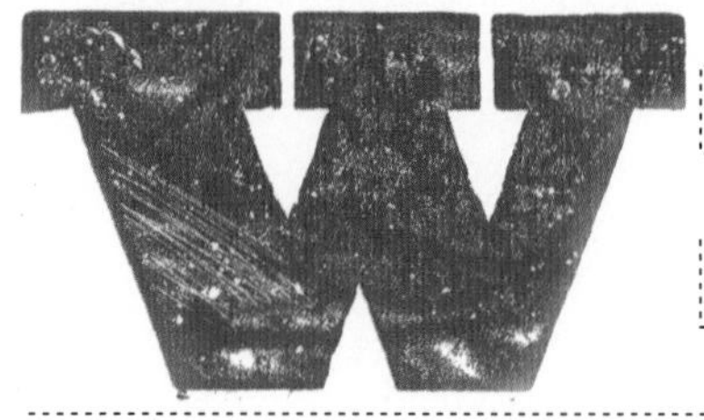

WITH ITS COMMITMENT TO BEING THE MOST DEPENDable supplier of basic maintenance products to America's farmers—whether full-time, part-time, or hobby—Tractor Supply Company (TSC) pledges to do whatever it takes to keep its customers happy.

TSC was founded in 1938 by Charles E. Schmidt in Minot, North Dakota. Schmidt started with a 24-page farm supply mail-order catalog and one retail store in the nation's Midwest. By the mid-1950s, Schmidt had opened 29 retail stores, the catalog had 116 pages, and national sales had exceeded $4.5 million.

In 1959 the company went public, and within one year expanded to 44 retail centers and moved its headquarters to Chicago. While public and private ownership have changed hands over the years and multiple acquisitions and mergers have taken place, the mission to serve the American farmer has remained the same.

TSC's national headquarters moved to Nashville in 1979 because of the city's central location. In 1991, TSC announced a plan to double in size within five years. By 1995, the company had reached its goal—income from operations exceeded $22.5 million and more than $383 million in net sales was realized. A $400 million net sales goal was set for 1996. In the next five years the company is aiming for $1 billion in net sales and is hoping to add 25 to 30 new stores a year.

In addition to the traditional American farmer, target consumer groups now include gentlemen farmers—professionals during the week and farmers in their spare time—as well as suburban customers, contractors, and tradesmen.

Today, with approximately 2,300 employees and 185 retail stores in 22 states, TSC is a category killer in items essential to the American farmer. TSC, Inc., is publicly held and its stock is traded on NASDAQ under the symbol TSCO.

LOOKING TO THE EXPERTS

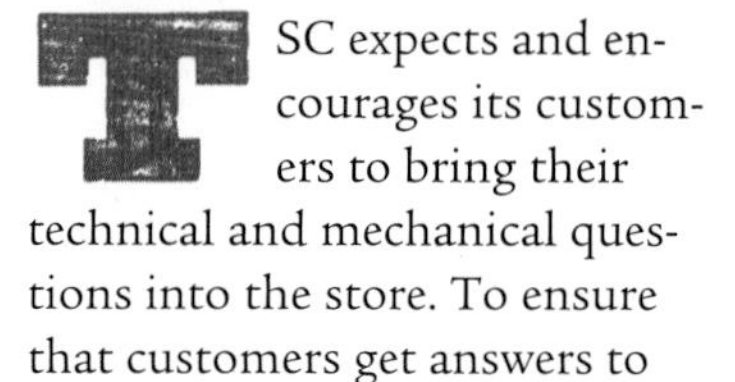

TSC expects and encourages its customers to bring their technical and mechanical questions into the store. To ensure that customers get answers to their often complicated questions, each TSC sales associate is provided with extensive technical training.

The idea behind the training started a few years back when all sales associates were trained in the craft of welding and taught how to efficiently use and repair an

TRACTOR SUPPLY COMPANY WAS FOUNDED IN 1938 BY CHARLES E. SCHMIDT IN MINOT, NORTH DAKOTA. BY THE END OF 1996, THE COMPANY OPERATED 208 RETAIL FARM STORES IN 24 STATES.

air compressor. TSC found that customers began to rely heavily on the expertise of the sales associates. As sales of related items increased, additional training sessions on reciprocal saws and sanders were initiated.

TSC realizes that while equipment training can be uniform, regional farming issues and needs are quite diverse. Sales associates are expected to be experts on the seasonal, climatic, and agricultural needs of their customers. By knowing the intricate differences between what's needed on a Tennessee farm versus an Iowa farm, TSC's sales associates rise above the competition.

Success stories of sales associates are numerous and highly valued. For example, the entire company benefited when one TSC store manager in Illinois encouraged a local manufacturer to expand its product line; another manager in South Dakota lined up special delivery truckloads of generators and heating equipment when an early 10-inch snowstorm threatened her customers' livelihoods.

In TSC's retail farm stores virtually every foot is preplanned and arranged for the best mix in products and services. The walls are strategically merchandised with tractor parts, air compressors, welders, work clothing, footwear, lawn mowers, power equipment, bale feeders, harnesses, fencing, feed, animal health products, truck accessories, and much more.

Also noticeable is the motto printed on a banner in every store: "Customer Satisfaction Guaranteed. Every associate in the store has been empowered to do whatever it takes to satisfy the customer."

Looking Toward the Future

SC makes certain promises to its customers: to provide the best customer service; guaranteed satisfaction; and low prices every day. To accomplish these goals, TSC's business plan is to be the most dependable supplier of basic maintenance needs to farmers and other residents of rural areas, and to continuously improve all operations so that TSC is the most efficient operator. TSC also makes promises to its employees: to provide an environment where the free exchange of information is a way of life, and where personal growth and achievement are based on individual initiative and achievement.

TSC has taken the words of success and put them into action. The company stands behind its people and its manufacturers' products while serving its target consumer. In addition, TSC invests in America's future by providing $100,000 annually in scholarship programs to the Future Farmers of America (FFA).

Since 1938, a lot has changed at TSC, most notably the company's size and profits. But its mission to serve the customer and provide a desirable place to work has remained the same, boosting the company's place in the market as the store where America's farmers shop.

An average TSC store displays a wide selection of more than 12,000 different items from animal supplies to lawn and garden products.

Davis-Kidd Booksellers, Inc.

In 1980, social workers Karen Davis and Thelma Kidd envisioned an independent bookstore that would serve Nashville like no other. Today, that dream is manifested in an overwhelmingly successful reality: Davis-Kidd Booksellers, Inc. From its early days, Davis-Kidd has grown into the dominant force in Nashville's book trade. Its 24,000-square-foot, two-story facility in Grace's Plaza—just across Hillsboro Road from its original 3,500-square-foot site—has become a local institution, a magnet for people who love books, and the hands-down winner among bookstores in "best of" polls by media outlets, year after year.

A Welcoming Place

Thelma Kidd remembers the dream. "I had lived in Ann Arbor, Michigan, for a period of time, and there was a wonderful bookstore there that became the image in our minds," she recalls. "We wanted a large, general bookstore that was a comfortable place for people to spend time."

Kidd and Davis imagined the store as a welcoming, warm environment that would encourage folks to come in and stay a while. "Our assumption was that if the customer felt comfortable enough to hang out and look at whatever book they were thinking of buying, then they would buy books eventually," Kidd says. Davis and Kidd pursued their vision, becoming pioneers in a wave of independent booksellers that now challenge the chains in many American cities.

The store has gained a reputation in Nashville for attracting fascinating visitors. The personalities who have come to the store for book signings represent a cross section of American life, including Newt Gingrich, Jesse Jackson, Greg Louganis, Jeff Foxworthy, Anne Rice, Rosa Parks, Ray Bradbury, Don Henley, George Jones, Gloria Steinem, and Stephen King.

Davis-Kidd's physical growth has mirrored its growing popularity, as the store moved from its birthplace to a larger facility in the Mall at Green Hills in 1983 and then opened its current Nashville location on September 1, 1988. Meanwhile, Davis-Kidd has expanded across Tennessee, moving into the Memphis market in 1985, Knoxville in 1986, and Jackson in 1995.

Keeping the Dream Alive

Community involvement has been part of Davis-Kidd's mission from the start. A participant in the Project PENCIL literacy program, the Nashville store has adopted a local school. Other schools and organizations reserve the store after hours for book fairs, through which they can raise money for libraries and other needs. Davis-Kidd's support of public radio has earned it the National Public Radio/WPLN Mic Award.

In one sense, Davis-Kidd today is a retail enterprise with more than 115,000 different book titles in stock, over 1,000 different periodicals, a 96-seat café serving delicious food in a relaxing atmosphere, a toy department, and a stationery department. In another, Davis-Kidd is something less tangible—a realization of the founders' original vision. "We will always want to be sure the store appeals to a broad range of people, regardless of their level in society, their political beliefs, or their religious beliefs," Kidd says. "They can all feel that 'This is my store,' " says Davis.

Davis-Kidd today is a retail enterprise with more than 115,000 different book titles in stock, over 1,000 different periodicals, and a 96-seat café serving delicious food in a relaxing atmosphere.

In 1980, Karen Davis (left) and Thelma Kidd fulfilled their dream of owning a large, general bookstore that was a comfortable place for people to spend time.

NISSAN MOTOR MANUFACTURING CORPORATION U.S.A.

WHEN NISSAN MOTOR CO. LTD. ANNOUNCED ITS decision in 1980 to build a facility in Smyrna, Tennessee, 20 miles south of Nashville, its goal was to bring together the best of both Japanese and American manufacturing. Nissan Motor Manufacturing Corporation U.S.A. has helped forge new economic growth in Middle Tennessee while providing products for American consumers.

Smyrna's proximity to the major American markets, a good climate, the sound work ethic of Tennesseans, and supportive state government helped seal the deal for the U.S. manufacturing venture. Nissan's initial $760 million investment has grown into a $1.43 billion capital investment in Middle Tennessee. The company, which is located in a 5.2 million-square-foot facility, today employs 6,000 people and has the capacity to produce approximately 465,000 light trucks and cars annually.

PARTICIPATIVE MANAGEMENT

The framework for Nissan was established by visionary Marvin Runyon, the manufacturing company's first president and chief executive officer. He sought to combine the best American managerial know-how with the best features of Japanese technology, process design, and creative approaches.

Runyon and Jerry Benefield, who has served as president and chief executive officer since 1987, modeled the company's participative management style—now a buzzword in corporate America. The bottom line of this simple operating philosophy is that people are treated with dignity and their ideas and involvement are encouraged.

"Respecting others and remaining loyal to the company are the most important characteristics of the people who work here. We know our roles, and we perform well together," remarks Benefield.

This performance has been recognized with the Tennessee Quality Award, which emphasizes standards of excellence in total quality management. And Nissan's Smyrna plant was named in both editions of *The 100 Best Companies to Work for in America*, with authors Robert Levering and Milton Moskowitz praising the company's sensitivity to its employees.

GOOD VEHICLES BUILT BY GOOD PEOPLE

Nissan built its first truck in Tennessee in June 1983. In 1985, the company added Sentra production, and Altimas were launched in 1992. The Altima was a success from its start. *Family Circle* magazine named the Altima the 1993 Family Car of the Year, and the Altima was named Best in Class by both the 1996 and 1997 J.D. Power and Associates Initial Quality Study.

In 1994, the Smyrna plant began manufacturing the 200SX. In May 1997, Nissan dedicated an $80 million facility in Decherd, Tennessee. The plant's 240 employees build engines for the Altima, with transaxle production to begin in the spring of 1998.

For the past four years, the *Harbour Report*, a North American survey of the auto industry, has named the Smyrna facility the nation's most productive plant for both car and truck manufacturing. Benefield attributes this steady growth and success to the company's good employees, maintaining that Nissan hires well, invests heavily in training, and encourages active involvement from everyone.

INVESTMENT IN TENNESSEE

Nissan's investment in Tennessee goes far beyond its investment in facilities. In addition to the substantial federal, state, and local taxes the company pays each year, Nissan's payroll is approximately $280 million. Since 1981, Nissan has contributed more than $6.5 million to 200-plus nonprofit organizations in Middle Tennessee that are improving the quality of life in communities where Nissan employees live.

The company not only respects the people within the community, but respect for the environment is also a priority. Nissan has initiated numerous environmental programs, vigorously recycling everything from paint solvents to office paper to industrial waste.

Nissan's solid corporate citizenship, skilled employees, and advanced technology have enabled its original vision to thrive; the company now stands as a model for manufacturing excellence. Nissan Motor Manufacturing Corporation U.S.A. is proud to call Middle Tennessee home.

CLOCKWISE FROM TOP:
WITH NISSAN'S PATENTED INTELLIGENT BODY ASSEMBLY SYSTEM, ALTIMA BODIES ARE WELDED WITH INCREDIBLE ACCURACY.

THE SPRAWLING NISSAN PLANT IN SMYRNA COVERS 5.2 MILLION SQUARE FEET.

TECHNICIAN THOMAS PALMER INSTALLS A SEAT IN A NISSAN TRUCK IN THE TRIM AND CHASSIS PLANT.

TECHNICIAN JEFF GEORGE INSTALLS AN INSTRUMENT PANEL IN A NISSAN TRUCK.

▶ JIM DEVAULT

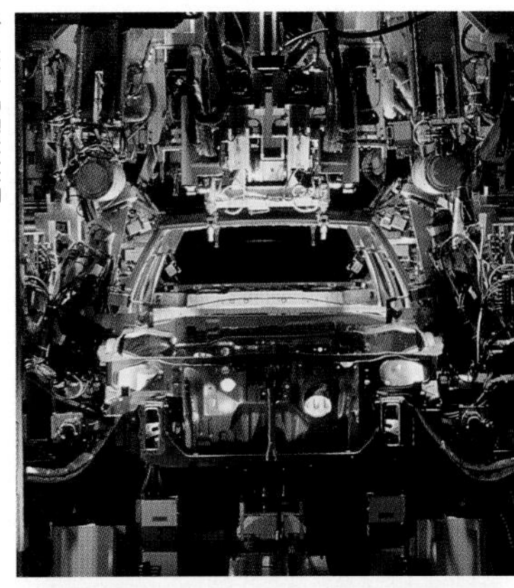

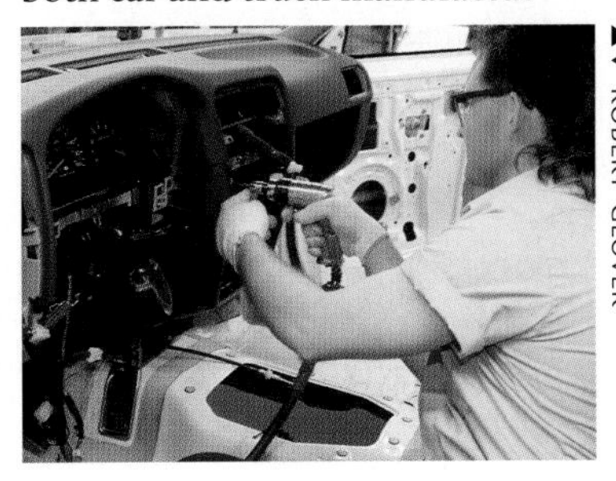

◀▼ ROBERT GLOVER

Gould Turner Group, P.C.

It's not that Gould Turner Group, P.C. keeps a low profile in Nashville. When architects design local landmarks like the Palmer Plaza office building on West End Avenue and One Belle Meade Place on Harding Road, they get noticed. Yet Gould Turner Group is better known in certain nationwide circles than it is at home.

Since its founding in 1980, the firm has acquired a national reputation for design excellence in the health care facility field. Still, it's more than a niche firm. In Nashville and around the country, Gould Turner Group has become known for its architects' down-to-earth, no-nonsense approach—their ability to strike a balance between creativity and practicality—in designing a wide variety of structures.

A Diversity of Specialties

The firm has blueprinted more than $1 billion worth of buildings in its history, and it takes on roughly 120 new projects a year. Gould Turner Group's staff of 45 includes 15 architects—a high ratio that ensures the firm's standard of excellence. The involvement of principals in each project provides a comprehensive and knowledgeable approach to planning and problem solving in an environment of ever increasing regulatory and economic constraints.

"Our job is to help our client create a building that projects an appropriate corporate image in the community, markets the client to the outside world, and allows for future growth and evolution," explains President Steve W. Turner. "We are committed to designing environments that are functional, yet aesthetically compelling and economically constructed and durable."

The firm's architects are licensed in almost every state, and they bring to their work a variety of specialized talents: facility master planning, site planning, medical planning and programming, medical-certificate-of-need preparation, commercial design, multifamily residential design, hotel planning and design, education and collegiate planning and design, corrections planning and design, and construction administration.

Each project at the firm begins with a careful assessment of the client's needs to ensure compatibility with budget constraints. Through a sophisticated method of interpreting and assimilating planning strategies and concepts into a working program that defines the goals of the project, the programming phase produces a clearly

TOM GATLIN

TOM GATLIN

TOM GATLIN

Gould Turner Group has become known for its ability to strike a balance between creativity and practicality. Local projects include (from top) the Overlook One office building, the BMG office building, and the national headquarters for Alpha Omicron Pi.

▲▼ TOM GATLIN

documented rationale for the design process, as well as a preliminary evaluation of construction costs.

More than Skin Deep

Gould Turner Group also offers a broad array of interior architecture services. "In buildings, as with people, beauty is not merely skin deep," Turner observes. "Ultimately, structures are judged not only by how they look on the outside, but also by what's inside—how functional and user friendly the interior is and the image it projects to its users and visitors." To that end, Gould Turner Group maintains a staff of interior architecture professionals with decades of combined experience.

In terms of future projects, Turner anticipates more local work on the firm's horizon—even as it remains nationally prominent in certain fields. "Though we have become a large firm, we will still strive to deliver the personalized service typical of a smaller shop," Turner vows.

The firm has acquired a national reputation for design excellence in the health care facility field, designing such facilities as Henrico Doctors Hospital in Richmond, Virginia, (left) and Texas Orthopaedic Hospital in Houston, Texas (right).

▲ TOM GATLIN

Gould Turner Group's corporate headquarters in Nashville reflects the talent and innovation of the firm.

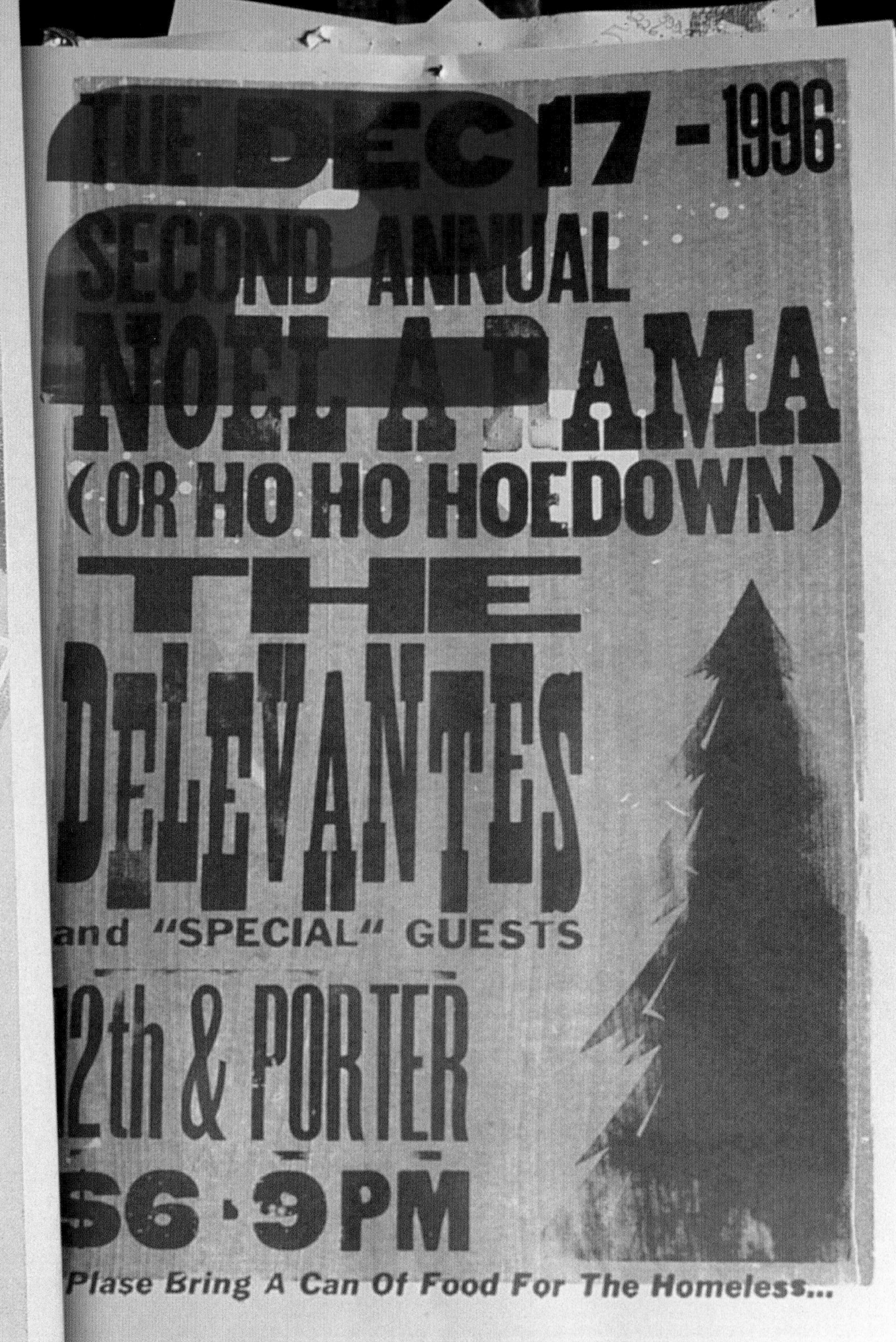
TUE DEC 17 - 1996
SECOND ANNUAL
NOEL A RAMA
(OR HO HO HOEDOWN)
THE
DELEVANTES
and "SPECIAL" GUESTS
12th & PORTER
$6 · 9PM
Plase Bring A Can Of Food For The Homeless...

COPYRIGHT 1996 HATCH SHOW PRINT CO.

▼ JONATHAN POSTAL / TOWERY PUBLISHING, INC.; POSTER DESIGN: JIM SHERRADEN / HATCH SHOW PRINT

★

1981
ENVOY Corporation

1982
ADT Automotive, Inc.

1982
Tennessee Managed Care Network

1983
Bridgestone/Firestone, Inc.

1983
O'Charley's, Inc.

1984
American Fabricators, Inc.

1984
Loews Vanderbilt Plaza Hotel

1984
PMT Services, Inc.

1984
Whirlpool Corporation

1985
French, Clayton, Johnson & Assoc.

1985
Saturn Corporation

1985
Sheraton Music City Hotel

1986
Reemay, Inc.

1987
Renaissance Nashville Hotel

1988
Cytometry Associates, Inc.

1988
IPN Network

1988
Lovell Communications Inc.

1989
Aegis, Inc.

1989
Akersloot, DePriest, Wall & Associates, PLLC

1989
Cambridge Equity Advisors

1990
Gold Skin Care Center

1990
Kyzen Corporation

1991
Caterpillar Inc.

1991
LifeView Resources

1991
Logan's Roadhouse Restaurants

1991
Middle Tennessee Motor Cars, Inc.

1992
American Transitional Hospitals, Inc.

1992
Curb Records

1993
Electric Picture Company

1994
InterMedia Partners

1994
MagneTek, Inc.

1995
Speer Communications, Ltd.

ENVOY Corporation

NVOY Corporation has carved an impressive niche among health care and health-care-related companies emerging in the Nashville area. As one of the largest electronic data interchange (EDI) clearinghouses for the health care industry, ENVOY has effectively facilitated the shift in the industry from paper-based information processing to easily implemented and utilized computerized electronic systems. Quite simply, the company has streamlined the process for sending and receiving health care information.

Currently, ENVOY Corporation stands as one of the strongest electronic health care clearinghouses of its kind, with links to more than 220,000 providers, 600 authorized EDI service vendors, and 550 managed care plans and insurance carriers, processing more than 750 million health care transactions each year.

Evolution

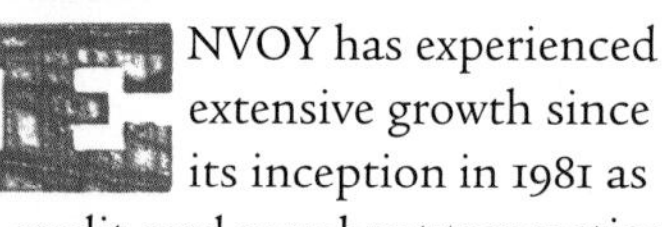

NVOY has experienced extensive growth since its inception in 1981 as a credit card merchant transaction processing company. The technology to authorize a credit card purchase and settle the funds to the merchant electronically revolutionized the credit card industry. ENVOY began applying this technology to health care in 1989, when the corporation began processing pharmacy transactions. In 1990, the corporation developed a Medicaid eligibility verification system, and in 1991, ENVOY completed a successful initial public offering.

By 1994, the corporation enjoyed a strong presence in the health care field, processing more than 302 million health care transactions from more than 28,000 pharmacies. This success, coupled with the evolution and growth of the health care market, encouraged ENVOY to sell the credit card processing system in 1995 and focus solely on health care.

ENVOY's clients now include hospitals and clinics; physicians, dentists, and pharmacists; practice management system vendors; managed care organizations; such government agencies as Medicare, and Medicaid; Blue Cross/Blue Shield; and commercial insurance companies.

With the acquisition of National Electronic Information Corporation (NEIC) in 1996, as well as a variety of other companies related to the EDI field, ENVOY has created one of the strongest and most functional networks for health care electronic data interchange. In the process, ENVOY has created more than 400 jobs for area residents in the Nashville-based corporate offices and established eight regional branches across the United States that serve a nationwide clientele.

Revolution

pioneer in health care electronic data interchange, ENVOY has developed products and services that have helped revolutionize the health care EDI field. Dedicated to quality service, product innovation, and market leadership, ENVOY eliminates the administrative headaches of paper processing by providing an electronic data interchange solution.

Traditionally, claims processing involves paper copies generated by hand, typewriter, or computer. The paper forms are mailed to the payer, microfilmed, sorted, and sent for data entry. The potential for human error and delays is enormous.

With links to other health care partners over the telephone electronically via modem, participants send and receive vital health care information as well as transmit many transactions, including claims, referral inquiries, encounters, and financial transactions in a cost-effective and efficient manner.

Providers and payers reduce operating costs and the number of rejected entries while increasing efficiency, productivity, and data accuracy. Furthermore, such interchange reduces payment turnaround time and improves communication between the providers and payers.

ENVOY continues with resourcefulness and drive to handle a large transaction volume and revenue, offering an extensive variety of health care EDI services to all participants in the industry. The corporation remains strategically committed to a growth strategy based on the innovative application of technology, quality services, and strong partnerships with its payer, vendor, and provider partners. ENVOY has created for the health care industry a full-service, national transaction network. This network provides the flexibility and breadth of services necessary to achieve significant and ongoing administrative savings for all participants.

From its headquarters in Nashville, ENVOY Corporation has streamlined the process for sending and receiving health care information.

Renaissance Nashville Hotel

LOCATED IN THE HEART OF DOWNTOWN NASHVILLE, THE Renaissance Nashville Hotel has been providing first-class facilities and services to business and leisure travelers, convention groups, and local organizations since 1987. A recipient of AAA's prestigious Four Diamond Hotel award for the last eight years, the Renaissance Nashville is wholly owned by Renaissance Hotels & Resorts, an upscale chain with 146 properties in 38 countries. The ultramodern 25-floor hotel features 673 deluxe guest rooms, including 24 luxury suites, and a dramatic, four-story atrium.

The Renaissance of Nashville

The hotel's name is uniquely suited for a city enjoying a renaissance of its own. Within walking distance of the hotel is the Second Avenue Historic Entertainment District, historic Ryman Auditorium, Country Music Hall of Fame, Tennessee Performing Arts Center, and Riverfront Park. From the park, visitors can ride water taxis down the Cumberland River to Opryland Theme Park and the Grand Ole Opry or enjoy a cruise on the *General Jackson*, the world's largest river showboat. The Renaissance Nashville Hotel offers a variety of weekend packages for family vacations and romantic weekends.

After taking in the sights and sounds of Nashville, guests can retreat to the comfort of the hotel, unwinding in the heated indoor pool, working out in the fully equipped fitness center, or simply enjoying the excellent cuisine and stunning views of the cityscape from the hotel's two restaurants and two lounges.

Just 15 minutes from the Nashville airport, the Renaissance provides a number of services and amenities designed to surround guests in comfort. Fifty-four private access club floor rooms feature an elegant private lounge and concierge service, as well as complimentary continental breakfast and evening hors d'oeuvres daily.

All of the spacious guest rooms are well appointed and offer amenities such as coffeemakers, complimentary *USA Today*, 24-hour room service, no surcharge on toll free and credit card calls, in-room movies, computer dataports, and cable television.

Ideal Venue for Meetings and Events

Setting the standard as a first-class business and convention hotel, the Renaissance Nashville Hotel has been honored with the *U.S. Association Executive* magazine's prestigious Aster Award—bestowed upon the top 10 new convention hotels—for five consecutive years.

The hotel connects to the Nashville Convention Center and the new, 20,000-seat arena, affording its guests a total of 205,000 square feet of meeting space—the most in downtown Nashville. The complex features a 119,000-square-foot exhibition hall, 18,000- and 11,000-square-foot ballrooms, and 45 additional meeting rooms. An outstanding team of culinary, banquet, and audiovisual professionals attend to all details to ensure a successful event.

Unique to the Renaissance properties are its Club Express and Meeting Express services. Club Express allows patrons worldwide to earn free stays through frequent use of Renaissance Hotels & Resorts. Meeting Express is designed to facilitate the needs of small meetings as a one-stop shopping service that provides 24-hour turnaround on requests for prices and information including catering, audiovisual facilities, function space, and guest rooms.

The Renaissance Nashville Hotel provides the best the Music City has to offer through its excellent meeting and convention services as well as its proximity to many of the area's renowned attractions.

THE RENAISSANCE NASHVILLE HOTEL'S SALES AND CATERING PROFESSIONALS CAN ASSIST WITH ALL THE IMPORTANT DETAILS FOR SMALL MEETINGS OR LARGE CONVENTIONS (TOP).

THE HOTEL IS CONVENIENTLY LOCATED IN THE HEART OF DOWNTOWN NASHVILLE, NEAR ALL THE ATTRACTIONS THAT HAVE MADE NASHVILLE FAMOUS (BOTTOM).

ADT Automotive, Inc.

In recent years, as new cars have become more expensive while the quality of cars has continued to improve, used cars have moved to center stage in the automotive industry. Central to the used car industry is the auto auction. As the nation's most progressive auto auction company, Nashville-based ADT Automotive, Inc. has earned a reputation as a national leader in the field of vehicle redistribution, providing a service vital to this growing industry.

Clockwise from right:
ADT played an important role in the nationwide sale of more than 41 million used cars in 1996 for almost $365 billion.

ADT Automotive plays a vital role in the Nashville community as the corporate underwriter of Un Été du Vin, an annual wine auction that benefits the American Cancer Society.

Michael J. Richardson, president and CEO of ADT Automotive

People love to buy used cars, and dealerships love to sell them. Consumers increasingly see used cars as a more attractive, acceptable purchase than an expensive new car, due in part to the increase in vehicle quality since the start of the decade. In addition, car dealers have found that they make a much higher profit selling a used car than a new one. The result? More than 41 million used cars were sold in 1996 for almost $365 billion.

Wholesale Auto Auctions Nationwide

Auto auctions provide a service through which institutions with a large volume of used cars—such as manufacturers, rental companies, lending organizations, leasing companies, state and federal governments, fleet operators, and auto dealerships—can remarket their vehicles to dealers in a competitive bidding environment. In 1996, ADT Automotive handled more than 1.9 million vehicles. ADT Automotive operates 28 wholesale auto auctions nationwide, in cities such as Dallas, Chicago, Detroit, Honolulu, Miami, Nashville, and San Francisco.

While auctioning cars is ADT Automotive's core business, the company also offers its clients a variety of other programs to assist them in the vehicle redistribution process. These include vehicle title processing, repossession, transportation, reconditioning, repair, and lease termination.

Heritage in Postwar England

The origins of ADT Automotive reach across the Atlantic Ocean and back half a century. At the end of World War II, a young English veteran named David Wickins decided to sell his car. With the war over and the demand for cars on the rise, so many responded to his advertisement that he held an impromptu auction. After this successful effort, Wickins and his brothers began auctioning cars throughout England. That effort would eventually become the United Kingdom's first and largest car auction company, British Car Auctions (BCA).

In the early 1980s, BCA Managing Director Mike Richardson traveled to cities in the United States, including Nashville, to assess the U.S. auto auction industry, which then was a series of independent auctions. He quickly realized two things: The U.S. auto industry could be better served with an auction chain, and the southern charm of Nashville reminded him of the pleasant ambience of his native southern England. In 1982, BCA established its U.S. headquarters in Nashville and bought its first American auctions, and ADT Automotive was born.

ADT Automotive grew rapidly in its early years, quickly expanding the number of auctions it owned and introducing practices that are now industry standards. These include recruiting national clients and protecting dealers from buying cars with altered odometers or fraudulent titles. Today, ADT Automotive employs more than 6,000 nationwide, including 200 at its corporate office and 300 at its 100-acre Nashville Auto Auction, located on Lebanon Road and founded in 1947.

ADT Automotive has also done much to improve the automotive industry. In 1986, the company played a key role in the contents and passage of the federal Truth in Mileage Act, a law designed to curtail odometer tampering. In recent years, the company has lobbied Congress extensively for uniform titling legislation, which would prevent consumers from unknowingly buying a rebuilt car that had previously been seriously wrecked or totaled.

As the nation's most progressive auto auction company, Nashville-based ADT Automotive, Inc. has earned a reputation as a national leader in the field of vehicle redistribution, providing a service vital to this growing industry.

CHARITABLE CONTRIBUTIONS

ecause ADT Automotive is primarily a wholesale operation for dealers, it offers few services directly to the general public (although some auctions offer regular public sales of government vehicles). Nevertheless, ADT Automotive plays a vital role in the Nashville community as the corporate underwriter of Un Été du Vin, an annual wine auction that benefits the American Cancer Society. ADT Automotive began sponsoring the auction in 1989, and since then it has raised more than $3.8 million for the American Cancer Society. Last year, the event raised $823,000, which was used locally and statewide for research fellowships and grants at Vanderbilt University; Camp Horizon, a camp for children with cancer; and local education, prevention, and patient services. Richardson, ADT Automotive's president and CEO, is a past president and a current board member of the American Cancer Society.

Most recently, in late 1996, ADT Automotive had a senior executive appointed to the 1996-1997 Leadership Nashville class. This class is comprised of an elite group of Nashville businesspersons who meet to address community concerns such as crime and education.

Although the company is headquartered in Nashville, ADT Automotive's active involvement in charitable causes extends well beyond the Nashville community. Many of the company's auctions hold special sales to raise money for organizations in their local areas. The auctions' charity contributions range from donations to local chapters of such nationally recognized organizations as United Way, Make-A-Wish Foundation, Easter Seals, NAACP, and American Red Cross to area children's homes and food banks.

ADT Automotive looks to the future with excitement and anticipation. As the $365 billion used car industry continues to grow, ADT Automotive has positioned itself a step ahead of the competition, currently pioneering electronic vehicle redistribution via personal computer. Wherever the next century takes ADT Automotive, it is proud to have both its beginnings and its future firmly anchored in Nashville.

From its Nashville site on Metroplex Drive, ADT Automotive operates 28 wholesale auto auctions nationwide, in cities such as Dallas, Chicago, Detroit, Honolulu, Miami, Nashville, and San Francisco.

Tennessee Managed Care Network

N the managed health care furor of recent years, the Tennessee Managed Care Network (TMCN) and its offshoots have emerged on top. When doctors kept their distance, when patients shied away, and when some said it couldn't be done, TMCN kept the faith and was there to lead the way when the advantages of managed care for everyone became apparent.

"We feel that if managed care is good enough for wealthier populations, it should also be good enough for folks who don't have as many resources," explains President and CEO Anthony J. Cebrun. "Our mission is to make sure that high-quality health services are accessible to everyone."

The Incredible Paradox

ennessee Managed Care Network's mission rests on what Cebrun calls "an incredible paradox." TMCN addresses a full range of needs—not just the narrow dimensions of surgery or pharmacology—for the state's medically underserved population. Yet this expansive and ambitious view of health care is coupled with the imperative of cost savings that is managed care's reason for being.

The network has successfully straddled that paradox since it first came off the drawing board in 1982. For TMCN, managed care is the Good Shots campaign, taking busloads of children to see NBA basketball games—but only if they have their immunization certificates. Managed care is Never Ever Never Town, a comic-book land that sends a strong anti-drug-abuse message to children. Managed care is the Mom 2-B Club, an educational and wellness group for pregnant women of all ages. It's Healthy Lifestyles, a new frontier in wellness promotion and disease prevention, which is a collaborative effort with the AHEC of Meharry Medical College.

Good Shots winners take a vow not to take illegal drugs (top).

TMCN participates in many health fairs throughout the state promoting preventive health measures (bottom).

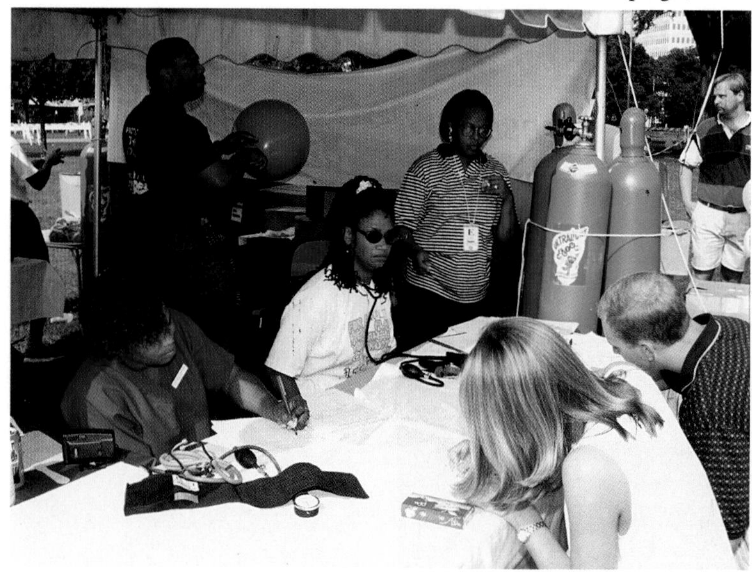

There are other outreach programs, too. There are community health fairs, offering preventive health education, cholesterol and blood pressure screening, and diagnosis of possible problems. There are educational efforts aimed at heightening awareness about nutrition, hypertension, breast cancer, and sickle-cell anemia. There's the Top Hats program, combating head lice among children. There has been cooperation with state and local health officials to cope with outbreaks of hepatitis. There's a statewide calendar art contest in schools, used by teachers as a springboard for health and safety lessons.

These efforts creatively approach people and communities that have historically lacked the opportunity for comprehensive health care. Through its emphasis on preventive care of all kinds, Tennessee Managed Care Network treats health problems when they are most treatable—in their early stages.

"We're trying to address the underlying conditions—financial, behavioral, and physiological—that create the need for acute care and sometimes for unnecessary utilization of services," Cebrun says. "You have to change people's perceptions and ultimately their behavior."

Often the resources that underserved communities lack are monetary, but just as often they are informational. TMCN's outreach initiatives place the power of information in the hands of people who need it. In many cases, the conduits of that information are health outreach workers living in the community who are former welfare recipients themselves. With the trust of their neighbors

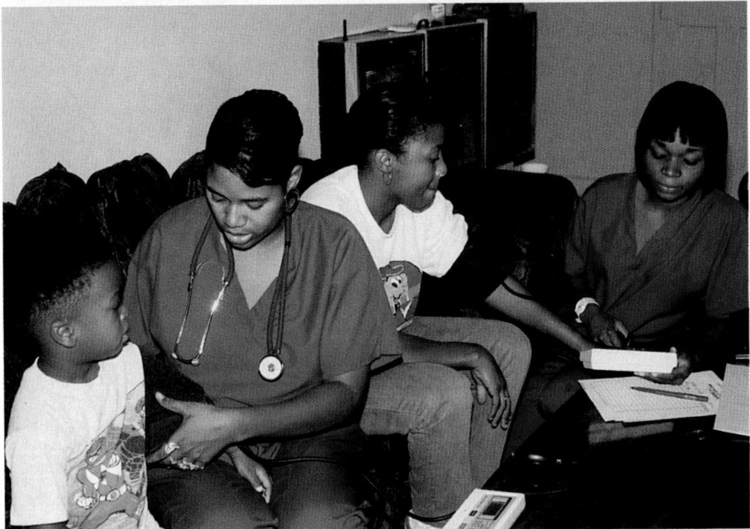

and training from the network, the outreach workers can connect needy individuals with information resources.

A Vision Shared

TMCN originated as the Tennessee Primary Network, funded by grants from several major foundations and the State of Tennessee. Cebrun and like-minded visionaries approached the state and the foundations, convincing them that managed care was a viable approach to the health needs of underprivileged people. By 1994, TMCN's success as a pilot program had emboldened the state to launch its innovative TennCare health insurance program, a trailblazing effort in health care reform. Tennessee Managed Care Network is the linchpin of the entire TennCare effort.

With more than 250,000 members in the state, TMCN is now the largest Medicaid-based health maintenance organization in the United States. Most of the members are in the Access MedPlus program—the health plan available to all Tennesseans eligible for TennCare. It's a prepaid, capitated plan, meaning that the state pays the network a set amount per person at the beginning of each month—and the network must deliver its services within that budget. Other members are in MedTrust, a plan oriented to small business, and Access Health, an emerging statewide commercial plan.

TMCN is managed by a for-profit management company, Medical Care Management Company, but the network itself operates autonomously as a not-for-profit corporation. Its principals have been approached by representatives from some 25 states about how they can cooperate in carrying the TMCN vision forward to the nation at large. The network is also exploring the possibility of partnering with a for-profit health care corporation to expand its activities in commercial health care.

Cebrun envisions the TMCN of the future as "the major planet in our solar system," the hub of a nationwide network providing affordable health care to people and communities long in need of it. "Sometimes people want a panacea out of managed care and it is not that," Cebrun admits. "It is only as good as the people and systems involved. And we are constantly striving to improve the quality of our operations."

Clockwise from bottom right: Good Shots winners represent the brightest of students and the best citizens.

Captain Victory of Never Ever Never Town and his assisting nurse remind their audience to practice good health habits and have their children immunized.

TMCN's Outreach Program helps monitor the health of citizens enrolled in the program.

TMCN has an Access MedPlus Walking Club to promote good health to all who participate.

Bridgestone/Firestone, Inc.

The roads of Music City sing with the sound of tires made by Bridgestone/Firestone, Inc., a wholly owned subsidiary of Tokyo-based Bridgestone Corporation, the world's largest tire and rubber company. ★ Since 1983, when Bridgestone purchased a truck tire plant in LaVergne some 20 miles southeast of Nashville, the company has invested more than a billion dollars in middle Tennessee. Following Bridgestone's 1988 purchase of the Firestone Tire and Rubber Company, it moved its sales and marketing headquarters to Nashville. In 1990, operations were consolidated into Bridgestone/Firestone, Inc. and in 1991, a state-of-the-art radial tire plant was completed in Warren County. The road was once again paved to middle Tennessee in 1992 when corporate headquarters for Bridgestone/Firestone, Inc. moved from Akron to Nashville.

Bridgestone's Potenza ultra-high performance tire line incorporates several advanced tire technologies and is the tire of choice for many of the world's most prestigious vehicles.

Blending Our Heritage

One would hardly imagine that a company with roots on the southerly island of Kyushu in Japan would ultimately settle in Nashville. But Shojiro Ishibashi had dreams of a global enterprise when he began making tires in 1931. He even christened his new venture with an English version of his name (Ishibashi translates as "stone bridge"). With his credo "to serve society with products of superior quality," Ishibashi quickly built Bridgestone into a leading tire maker in Japan, providing tires to the three leading automakers there. In 1967, poised for international growth, Bridgestone arrived in the United States.

Meanwhile, Akron-based Firestone Tire and Rubber Company had emerged as a leading U.S. tire maker. Founded at the turn of the century by Harvey Firestone, the company originally made solid rubber tires for carriage wheels. A few years later, Firestone tires were chosen by Ford for the first mass-produced automobiles in America. Firestone's motto "Best Today—Still Better Tomorrow" continues to ring true.

Worldwide Presence

The merger of Bridgestone and Firestone resulted in the largest tire and rubber company in the world, with more than 90,000 employees. Its largest subsidiary, Bridgestone/Firestone, Inc., represents an investment of more than $4 billion to America's research and development, manufacturing, and commercial infrastructure. A prime example of this investment is the truck tire plant built on 900 acres in Warren County at a total cost of almost $500 million.

Bridgestone Corporation has technology centers on three continents. Its sales and marketing divisions span the globe with a presence in virtually every country. Bridgestone/Firestone maintains 14 tire plants (seven in the United States) and 20 other manufacturing facilities worldwide. The company's annual sales exceed $6 billion.

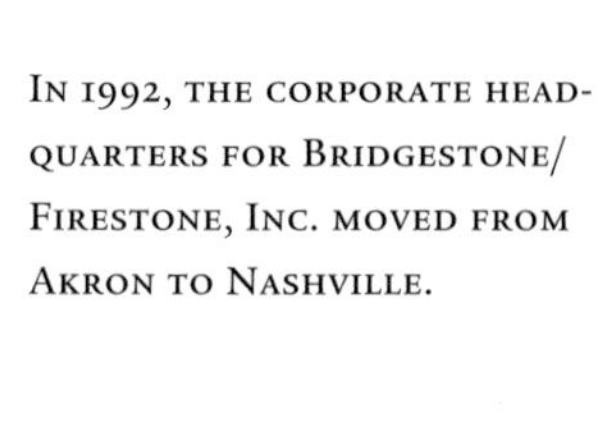

In 1992, the corporate headquarters for Bridgestone/Firestone, Inc. moved from Akron to Nashville.

Providing High-Quality, Innovative Products

Bridgestone/Firestone, Inc. designs, manufactures, and markets tires for every application, producing more than 50 million tires per year. The company also manufactures Firestone air springs, tubes and retread products, synthetic rubber, industrial fibers and textiles, and roofing materials.

Bridgestone offers the "Next Revolution in Tires" with its technology-driven tires. Its Potenza ultrahigh performance tire line incorporates several advanced tire technologies and is the tire of choice for many of the world's most prestigious vehicles. Bridgestone's truck tires have been voted first in retreadability for 11 consecutive years by the American Retreaders Association. And the patented UNI-T™ technologies found in both Bridgestone and Firestone tires offer unprecedented performance capabilities.

Firestone tires merit recognition as America's Tire since 1900, representing quality, value, and maximum performance. Its legendary Firehawk tires are responsible for giving the company bragging rights for 49 victories at the world-famous Indy 500 and an unparalleled 43-race winning streak. Firestone...the Legend is an appropriate slogan for the brand that won its first Indy victory in 1911. Following a 21-year absence from the Indy 500 in the 1970s and 1980s, Firestone revived participation in the race in 1995 and won again in 1996.

All of the company's U.S. tire plants have met the stringent standards for quality established by Bridgestone in Japan, and all production operations are being certified under the international ISO 9000 standards for quality assurance.

Both Bridgestone and Firestone brands are sold through the 1,500 company-owned stores, including the Firestone Tire & Service Centers, as well as more than 8,000 independent retailers.

Commitment to Tennessee

Bridgestone/Firestone, Inc. credits Nashville's proximity to its customers and markets, low tax rate, and low cost of living as prime reasons for having its operations here. Bridgestone/Firestone, Inc. has been good to middle Tennessee, employing 3,800 in its two plants and in corporate headquarters.

In addition to bringing jobs to Tennessee, Bridgestone/Firestone, Inc. rolled in a priceless collection of French impressionist art from the Bridgestone Museum of Art in Japan for the *Masterworks* exhibit at the Tennessee State Museum, its exclusive showing in North America. The exhibit was just one more piece of Bridgestone's global plan to make a real contribution to the happiness of people worldwide, and to make a lasting commitment to serving society, through public interest activities as well as through products of the highest possible quality.

Through its trust fund, the company spreads its charitable arms across the United States and provides millions of dollars in donations and sponsorships for education, health and welfare, culture and arts, and civic and community causes. The Bridgestone/Firestone EnviroLeader program encourages and supports environmental improvement projects by young people across the United States.

Diversity is the road map for the future at Bridgestone/Firestone, Inc. as it responds to an increasingly sophisticated market with continued development of technologically advanced products.

Clockwise from top: The Bridgestone Blizzak ice and snow tire is a perfect example of the company's technological prowess.

Bridgestone/Firestone manufactures the world's largest tires for off-the-road use, with engineers providing technical support to users around the globe.

Following a 21-year absence from Indy car racing, Firestone returned to the competition in 1995, reclaiming its dominance in this exciting arena.

O'Charley's, Inc.

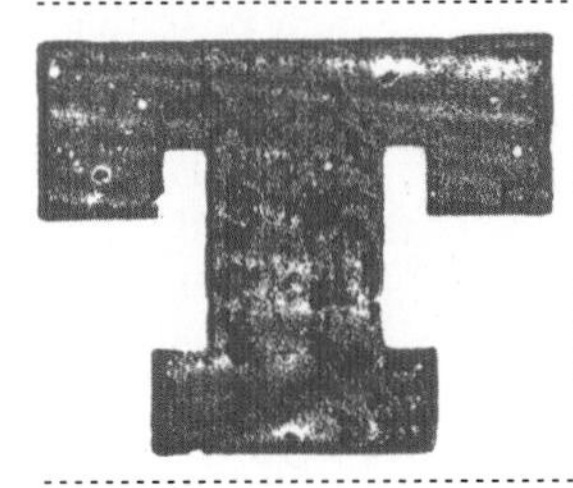

The menu at O'Charley's bears this message for its customers: "O'Charley's guarantee is total satisfaction. We promise a great meal prepared with care and served with genuine hospitality each and every time you dine with us." This simple message sums up the company's customer service focus.

By consistently delivering on this guarantee, O'Charley's has flourished since its founding in Nashville in 1983. Currently, O'Charley's operates 79 restaurants in 10 states throughout the Southeast and Midwest with 6,000 total employees, 1,200 of whom are in the Nashville area.

In the highly competitive restaurant environment, O'Charley's has refined its niche within the casual dining segment and posts more than $200 million in annual revenues. Since 1991, revenues and earnings have increased in excess of 20 percent per year.

"Our concept has successfully evolved as we work to meet the changing preferences of our customers. We listen to all ideas and address all facets of our operations from food to service to atmosphere," says Gregory Burns, company chairman and president. "We are continually trying to make O'Charley's better."

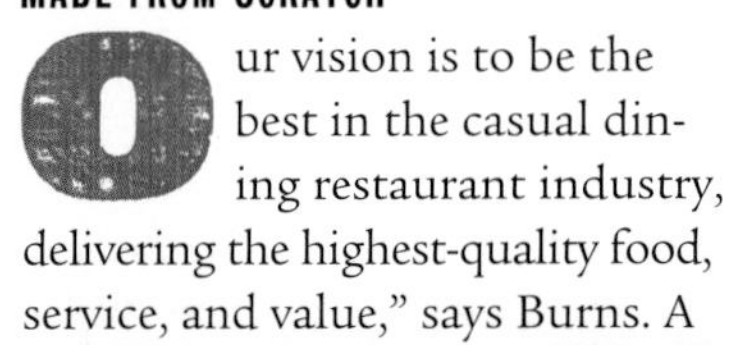

Made from Scratch

"Our vision is to be the best in the casual dining restaurant industry, delivering the highest-quality food, service, and value," says Burns. A devoted clientele frequents the restaurant for its affordable, and broad, menu selection featuring made-from- scratch meals. One of the first to offer entrée dinner salads, O'Charley's is also known for its prime rib, pasta, fresh-baked breads, soups and salad dressings from scratch, and caramel pie.

O'Charley's food preparation commissary, located behind its corporate headquarters in Nash-

Clockwise from left:
O'Charley's is famous for its Southern-fried-chicken salad.

In addition to good food, customers at O'Charley's find a casual atmosphere and fun dining.

From great steaks to seafood to chicken, there is something for everyone at O'Charley's.

ville, prepares the salad dressings and bread dough daily. The culinary team also ages and cuts all the steaks at the commissary before they are sent to the restaurants. By utilizing its own commissary, O'Charley's can regulate pricing and monitor superior quality control.

The restaurant's menu selection, liquor service, and ambience are appealing to a diverse audience—families, kids, singles, couples, and seniors. Its Kids Eat Free All the Time policy wins praise from parents and creates O'Charley's devotees out of even the youngest patrons.

As the company moves forward, the restaurant furniture and fixtures are evolving into a more upscale look; however, Burns maintains O'Charley's will stay a casual concept, never turning into a white tablecloth restaurant. "We want everyone to feel comfortable coming into our restaurants, and we want our employees to feel and be comfortable working here," adds Burns.

A Neighborhood Restaurant

One strategy that the company has successfully employed is clustering—or fully penetrating a market by operating multiple restaurants in that one market. For example, there are 12 O'Charley's locations in the Nashville/Middle Tennessee market. No other casual dining restaurant has as many locations as O'Charley's does in the Volunteer State.

O'Charley's prides itself on being an employee-driven restaurant chain. Through the Impact program, the senior management team holds in-store meetings at each location to discuss the impact each coworker and manager has on the success of the company. O'Charley's believes these meetings are invaluable for maintaining a single-store focus and opening two-way communication with coworkers. The meetings include discussions regarding ways to improve the O'Charley's concept and operations. Employees' ideas and suggestions are encouraged and often implemented. In addition to improved operations, the end result is a sense of employee ownership and pride in the company.

Senior management also encourages the managers and each of the store's 125 employees to be active in their community and support local causes. The list of charitable and civic causes they advocate is countless, as well as representative of O'Charley's diverse workforce. The list ranges from the Boy Scouts to local schools and sports programs to the March of Dimes, American Cancer Society, United Negro College Fund, and Salvation Army.

Training and Technology

he company firmly believes in being a people-oriented, coworker-run company," says Burns. "We think we do a good job of training our employees, and we know that's an important area on which to focus in order to stay competitive." In addition to strategic and ongoing in-store training, O'Charley's is adding a central training facility to its Nashville headquarters. There, trainees will learn detailed operating policies and procedures, as well as develop management and leadership skills, thereby gaining an understanding of the importance of teamwork in the restaurants.

O'Charley's also strives to provide its managers and coworkers with the best possible systems so they can focus on customer service, quality, and satisfaction. With advances in technology, the company has upgraded all its computers. This not only enables servers to place orders more quickly, but allows managers to monitor labor and product costs more effectively, as well as transfer data to and from the home office and commissary.

Remarkable Growth

s a whole, O'Charley's restaurants have posted same-store sales increases for every quarter for the last five years, a remarkable feat by restaurant industry standards.

O'Charley's, which went public in 1990 and is traded on NASDAQ under the initials CHUX, is well capitalized for future expansion. Its operating philosophy—"if it's not good enough for our customers and our coworkers, it's not good enough for O'Charley's"—has helped to build a loyal customer base and puts the company on track to continue its successful operation well into the 21st century.

O'Charley's has refined its niche within the casual dining segment and posts more than $200 million in annual revenues (top).

Management and staff are prepared to make the dining experience at O'Charley's the best ever for their customers (bottom).

AMERICAN FABRICATORS, INC.

MERICAN FABRICATORS, INC. (AFI) DIDN'T BECOME THE largest sheet metal fabrication shop of its kind in the United States by doing jobs at its own speed. The company has reached that milestone by focusing on the needs of its customers—and doing whatever it takes to satisfy those needs. With more than $30 million in sales in 1996, American Fabricators creates metal parts for manufacturing clients all over the country. The workmanship skills of its 115 employees go into products ranging from truck floorboards to the walls of heating and air-conditioning units to the decks of lawn mowers. All those items share two qualities in common: They are done quickly, and they are done right.

CRAFTING A VISION

Milton Grief, president and cofounder of American Fabricators, built on the less-than-ideal experience of a former employer when he started the company in 1984. Trained as an accountant, Grief knew that time is money. He saw that his old shop's hodgepodge of machinery slowed the process of turning raw metal into finished parts, and he imagined how much more productive a fabricating shop could be with standardized, integrated, strategically deployed machinery.

Grief's approach won customers for the new company as soon as it opened its doors. A restaurant chain needed kitchen tables and exhaust hoods. Then an automaker needed parts for dealership signs, and later body and chassis parts. Then came a big order from a lawn mower manufacturer. By 1986, the company's volume had doubled.

Over the years, American Fabricators has accumulated a fair assortment of war stories. There was the time one of the major auto manufacturers decided to consolidate purchasing for its North American facilities, reducing its vendor list from about 2,000 to 20. American Fabricators made the cut, doubling the amount of business it did with the carmaker. And then there's the customer whose costs have remained flat for 12 years because the company has been able to employ advances in technology to do the work more and more efficiently.

Like so many other companies whose business requires the shipment of goods all over the

CLOCKWISE FROM TOP:
AMERICAN FABRICATORS, INC. HAS A VARIETY OF AMADA TURRET PUNCHES THAT CAN ACCOMMODATE A WIDE RANGE OF SHEET SIZES AND MATERIAL THICKNESS.

AFI USES MULTIAXIS UP-ACTING PRESS BRAKES THAT ARE COMPUTER CONTROLLED AND HAVE MEMORY CAPACITY FOR 99 POSITIONS. THESE MACHINES ARE VERY VERSATILE AND ACCEPT A WIDE VARIETY OF TOOLING. MOST IMPORTANTLY, THEY ARE EXTREMELY ACCURATE.

THE PULSAR LASER HELPS STREAMLINE INTERNAL OPERATIONS.

continent, American Fabricators makes its Nashville location a major selling point. The convergence of three interstates in the city, and the fact that half of the U.S. population lives within a 600-mile radius of it, makes Nashville an attractive supplier location for any manufacturer that needs parts on a short-order basis.

Return on Investment

Throughout its history, American Fabricators has been first with the latest and best in metalworking hardware and control technology. The company understands the importance of being equipped to give customers what they want, right away. "When they call, they want it done yesterday," Grief says. "We deliver."

The company's manufacturing facilities on Metroplex Drive, covering more than 100,000 square feet, are outfitted with a dazzling array of turret punch presses, band saws, a tool grinder, the first laser-cutting machine to be put into operation in Tennessee, and myriad other pieces of specialized, state-of-the-art, computer-operated equipment. American Fabricators invests more than $1 million a year in new machinery—and some years as much as $4 million.

In 1996, the company purchased an automated punching cell that has already revolutionized its work flow. This item is only the latest of many investments in technology to pay immediate dividends for the firm. One new turret punch increased production speed by 40 percent. The company's investments in laser-cutting equipment have allowed it to shape nonmetal materials such as acrylics, so that it can produce complete signs instead of just the metal portions. A new press purchased to make parts for fireplaces turned out to be ideal for lighting and appliance parts as well, opening another new market.

Computerized automation is another linchpin of American Fabricators' success. Since every order is built to customers' specifications, it is essential to set up those engineering coordinates as quickly as possible on each piece of machinery—and with no margin for error. American Fabricators manages this challenge by loading the product designs directly from the customer's computer-aided-design system into its own, thus programming the designs into computer-controlled machinery on the shop floor.

All those fancy tools represent large capital outlays, but the company has never flinched from paying the price for excellence. "Those investments are always cost effective," Grief says. As he sees the issue, failing to invest would send a signal to existing customers that the firm is not prepared to keep up with demand. On the other hand, maintaining the technical capacity to take on new challenges can bring new business to the company's door.

"The status quo is unacceptable," Grief tells the people of American Fabricators. "In order for us to grow, change must be a constant."

Clockwise from top left:
The founders of American Fabricators, Inc. are Clarence M. Bain, vice president of manufacturing; Milton R. Grief, president; and Freddie Hobbs, director of manufacturing.

An AFI technician programs parts for the computer numerical controlled turret punches and laser.

AFI conducts the precision welding of various metals, including stainless steel enclosures.

The speed and capacity of the Pega King turret punch helped the company win new customers within the automotive industry. The punch has specialized forming capabilities and operates at a much higher cyclic speed than many other turret punches.

Loews Vanderbilt Plaza Hotel

Corporate executives playing a competitive Monopoly game for charity, chefs creating decorative gingerbread houses, and children filling holiday gift baskets for other children are the true embodiment of the corporate Good Neighbor Policy program and the heart of Loews Vanderbilt Plaza Hotel. One of the most successful enterprises in the Loews hotel chain, Loews Vanderbilt Plaza Hotel has made a business of being neighborly. With a community spirit that is unparalleled, the hotel has initiated such programs as the Monopoly Power Breakfast in which local business executives play a competitive game of Monopoly, raising more than $100,000 for numerous organizations, including the Nashville Symphony, National Foundation for Cerebral Palsy, Ronald McDonald House, and Junior Achievement.

A Gingerbread World, an annual competition and display of gingerbread houses, has taken place every year since the hotel opened in 1984. In 12 years, the program raised more than $200,000 for local charities, including the Dede Wallace Center.

Loews Loves Kids is another outstanding example of Vanderbilt Plaza's commitment to being a good neighbor. Since 1994, the hotel has invited children to create and build special holiday gift baskets for families with an HIV-positive parent or child.

This spirit of giving is obviously apparent to the hotel's business and leisure travelers, as occupancy has increased 10 points in the years since Loews purchased the hotel in 1990. Revenues have almost doubled in that same time frame.

A Business-Class Hotel

Nashville's true business-class hotel features rooms and amenities that are designed with the business traveler in mind. There are designated business-class floors, in which each room is equipped with fax machines, dual phones, voice mail, and a data port.

State-of-the-art office equipment, as well as the most current software packages, is available for guests' use at the Executive Business Center. Another service presented to small groups is Loews Access—a personalized one-stop shopping service. One hotel representative makes all the arrangements for groups, from booking guest rooms to organizing banquet functions to securing meeting space.

From blue-chip meetings to black-tie balls, the Vanderbilt

Loew Vanderbilt Plaza's 17,000 square feet of meeting and function space includes an elegant, 8,500-square-foot ballroom (top).

The hotel's entrance and lobby showcase original fine art and Aubusson tapestries in a faux marble colonnade (bottom).

Plaza is superbly prepared to accommodate group functions for 12 to 1,200 people. The 17,000 square feet of meeting and function space available includes two boardrooms with conference tables; broadcast quality lighting and sound systems; an elegant, 8,500-square-foot ballroom; and an expansive, 3,900-square-foot prefunction promenade.

NASHVILLE'S TRUE BUSINESS-CLASS HOTEL FEATURES ROOMS AND AMENITIES THAT ARE DESIGNED WITH THE BUSINESS TRAVELER IN MIND.

SOPHISTICATED ELEGANCE

touch of elegance is evident in every corner of the Loews Vanderbilt Plaza. The hotel's entrance and lobby showcase original fine art and Aubusson tapestries in a faux marble colonnade. In addition, an exclusive lounge area and full concierge service are dedicated to the top two floors, and the 11-story hotel boasts 338 rooms, each of which has hair dryers, irons and ironing boards, coffeemakers, and minibars. Loews Vanderbilt Plaza also maintains 12 magnificent suites—some of the finest in the city—that have a private French balcony, working fireplace, wet bar, and stunning views of Nashville.

Vanderbilt Plaza's new Snaffles Cigar Bar—the first in Nashville—has been wildly popular since opening in 1996. Not only are fine cigars presented in the clublike ambience, but spirits including single barrel bourbons, single malt scotches, microbeers and stouts, and an impressive list of ports and wines delight even the most discriminating connoisseur.

The Plaza Grill is the hotel's full-service restaurant featuring American/New South cuisine. The Garden Bar, with its live piano entertainment, offers beverages and light snacks every evening. Ruth's Chris Steakhouse, the well-known chain, opened a location in 1996 in the hotel's lower level, with an entrance onto the street.

Conveniently situated in Nashville's midtown, Vanderbilt Plaza is in the heart of the city's medical community, directly across the street from Vanderbilt University and within one and a half miles of downtown. In the summer season, guests can hop on the trolley for easy access to downtown's entertainment district. Within close proximity are such major attractions as the Parthenon, Music Row, Cheekwood Fine Arts and Botanical Gardens, the State Capitol, Ryman Auditorium, and Bicentennial Mall. Guests can also walk to the numerous restaurants—from fast food to fine cuisine—located in the area.

ENHANCING GUESTS' EXPERIENCE

ith a constant focus on enhancing customer service, the Vanderbilt Plaza initiated an advisory council in 1990. Comprised of a group of customers representing all facets of the market, the council meets quarterly to discuss, analyze, and make recommendations for the hotel, reviewing everything from the menu to profit-and-loss statements. The hotel also sponsors two focus groups each year outside the Nashville area to keep abreast of trends in the business and leisure travel market.

Loews Vanderbilt Plaza Hotel is part of Loews hotel chain, which owns and/or operates 14 hotels and resorts in the United States, Canada, and Monaco. Loews' management continually propels the Vanderbilt Plaza property forward, showing a willingness to invest in its property to meet customers' needs and improve their experience. Whether it's expanding the health facility, adding turndown service and bathrobes to rooms, or adding new features to the executive business centers, the Loews Vanderbilt Plaza strives to be a good friend to its clientele and a good neighbor to Nashville.

THE PLAZA GRILL IS THE HOTEL'S FULL-SERVICE RESTAURANT FEATURING AMERICAN/NEW SOUTH CUISINE.

PMT Services, Inc.

E ARE EXTREMELY FORTUNATE TO CALL NASHVILLE home," says Chairman and Chief Executive Officer Richardson M. Roberts of PMT Services, Inc., a provider of credit card terminals to small retailers. "For us to have started this company from scratch and built it to several hundred million in revenues is testament to the entrepreneurial spirit prevalent in Nashville in a variety of industries, which has helped pave the way for our good fortune."

An entrepreneur, who at the age of 26 started the company with his friend and coworker Gregory S. Daily, Roberts marvels at the phenomenal growth and success the company has enjoyed since it opened for business in 1984. "The old adage 'the harder you work, the luckier you get' certainly applies in our case," he concludes.

PMT'S RAPID GROWTH HAS REQUIRED THE COMPANY TO MOVE FOUR TIMES OVER THE YEARS, THE MOST DIFFICULT OF WHICH WAS LEAVING ITS ACCLAIMED RENOVATION OF THE HISTORIC ELM STREET METHODIST CHURCH.

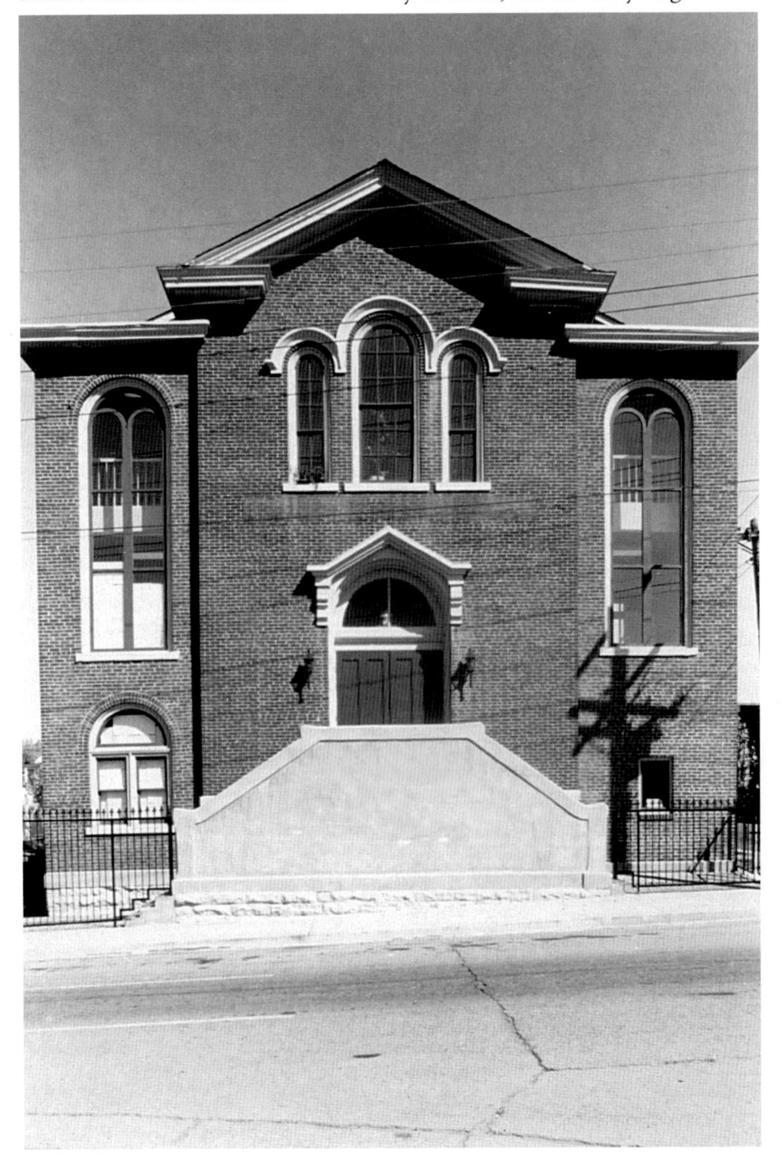

Entrepreneurial Beginnings

aving witnessed the early-stage development of the electronic transaction processing industry while at another company, Roberts and Daily started their business in a renovated, 1,200-square-foot house behind Mrs. Grissom's Salads in Nashville. Those early, lean years were especially meaningful to PMT while surviving leaky roofs and faulty HVAC systems, and making payroll on personal credit cards. Roberts points out that PMT Services captured the watchful eye of some extraordinary guardian angels, one of these being Nashville-based Massey-Burch Venture Capital, which infused the fledgling business with equity in 1987.

PMT reached a major milestone in 1990, breaking even after reaching 10,000 merchant accounts. Since then, the company has acquired more than 100,000 additional accounts in 30 separate transactions. The company's ability to meld these acquisitions into its own operation is a unique talent, which sets it apart from its major competitors. As a result, PMT Services today has approximately 400 employees and has added subsidiaries in Chicago, Dallas, New York, and Tampa, all of which service a diversified national customer base.

In an unprecedented move for an independent service organization in the merchant processing industry, PMT completed an initial public offering in August 1994. At the time, the company had 37,000 accounts. With the capital raised in that and subsequent equity offerings, the firm grew rapidly, processing more than 100,000 accounts in 1996.

"I think I am most proud of going from a complete start-up in 1984 to a $25 million company in 1994 to a $200 million-plus company in 1996," says Roberts. "I would certainly encourage other would-be entrepreneurs to take a chance and pursue their dream. We certainly didn't start with the skill to be a public company. We benefited from on-the-job training and received good advice from our attorneys, accountants, venture capitalists, and investment bankers. Nashville is unique to have such a high level of talent in areas such as these, which provides a springboard for the entrepreneurial spirit in this town. We have enjoyed this opportunity to personally grow with the company, and it has been both a fascinating challenge and a very rewarding experience."

Building the Business

hile PMT's numerous acquisitions have contributed to its growth, the firm also has taken a highly proactive approach to sustaining its strong foundation by placing heavy emphasis on the customer service side of the business. "If there's one cornerstone approach for the company's actions, it is 'relationships count,' " notes Roberts. "We're in a relatively small industry and Nashville is still a small town in many ways, so we've always tried not to burn any bridges. It's vital to our business to maintain relationships, to treat our customers and our employees with dignity and respect. We've benefited by

South Central Bell's former headquarters in the heart of Green Hills will serve as the company's new offices beginning in the fall of 1997.

surrounding ourselves with talented people we have tried to treat as equals. Also, we try to have fun while still accomplishing our goals."

With that perspective in mind early on, PMT has established an affinity with business associations by offering a comprehensive marketing program for its members. With the endorsement of the association, the door is open for PMT to contact the association's members, who are potential customers for PMT's point-of-sale processing services. Historically, PMT has utilized telemarketing to establish and maintain these relationships with clients, offering a relatively inexpensive means to build a strong, recurring base of revenues. In 1996, PMT focused on strategic acquisitions of companies with direct sales presence in the field and, subsequently, increased its internal growth fourfold within one year.

As both a sales and a service company, PMT has increasingly focused its resources on protecting its existing merchant portfolios with superior customer service. Remaining highly focused on its marketplace and skill sets has allowed PMT to leverage its growth and use its capital to quickly grow a large, profitable account base. PMT's past and future success hinges on its ability to continually invest in its people and systems. The company maintains it doesn't invest in glitzy office environs, although its rapid growth has required the group to move offices four times since inception, including a recent move to its new headquarters.

As PMT has matured as a company, the opportunity to give back to the Nashville community has expanded as well. A number of local events and charities have benefited from the firm's goodwill, including blood drives, Swing for Sight, Swan Ball, and Second Harvest Food Bank.

Mission for the Future

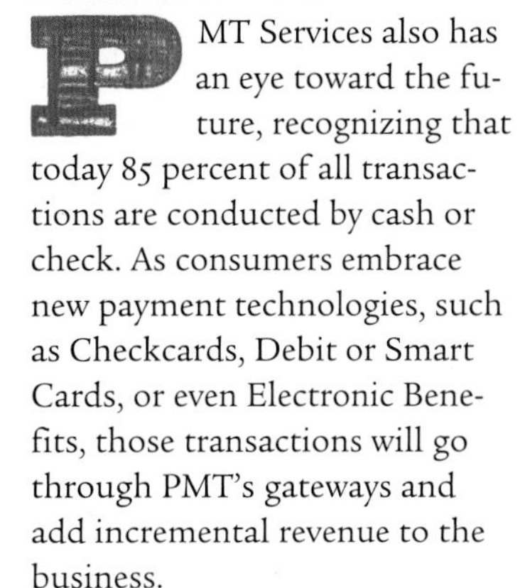

PMT Services also has an eye toward the future, recognizing that today 85 percent of all transactions are conducted by cash or check. As consumers embrace new payment technologies, such as Checkcards, Debit or Smart Cards, or even Electronic Benefits, those transactions will go through PMT's gateways and add incremental revenue to the business.

Striving toward its goal of several hundred thousand merchant accounts, PMT aims to dominate the small sector of the merchant-processing industry. With access to capital, superior service platforms, and a talented management pool, PMT is primed to accomplish that mission.

In January 1995, PMT settled into offices in Brentwood's Maryland Farms, but with explosive expansion from its August 1994 IPO, the company quickly outgrew this space.

Whirlpool Corporation

VERYTHING'S COOL AT WHIRLPOOL—FROM THE HOUSEHOLD appliances rolling off the assembly line to the smooth teamwork between labor and management. ★ Whirlpool/LaVergne is the largest producer of room air conditioners in North America, selling its wares through retailers like Sears and Home Depot. As a unit of Michigan-based Whirlpool Corporation, which has been building appliances since 1911, the local plant has been in operation since 1984. It originated as a facility of Whirlpool's former Heil-Quaker subsidiary, remaining a part of the Whirlpool family after Heil-Quaker was sold in 1986.

In addition to its air conditioner business, the roughly 2,000 people of Whirlpool/LaVergne also manufacture thousands of dehumidifiers and KitchenAid built-in refrigerators every year at the 1 million-square-foot plant on Nashville's southeastern fringe. "We lead in technology and in establishing value in what we deliver to the consumer—excellent durability, quality, and service," says Doug Hutchins, Whirlpool Corporation division vice president, who has been at the helm of the local operation since 1986.

RANDY FOX, FOX STUDIO

WHIRLPOOL/LAVERGNE IS THE LARGEST PRODUCER OF ROOM AIR CONDITIONERS IN NORTH AMERICA. AS A UNIT OF MICHIGAN-BASED WHIRLPOOL CORPORATION, WHICH HAS BEEN BUILDING APPLIANCES SINCE 1911, THE LOCAL PLANT HAS BEEN IN OPERATION SINCE 1984.

Unlimited Partnershop

"We use the word 'we' a lot here, and both management and labor work hard to make our relationship as productive as possible," Hutchins says. Jim Romines, president of local S-272 of the International Brotherhood of Boilermakers union, which represents Whirlpool/LaVergne's workforce, echoes Hutchins' words: "We all realize that the nation's work communities are changing, and it takes more effort than ever for management and the workforce to meet the demands of the customer."

At Whirlpool/LaVergne, that effort takes its focus from Partnershop, a labor-management council cochaired by Romines and Hutchins. Since April 1993, the Partnershop group has met at least once every month. "That's actually the way we run the business and make key decisions," Hutchins says. The Partnershop structure permeates all levels of the organization. On the shop floor, goal-directed work teams of employees work to meet cost and quality objectives. "Each employee is the expert within 50 feet of his or her job, whether that job is machine operator, utility operator, or material handler," Hutchins explains. "They know more about their positions than anybody. That's one of our guiding principles."

Through Partnershop, the Whirlpool facility has successfully implemented a state-of-the-art manufacturing process—demand-flow technology. Hutchins describes the process as "a pull system rather than a push system" for managing the flow of assembly work through the plant. At the core of the system is the individual authority of employees. "We give production operators the time and control to perform their job and perform quality checks," Hutchins explains. "The product does not move from operator to operator until they release it. They have total control."

Romines admits that there was a lot of uncertainty about the process when it was first implemented, but the employees involved in the system are very appreciative of it today. He adds, "They do their job and verify quality before releasing the product. The system also gives employees input into what goes on in work areas and how day-to-day activities are conducted."

A Hub of Activity

Like many other businesses that have chosen to locate in Nashville, Whirlpool was drawn by two of the city's strengths: the place and the people. Hutchins describes the Music City as ideal for its proximity to distribution channels, transportation, and delivery options, noting that Nashville is within 500 miles of half the population of the United States. At the same time, Hutchins says, Nashville offers a labor force with a good work ethic.

The LaVergne facility has received widespread recognition for the superior quality of its products. Whirlpool is the recipient of numerous quality awards bestowed by such major customers as Sears and by the state of Tennessee. *Home Mechanix, World Trade,* and *Consumer Reports* have also recognized the quality and value of products made by the workers of Whirlpool/LaVergne.

Other plaudits have come from Inroads, an organization devoted to helping disadvantaged young people excel in business. It named Whirlpool/LaVergne the 1994 Company of the Year, recognizing the internships and other support Whirlpool has provided to Inroads. The LaVergne Division has also been recognized locally and nationally for its commitment to the environment, winning state and governor's awards and being named a Best Practice by Whirlpool Corporation for its environmental efforts.

The Commitment of Partners

Even though Whirlpool/LaVergne has almost doubled its market share in the last six years, posting record numbers of units shipped year after year, it shows no signs of complacency. "We intend to increase that share and maintain our position," Hutchins says. "We intend to update and rejuvenate our products on a recurring basis. We plan to continue delivering a premium product, maintaining the number one manufacturing share in North America."

Hutchins cites two elements as keys to the company's strategy for staying on top: building customer loyalty—a relationship beyond mere customer satisfaction—and building employee commitment. "Commitment," he explains, "works two ways: employees committed to the business and the business committed to employees."

Romines seconds that thought. "We have every reason to expect continued success in building upon the partnership we have here, to ensure the continued growth of the division and the security of our employees," he says.

▲ RANDY FOX, FOX STUDIO

▲▼ RANDY FOX, FOX STUDIO

Clockwise from top:
At Whirlpool/LaVergne, cooperation between management and the workforce takes its focus from Partnershop, a labor-management council cochaired by Jim Romines and Doug Hutchins. Since April 1993, the Partnershop group has met at least once every month.

The LaVergne facility has received widespread recognition for the superior quality of its products, which are tested in the on-site laboratory.

The Whirlpool facility has successfully implemented a state-of-the-art manufacturing process—demand-flow technology, which gives employees control over the assembly line.

French, Clayton, Johnson & Associates

Breaking the trend in residential real estate brokerage toward large multioffice and franchise firms, French, Clayton, Johnson & Associates was formed in 1985. Instead of trying to be all things to all people, the aggressive team of 20-plus full-time brokers and affiliates specializes in the most sought after neighborhoods of Davidson and Williamson counties.

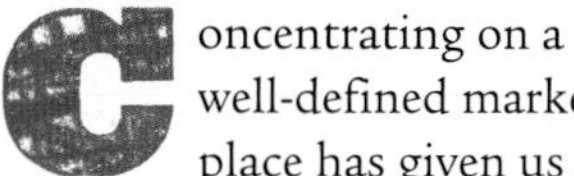

Meeting Market Needs

"Concentrating on a well-defined marketplace has given us an edge," explains Rick French, one of French, Clayton, Johnson & Associates' founding partners. "Thorough understanding and familiarity with our neighborhoods has given us the knowledge necessary to serve the increasingly sophisticated needs of the buyer and seller," French says.

"Further," adds Partner Neal Clayton, current president of the Greater Nashville Association of Realtors, "we have embraced the latest technology available in the industry without losing touch with the personal side of the business." Prospective buyers can even view active properties for sale through a computer program at their office or home.

According to Partner Ellen Johnson Christianson, "Our success lies with our associates. Twenty unique individuals, representing 20 different spheres of influence, join together to brainstorm for each client. Whether the client is buying or selling, a strategy is developed."

Specialized Treatment

For the buyer client, the home search begins by identifying appropriate neighborhoods. Then an exhaustive search of homes is undertaken. The firm explores properties even if they

The three founding partners—(from left) Ellen Johnson Christianson, Rick French, and Neal Clayton—remain active sales agents and monitor the market on a daily basis.

◀ Harry Butler

HARRY BUTLER

FRENCH, CLAYTON, JOHNSON & ASSOCIATES' MARKETING TEAM MAINTAINS THE HIGHEST STANDARDS OF PROFESSIONALISM, WITH ACTIVE MEMBERSHIP IN THE NATIONAL AND LOCAL ASSOCIATION OF REALTORS.

are not currently listed in the multiple listing system. If interim housing is required, the firm assists the client in finding it. French, Clayton, Johnson & Associates assumes responsibility for the smooth relocation of each client, as well as helping clients establish a connection with the community—from schools, banks, places of health care and worship to grocery stores and baby-sitters.

For a client desiring to sell, the property is evaluated and special features highlighted. Then a marketing plan is prepared along with a prospective buyer profile. The goal is maximum exposure to the most-qualified prospects. French elaborates, "Real estate is a numbers game. The more prospective buyers who see a property, the more likely the seller will recognize the maximum yield. With our efforts to search and reach prospects through personal contacts, as well as specifically targeted direct mail campaigns, we've earned the term 'aggressive.' " Clayton admits, "This approach has enabled us to control the lion's share of the market in the neighborhoods we serve."

PROFESSIONAL MARKETING

The firm's marketing team maintains the highest standards of professionalism, with active membership in the national and local real estate organizations. It enjoys the highest reputation in the business community, participating in the Nashville Area Chamber of Commerce and other civic, charitable, and professional organizations. Its commitment, experience, and technical skills are unsurpassed. The three partners remain active sales agents and participate in the market daily.

The firm has been chosen "Best Realtor" year after year in local readers' polls. When clients are looking for excellent service and quality real estate, French, Clayton, Johnson & Associates satisfies those needs.

Saturn Corporation

What began as a code name for General Motors' small-car project has today become an unprecedented automotive success story, a marketing phenomenon, and a role model for corporate America. Since the first car rolled off the Spring Hill assembly line in July 1990 through the one-millionth car in June 1995, Saturn has experienced double-digit sales increases annually, and achieved top sales and customer satisfaction rankings in the prestigious JD Power Surveys.

Saturn's site selection of Spring Hill, located 45 miles south of Nashville, in July 1985 began the company's contribution to Tennessee's economy. Saturn cites many factors regarding its decision to locate in Spring Hill, including Middle Tennessee's geographical proximity to 65 percent of the nation's population, good highway and rail systems, and a supportive climate in which to develop the company's new people systems concept. Today, the $1.9 billion manufacturing and assembly complex produces Saturn coupes, sedans, and wagons for the United States, Taiwan, Canada, and Japan.

Since the first car rolled off the Spring Hill assembly line in July 1990 through the one-millionth car in June 1995, Saturn has experienced double digit sales increases annually and achieved top sales and customer satisfaction rankings in the prestigious JD Power Surveys.

The Clean Sheet Approach

In 1981, after scrutinizing its American automobile production, General Motors (GM) posed a challenge to its Advanced Product and Design Team: Can GM build a quality small car in the United States that can compete successfully with imports? In response, the team established its small-car project, the Saturn Project, and adopted a "clean sheet" approach, meaning they would not be constrained by any industry practices or traditional thinking regarding automobile manufacturing.

Subsequently, GM and the UAW also recognized the need to explore new approaches to union-management relations. If Saturn was to successfully bridge the cost differential and quality perception with foreign imports, then all disciplines involved in the business would have to be integrated toward the common goals of quality, cost, and timing to assure the highest possible customer value. Donald Ephlin, then UAW vice president and director of the GM Department, helped form an unprecedented alliance of 99 GM and UAW people referred to as the Group of 99.

On January 7, 1985, the Group of 99 became a separate, wholly owned subsidiary of GM called the Saturn Corporation. Not since 1916, when Chevrolet joined the General Motors family, had GM added a new nameplate. Joseph Sanchez, was named president.

People Systems

artnership is the true heart of the Saturn culture and people are the company's greatest asset. Establishing partnerships with customers, members, suppliers, dealers, and neighbors in which everyone shares in the risks and rewards is the basis of the company's philosophy. Saturn's values call for an unparalleled commitment to excellence, teamwork, trust, and respect for the individual. The company strives to achieve not merely customer satisfaction, but rather customer enthusiasm, meaning the company meets and exceeds its customers' requirements and expectations on a consistent basis.

Saturn's organizational structure, consisting of work units, is dramatically different from typical hierarchical operations. Consensus decision making is the core of this operational structure. Each 6- to 12-person team is self-directed—making their own assignments, defining their own jobs, and resolving their own conflicts.

Environmental Initiatives and Industrial Innovations

Saturn Corporation is a model for environmentally compatible manufacturing, establishing a commitment to protect and preserve the environment from its grassroots beginning. To preserve the plant's rural and historical surroundings, strategic landscaping and creative building design and colors were used to make the facility nearly invisible from the highway. Saturn also created an on-site nursery for uprooted trees and later transplanted them for use in landscaping around the facilities.

Saturn also implemented the lost foam casing process, used for manufacturing several engine and transmission parts, which significantly reduces the amount of contaminated waste sand generated in the molding process. Specially designed hazardous materials docks also were installed in loading and unloading areas to contain potentially spillable materials.

Saturn has been duly rewarded for these environmental initiatives. The U.S. Department of the Interior presented Saturn with its 1989 Take Pride in America national award for outstanding contributions to protecting and enhancing public resources, and the Tennessee Association of Business recognized Saturn with the Overall Environmental Excellence Award in 1988.

Saturn Corporation has achieved many firsts in the automobile industry. The company was the first U.S. auto manufacturer to build both an automatic and a manual transmission on the same line. Saturn also developed the first thermoplastic exterior door panel, an effort that earned the company the 1991 Automotive Division Grand Award from the Society of Plastic Engineers.

The marketing of the Saturn brand has become a case history in successful product launches. The advertising campaign centers on the employees and buyers as much as it does the car itself. The no-hassle, no-haggle pricing policy is revolutionary and wildly popular with the buying public.

Perhaps the greatest testament to the quality and customer commitment Saturn embodies was the June 1994 Saturn Homecoming. The company invited Saturn owners and families to come to Tennessee to meet team members and other owners, tour the birthplace of their cars, and enjoy a weekend of family-oriented activities. Some 44,000 Saturn owners showed up in Spring Hill and another 130,000-plus attended regional events held by Saturn retailers.

As Donald Hudler, now president of Saturn Corporation, once said, "If we have any legacy at Saturn, it will be that we built an outstanding brand." There's no doubt that Saturn lives up to its motto: "A different kind of company. A different kind of car."

Partnership is the true heart of the Saturn culture and people are the company's greatest asset.

The $1.9 billion Spring Hill manufacturing and assembly complex produces Saturn coupes, sedans, and wagons for the United States, Taiwan, Canada, and Japan.

Sheraton Music City Hotel

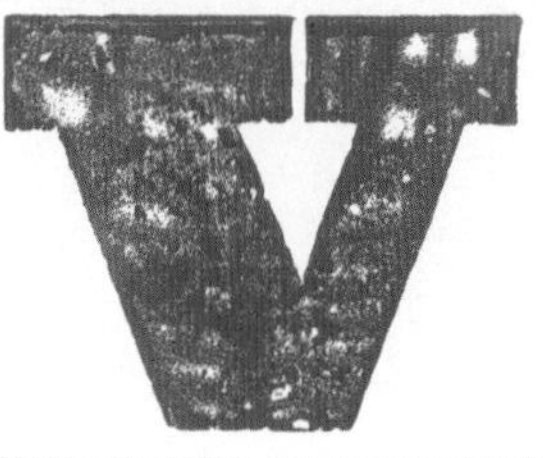

Visitors and locals alike have come to value Nashville's Sheraton Music City Hotel as something special. In a world of bustling convention hotels and take-a-number-and-wait travel destinations, the Sheraton is an oasis of gracious hospitality, quiet comfort, and personal attention.

The 412-room hotel, designed in 1985 in the tradition of a grand southern manor, crowns a 23-acre hilltop site off Elm Hill Pike in Century City, within easy access of Nashville's International Airport and major tourist and business destinations. Its tall, white columns, balconies, and traditional, Georgian, brick exterior evoke images of Nashville's history, a graceful counterpoint to Middle Tennessee's green, rolling hills.

The Lap of Luxury

Inside, the emphasis is on quality design, luxurious amenities, and unparalleled personal service. The impressive lobby welcomes guests with its rich, traditional colors and furnishings. The polished cherry paneling glows and a fountain whispers. Adjacent to this grand entrance, the wicker and greenery of the Veranda Lounge invite guests to linger over a cocktail and soft piano music with friends or business associates. Nearby, the award-winning restaurant Apples in the Field offers Nashville's best menu of regional specialties and seasonal continental cuisine. No ordinary restaurant, Apples has become a favorite dining spot for discriminating Nashvillians who savor such upscale fare as its elaborate Sunday brunch with its Nashville by the Sea buffet.

Those in search of upbeat, contemporary entertainment and good times flock to Coyote's, where fun-loving young Nashvillians gather for live and recorded music, videos, and good food in a casual atmosphere.

In its attractive and elegantly furnished guest rooms, the emphasis on quality and service continues. The hotel's luxurious rooms are private retreats for guests, and each offers two phones, a remote control television, hair dryers, coffeemakers, irons and ironing boards, video checkout, and even video games. Every room has a spacious, private balcony, where guests can relax in comfortable chairs while enjoying a view of either the beautifully landscaped pool courtyard or the surrounding hills.

Business travelers enjoy the 53 executive rooms and 60 club rooms designed especially for their needs. Three presidential suites are also available. On the special Club Floor, rooms offer free local calls, voice mail and data ports, and an executive lounge where guests can enjoy a complimentary continental breakfast and hors d'oeuvres.

Parking is ample, accessible, and always free. The hotel happily shuttles guests to and from Opryland USA or the airport. For recreation, the Sheraton offers its guests a fully equipped health club, massage therapy, outdoor jogging trails, and a choice of indoor and outdoor pools. The hotel is located conveniently near outstanding golf facilities.

Extraordinary Service

Since it was founded, the Sheraton Music City has earned an international reputation as one of the country's finest destinations for meetings and smaller conventions, with facilities accommodating from 12 to 1,200 people. Its

Sheraton Music City Hotel's tall, white columns, balconies, and traditional, Georgian, brick exterior evoke images of Nashville's history, a graceful counterpoint to Middle Tennessee's green, rolling hills (top).

The impressive lobby welcomes guests with its rich, traditional colors and furnishings. The polished cherry paneling glows and a fountain whispers (bottom).

26,000 square feet of beautifully appointed meeting space includes eight small meeting rooms, a paneled executive boardroom, and the sweeping Plantation Ballroom. The hotel's meeting and convention planning staff is among the best in the business, and its catering services can arrange everything from a boxed lunch to a theme buffet or formal multicourse dinner with ease and perfect attention to detail.

It is just that attention to service that has earned the Sheraton five prestigious Gold Key awards from *Meetings & Conventions* magazine. This award, the industry's most sought after, is based on seven criteria: meeting staff, meeting rooms, guest services, food and beverage service, reservations handling, audiovisual and other technical support equipment, and recreational facilities. The award is voted upon by the magazine's 80,500 subscribers, who include corporate, incentive, and association planners—a demanding and knowledgeable group to please.

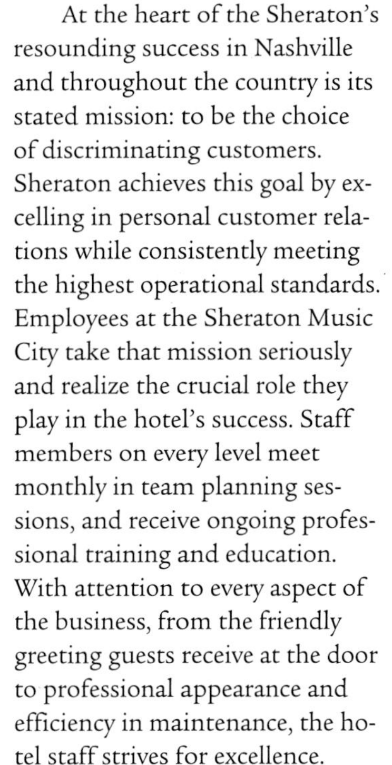

At the heart of the Sheraton's resounding success in Nashville and throughout the country is its stated mission: to be the choice of discriminating customers. Sheraton achieves this goal by excelling in personal customer relations while consistently meeting the highest operational standards. Employees at the Sheraton Music City take that mission seriously and realize the crucial role they play in the hotel's success. Staff members on every level meet monthly in team planning sessions, and receive ongoing professional training and education. With attention to every aspect of the business, from the friendly greeting guests receive at the door to professional appearance and efficiency in maintenance, the hotel staff strives for excellence.

Their success is measured in the Sheraton Music City's 95 percent customer satisfaction rating, setting the standard for the industry. One of only 63 corporate-managed Sheratons in North America, and the only one in Tennessee, the Sheraton Music City has also earned a place in the Sheraton Corporation's President's Club for properties with 90-plus percent customer satisfaction rating every year since opening.

Whether visiting Nashville for fun, traveling for business, or living right here in the birthplace of country music, visitors to the Sheraton Music City feel at home in this gracious southern manor.

Clockwise from top:
Since it was founded, Sheraton Music City Hotel has earned an international reputation as one of the country's finest destinations for meetings and smaller conventions, with facilities accommodating from 12 to 1,200 people.

The wicker and greenery of the Veranda Lounge invite guests to linger over a cocktail and soft piano music with friends or business associates.

The hotel's meeting and convention planning staff is among the best, and its catering services can arrange everything from a boxed lunch to a theme buffet or formal multicourse dinner with ease and perfect attention to detail.

REEMAY, INC.

STROLLING THROUGH A GARDENING SHOP, ANY NASHVILLIAN with a green thumb can usually tell how much of the merchandise is homegrown. Amid the potted geraniums and lily bulbs, however, there's a hardy perennial that not everyone would recognize as being native to Nashville: Reemay, Inc.

Products of Reemay, Inc., a member of the world's third-largest manufacturer of nonwoven fabrics, can be found in the finest gardens, landscape architecture, road building, agriculture, home construction, consumer products, clothing, automobile components, and heavy-duty wiring. And the list of possible applications continues to grow.

A WORLD LEADER IN NONWOVENS

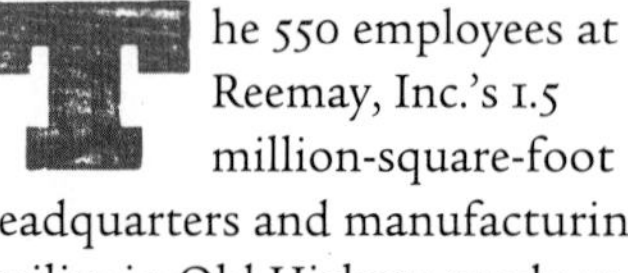

The 550 employees at Reemay, Inc.'s 1.5 million-square-foot headquarters and manufacturing facility in Old Hickory produce an increasingly diverse line of fabrics for customers throughout the world. "Middle Tennesseans purchase Reemay products without realizing they're manufactured in the area," according to Gil Rains, general manager of Reemay, Inc. "Typar® Landscape Fabric, Reemay® and Typar® Row Crop Covers, Biobarrier® II, Typar® HouseWrap, and Typar® Can Separator Sheets are all available locally. In addition, Reemay's fabrics are part of everyday items such as carpet backing, pool and spa filters, furniture and bedding, and fabric softener dryer sheets."

Typar Landscape Fabric is one of several Reemay, Inc. lawn

BIOBARRIER® II, GUARANTEED FOR 10 YEARS, IS USED IN AREAS WHERE WEED GROWTH IS NOT DESIRED (TOP).

REEMAY INC.'S BIOBARRIER® PREVENTS TREE ROOTS FROM INTRUDING INTO SIDEWALKS, STREETS, AND OTHER HARDSCAPED AREAS (BOTTOM).

and garden products designed to help plantings thrive and keep out unwanted weed growth. Placed in the area to be landscaped, and then covered with mulch, the landscape fabric keeps weeds from taking hold in gardens and ornamental beds, while allowing water, air, and nutrients to pass through for healthy soil and plants. It is also used for soil retention behind retaining walls, for support under brick walkways, and for a variety of other purposes. Other lawn and garden fabrics from Reemay, Inc. include the Germinator®, which retains warmth to promote early germination, and Biobarrier® Root Control System, which won an international award as a unique solution to the problem of the indiscriminate use of herbicides.

Reemay and Typar Row Crop Covers are to commercial agriculture what Reemay, Inc.'s lawn and garden fabrics are to landscape architecture. The row crop covers can inhibit insects and weeds, help crops germinate, and serve to prevent frost from affecting plants. Among the other agricultural products from the company are Typar® fabrics used for mud control, vapor control in poultry houses, and barn roofing. These products are in use on farms throughout North America.

Residential builders rely on Reemay, Inc.'s Typar HouseWrap as an essential construction material. Lightweight and easy to install, the fabric also has the advantage of being so strong that it will not tear or rip. Energy-saving Typar HouseWrap holds in a home's cool air in the summer and its heat in the winter so well that the product is the premier building wrap used in Sweden, where it has proved its mettle in subzero Scandinavian winters.

From the European construction market to the shoe industry in the Far East, Typar nonwovens are the materials of choice for a wide range of applications. All Typar products are composed of 100 percent polypropylene, while all fabrics sold under the Reemay brand are made of 100 percent polyester. Neither material includes any fillers or binders.

Gardeners with better things to do than pull weeds can get some help from Typar® Landscape Fabric.

The Fabric of Success

Since its founding in 1986, Reemay, Inc. has more than doubled its revenue base. Its reputation has grown, too. Within a number of global industries, Reemay, Inc. products are widely prized for their strength, purity, and versatility. In 1993, the company became wholly owned by BBA Group Plc, a London-based company, and is a member of its nonwoven division.

Throughout its history as an innovative nonwovens manufacturer, Reemay, Inc. has demonstrated a commitment to pursuing continual quality improvement. A thorough on-line quality measurement system, coupled with an extensive in-house laboratory facility, ensures that Reemay, Inc. products measure up to high standards. The company achieved ISO 9002 certification—an internationally recognized quality assurance standard—in 1995.

Research and development is a key element in Reemay, Inc.'s success. The company's R&D professionals are responsible for many of the innovations that have expanded the range of uses for Reemay and Typar fabrics. Additionally, this staff is developing a new technology for the production of a unique spunbonded fabric with characteristics that will lead the company into new markets.

Typar® Can Separator Sheets have found a niche in the beverage canning market. The sheets are used to separate empty cans during the trip from the can manufacturer to the facility where they are filled.

The people of Reemay, Inc. are striving hard to make the company's second decade as fruitful as its first. According to Rains, "Since 1986, Reemay has manufactured and shipped millions of yards of our fabrics around the globe. Our goal is to continue the rapid growth we've experienced, while maintaining our high standards of quality, employee safety, and customer service."

Cytometry Associates, Inc.

UST A FEW YEARS AGO, PEOPLE SPOKE OF A CURE FOR CANCER as something that might be hoped for in the distant future. Today, Cytometry Associates, Inc. is helping to make that once-faint hope a distinct reality. ★ Cytometry Associates functions as a trusted adviser and partner to physicians in the evaluation and treatment of cancer. The company offers testing, interpretation, and research concerning the many complex and esoteric issues that can confront a doctor and patient facing a cancer diagnosis.

Meeting Medical Needs

ounded in 1988 as an offshoot of the former International Clinical Laboratories, Inc., Cytometry Associates is a product of Nashville's booming health care industry. It is one of the many health care companies created in the ideal entrepreneurial environment that exists locally, which provides a wealth of expertise in starting, financing, and operating medical businesses.

The company's founders were medical technologist and clinical laboratory industry veteran Dennis Grimaud, now president and chief executive officer; health care investment analyst Andy May; diagnostic expert Dr. Gregory T. Stelzer, who now serves as vice president and scientific director; and cytometric specialist Keith E. Shults, now vice president of technology transfer. Grimaud recalls that the idea of starting the company came from the founders' recognition of a need in the marketplace: "We saw that physician specialists in pathology and oncology were underserved in the area of specialized testing."

From its earliest days, when the company had only nine employees, Cytometry Associates has grown by every standard. Its staff now numbers about 75, fulfilling the needs of doctors and hospitals nationwide from offices and laboratories in San Diego and Columbus, Ohio, and at its Brentwood headquarters. The company's sales exceeded $10 million in 1996.

Complex Procedures, Simple Results

e don't look at ourselves as a clinical laboratory," Grimaud explains. "We consider our service to be professional consultation in analytical

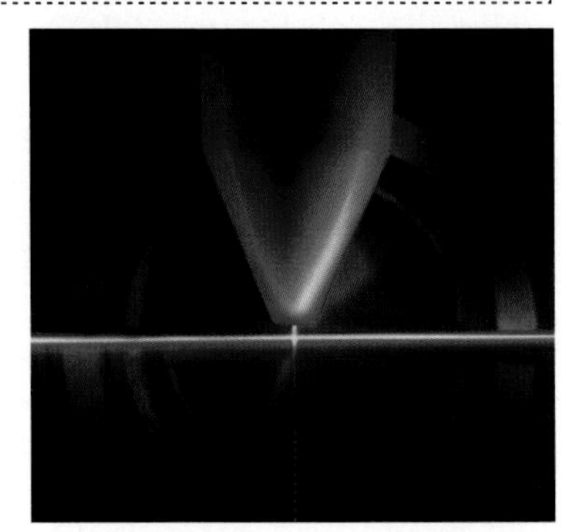

Clockwise from top:
Cytometry Associates, Inc. was the first independent laboratory to be certified to use flow cytometry, a powerful technology that provides accurate diagnostic information in most cancer patients.

Cytometry Associates integrates advanced cancer technologies through information systems.

Scientists at Cytometry Associates perform hormone receptor analysis to prognosis breast cancer.

cytology, providing value-added information to physicians about the disease state of the patient." Grimaud says that, in a typical case, "The physician may call us and ask, 'What have I got here? I know these are abnormal cells, but I can't determine what they are.' We walk them through the analytical process."

Physicians turn to Cytometry Associates to consult with its specialists in such disciplines as flow cytometry, immunocytochemistry, molecular biology, and cytogenetics. Drawing on a cumulative 50 years of experience in the clinical applications of cytometry, the experts at Cytometry Associates assist doctors in all aspects of diagnosis, prognosis, and monitoring therapy. The scientific staff uses state-of-the-art equipment, ranging from multilaser cell sorting systems to routine bench-top analyzers.

The business of Cytometry Associates is complex, but the impact the company's services can have on a single human life is simple. A case recently reported by one client physician is typical. The patient in question had been free from leukemia for two years. Normal microscopic screening of bone marrow cells had found no evidence of a recurrence of the cancer. But then Cytometry Associates called the doctor to inform him that its intricate analytical procedures had detected signs of renewed cancerous growth. Four months passed before the cancer became detectable by ordinary means. Cytometry Associates' early detection gave the doctor and patient a head start in their battle against the disease.

Searching for Answers

Research is an integral part of Cytometry Associates' overall mission. The company's specialists have had more than 60 articles published in medical journals in eight years in business, and they frequently appear at seminars and symposia throughout the United States. The company conducts much of its research in collaboration with academic institutions. "We're looking for answers," Grimaud explains. "Why are the cells doing what they're doing? Why is the cell functioning in this way? What is the best treatment for these patients?"

From its biopharmaceutical support services facility in England, Cytometry Associates provides clinical trials to pharmaceutical companies, helping them gauge the effectiveness of new cancer treatments. By doing so, the company becomes part of the search for a cure, and for improved care for those suffering from cancer. That segment of Cytometry Associates' business doubled in 1996.

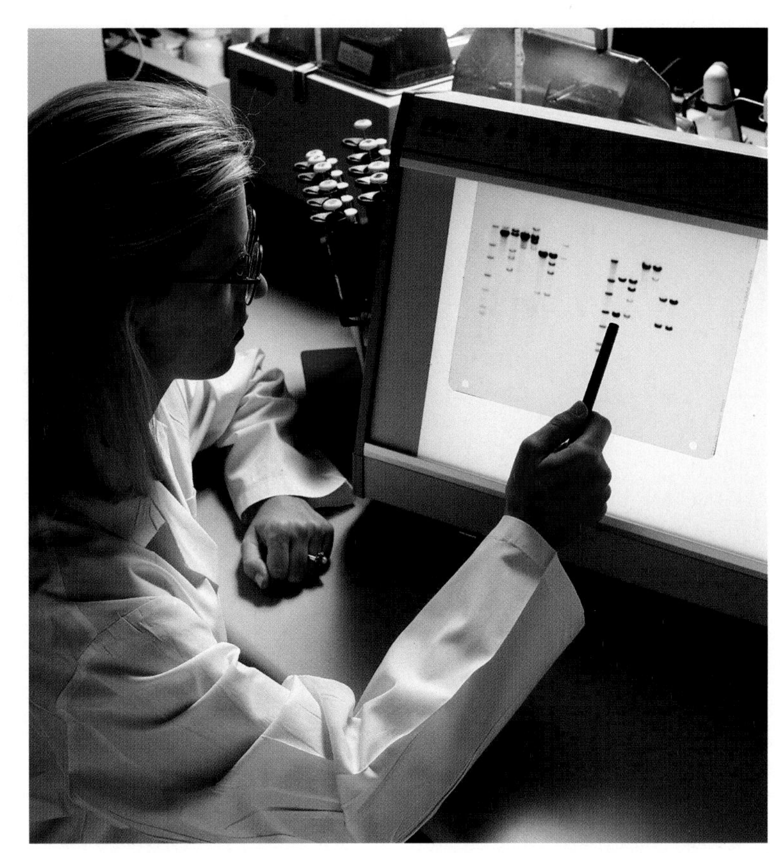

Cytometry Associates offers such molecular diagnostic services as immunoglobulin tests and T-cell gene rearrangements, which provide a precise diagnosis and establish a benchmark for tracking the progress of a patient.

The company's commitment to furthering understanding of issues related to cancer diagnosis and treatment is both deep and broad. It offers customized courses to educate medical professionals in both basic and advanced diagnostic applications, and maintains one of the nation's largest libraries on cytometric topics, making its holdings available to outside researchers and medical scholars.

In years to come, Cytometry Associates intends to move more and more deeply into the international market, especially through its pharmaceutical trials business. The company also expects that advances in telecommunications, such as videoconferencing, will allow for easier communications with physicians. Already, some clients have high-bandwidth telephone connections through which they can download information directly from Cytometry Associates' computers.

"We are a cutting-edge science and technology company," Grimaud says proudly. "The goal of this organization is to be a center of excellence. The way to do that is to provide integrated oncology solutions to the practicing physician for enhanced patient care."

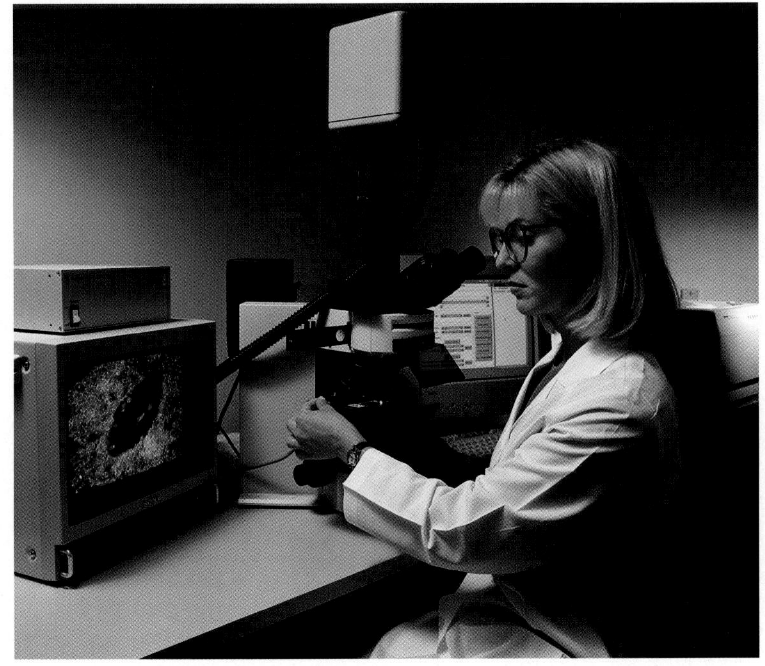

Scientists at Cytometry Associates are experienced in and focused on the prognosis and diagnosis of cancer, yielding information that surpasses the results of many other laboratories.

IPN Network

HE MORE THAN 400 EMPLOYEES IN THE IPN NETWORK FAMILY share a vision: An individual or a family receives a single monthly statement detailing all health care charges and payments—just like a credit card statement lists charges from several retailers. Compared to the paperwork generated by a single hospital visit today, this one family/one statement approach to health care receivables will eliminate volumes of paperwork through its simplified billing plan.

Building the Foundation

ealth care providers are looking for solutions, not just systems, to improve their operations. Hospitals, health systems, and physicians—all health care providers—are looking for methods to survive in an increasingly payer-driven environment.

IPN was founded in 1988 by Joe Hodge to provide billing and receivables management services to hospital business offices across the country. It is the company's totally integrated approach that has driven its rapid success. Its systems, services, focused management, and high standards of performance consistently achieve significant bottom-line improvement for its clients.

The IPN management team recognizes that health care providers must optimize their revenue and minimize their expenses as they are being forced to assume more and more of the financial risk in the delivery of patient care services. By working together in a partnership relationship, IPN enables its clients to realize immediate reductions in operating expenses and bad debts, and experience overall improved efficiencies in their business office operations. IPN's philosophy is quite simple—do what must be done.

Beyond Outsourcing

oday, IPN is the nation's leading provider of health care financial management services and a member of Irving, Texas-based UICI's Health-care Solution Partners (NASDAQ: UICI). The companies of the UICI network provide services such as underwriting, risk management, and consulting; health care administration and outsourcing; and paperless processing.

With IPN's acquisition of Rhode Island-based Healthcare Automation, Inc., one of the nation's leading suppliers of home health management software, and Oklahoma-based CompOne Services, Ltd., a leading provider of physician business management services, IPN provides a totally integrated approach to managing its clients' administrative and financial services. This combination of services offers the most cost-effective approach available for managing business office operations.

Hospitals, physician offices, and home health organizations all benefit from IPN's broad array of services, including claims processing, cash management, contracts administration, collections, employee leasing, surgery and anesthesia scheduling, transcription, and practice financial management. More efficient management of the billing and collections pro-

IPN IS THE NATION'S LEADING PROVIDER OF HEALTH CARE FINANCIAL MANAGEMENT SERVICES.

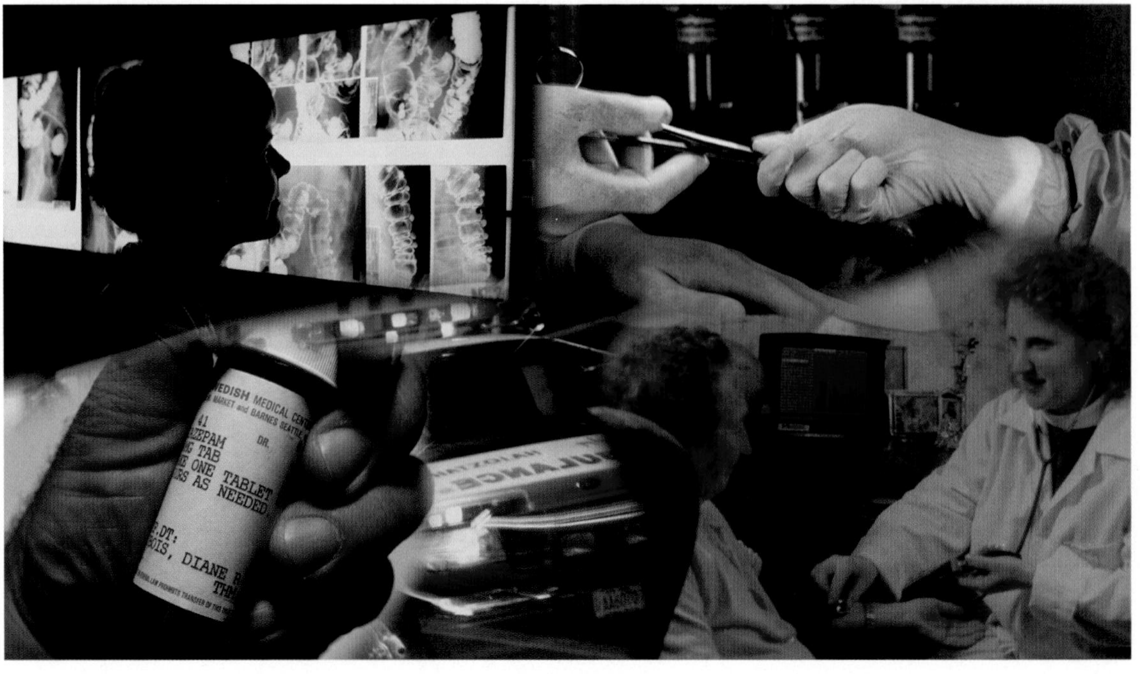

IPN was founded in 1988 by Joe Hodge to provide billing and receivables management services to hospital business offices across the country.

cess with less expense for the provider ultimately benefits the patient.

As part of its full-service approach to providing solutions, IPN's Strategic Finance Division offers innovative financing from institutional sources to hospitals, physician groups, home health, and long-term care organizations. It's all part of the company's commitment to helping providers survive in an increasingly complex health care delivery environment.

Making the Vision Reality

Now, IPN is entering the next realm of health care receivables management—a superstore approach that will ultimately result in the development of a one family/one statement system. By working with local hospitals, clinics, physician offices, and home health agencies within a community, IPN enables the politically neutral operational collaboration necessary to form shared services organizations (SSOs).

IPN provides a totally integrated approach to managing its clients' administrative and financial services.

SSOs will consolidate the administrative functions associated with health care delivery, reducing unnecessary paperwork and confusion for the patient while allowing providers to operate more efficiently. Providers will establish information networks throughout the local communities they serve.

As a result, when a patient goes to the emergency room at the local hospital, visits the family physician, is referred to a specialist, or needs a visit from a home health nurse, the patient's history and financial transactions will be available on the information superhighway, which must become reality if the company is to achieve the one family/one statement concept. IPN Network is positioned to be the driving force to make this happen.

Through its mission—Enabling Quality Health Care Through Optimal Cash Management—IPN has aggressively sought to bring together the critical elements necessary to accomplish this goal. It is IPN's philosophy, experience, and team approach that will result in success where others have failed. For after all, it's the carpenter, not the tools, that makes the difference.

Lovell Communications Inc.

S A MARKETING COMMUNICATIONS AGENCY PROVIDING PUBLIC relations and marketing support to a diverse list of companies across the United States, Lovell Communications finds Nashville's central location and rich reservoir of local talent compelling reasons to call this city "home."

Clients for Lovell range from very large publicly held companies to start-ups with a goal of going public to closely held family businesses. Industries represented by this team of communications specialists include health care, banking, food service and entertainment, hospitality, association management, retail, commercial real estate, and insurance.

Helping Clients Meet Business Objectives

"We work in the art of persuasion," says Paula Lovell, president of the firm she founded in January 1988. "Each of our clients has specific business objectives and they realize that effective communications with their employees, stockholders, customers, patients, or their referral base will be influential in helping achieve those objectives.

"Sometimes our clients will benefit from media relations and placing articles in national consumer publications like the *Wall Street Journal* or the *New York Times,*" Lovell continues. "At other times, it's from exposure in their industry's trade journals or by speaking to a national trade association or by making a world-class presentation to investors and analysts on Wall Street. Frequently, our clients need marketing materials including brochures, videos, slide shows, trade booths, company newsletters, direct mail, or advertising. Our efforts sometimes focus on internal communications functions and improving the flow of information throughout an organization so its vast numbers of employees are working with a common vision.

"In short, Lovell Communications helps identify each client's target audience and the messages they should receive, and then develops a strategic plan to influence those audiences. We rely on sound market research to formulate our action plans, and we utilize both traditional and nontraditional modes of communication to persuade or influence group and individual behaviors."

Lovell Communications is recognized by its peers and its several hundred clients as experts in managing the communications process during times of crisis. That process includes developing a strategic communications plan that addresses all stakeholders in an organization, including employees, customers, vendors, public policy makers, and the media.

"Our firm finds creative and effective ways to maximize the relationships between our business clients and their publics. We work in the art of persuasion," says Paula Lovell, president of the firm she founded in January 1988.

Decades of Experience

The diverse backgrounds of the staff at Lovell Communications complement the varied array of clients represented by the firm. Lovell employees have decades of experience as communications specialists in areas ranging from marketing national fast-food chains to naming and helping establish an identity for national health care providers and insurers. The firm includes specialists in the areas of print and TV production as well as desktop publishing and on-line computer marketing techniques.

Prior to forming the agency, Lovell, a graduate of Vanderbilt University, served as vice president of a local advertising and public relations agency, and spent 10 years as a print and electronic journalist for CNN, WTBS, ESPN, and national *P.M. Magazine*, and at a local newspaper and TV station. Using firsthand work experience, she conducts and supervises a variety of media training programs offered by the firm.

The agency has captured numerous national awards for its communications work, and Lovell has been honored with many business awards. Shortly after founding Lovell Communications Inc., Lovell was named Woman of the Year by Davidson County Business and Professional Women. She has served as a board member and as chairman of the Nashville branch of the Federal Reserve Bank of Atlanta, and on many civic boards, including the Nashville Chamber of Commerce and the Middle Tennessee Council of the Boy Scouts of America. She is an alumna of Leadership Nashville and an active member of the Nashville Rotary Club.

Lovell Communications Inc. continues to grow and prosper as a marketing communications firm committed to superior service and a creative approach to helping meet the business and communications objectives of the clients it serves.

Akersloot, DePriest, Wall & Associates, PLLC

"Anyone can add your numbers. We tell you how your numbers add up." That premise—that a CPA firm can and should help its clients understand where they are and where they can go—is the guiding principle of the partners of Akersloot, DePriest, Wall & Associates, PLLC (ADW).

The firm combines traditional accounting, financial, and tax skills with a unique insight—what small businesses need.

With offices in the Maryland Farms complex in Brentwood, Akersloot, DePriest, Wall & Associates' client roster represents a broad spectrum of companies in the Middle Tennessee and southern Kentucky areas, including many types of industries, not-for-profit organizations, and government entities. The principals handle all areas of auditing, accounting, and taxation, as well as strategic business planning, management information system consulting, business valuations, litigation support, and representation before the Internal Revenue Service.

Small-Business Savvy

Before forming their own company, the partners attended Austin Peay University in Clarksville, Tennessee, and then also worked together at a Big Eight accounting firm. The trio boasts a combined 50 years of experience in taxation and accounting, but specializes in a particular niche—small-business assistance.

"Some firms deliver a financial statement or a tax return, and that's it. But that's like telling someone to drive a car by looking in the rearview mirror," says Charles Akersloot, managing partner. "What our clients want is help with the road ahead, what's waiting around the curve." Backing their commitment to small business, ADW is a sponsor of the *Nashville Business Journal*'s annual Small Business Awards program.

Hands-On Approach

Critical to its success and mission, Akersloot, DePriest, Wall & Associates is committed to remaining a small, hands-on company. "While we will grow some, we do not want to become a 50-person firm. It's important to remain small to provide the high-quality service and expertise our clients need," adds Akersloot. "Small businesses don't always have small problems. We'll be there when there's a problem."

Akersloot also has extensive experience in tax planning and business consulting, with clients ranging from fledgling businesses to $500 million corporations. He received his bachelor of science degree in accounting at Austin Peay and a master's degree in tax from the University of Alabama. He is also certified by the NACVA as a business valuation consultant.

Richard L. DePriest has concentrated in tax preparation and review, tax planning and tax research, and client representation before the Internal Revenue Service. He received his bachelor of science degree in business administration from Austin Peay and his J.D. degree from Vanderbilt School of Law.

W. Thomas Wall has worked in tax preparation and review, tax planning, and estates and trusts, as well as audits, reviews, and compilations of financial statements. Wall, as well as Akersloot and DePriest, is a member of the American Institute of Certified Public Accountants and the Tennessee Society of Certified Public Accountants.

Dedicated to serving small businesses, Akersloot, DePriest, Wall & Associates will continue to use its unique skills to successfully meet the accounting needs of Nashville.

▶ Brad Gholson

Akersloot, DePriest, Wall & Associates, PLLC has its offices at Maryland Farms in Brentwood.

▶ Brad Gholson

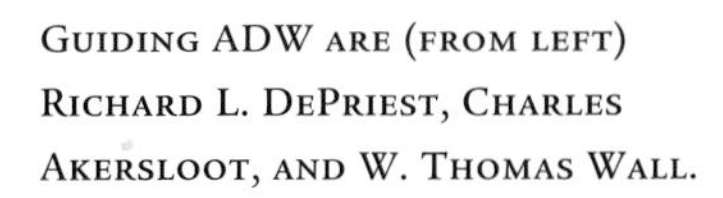

Guiding ADW are (from left) Richard L. DePriest, Charles Akersloot, and W. Thomas Wall.

Aegis, Inc.

A true 21st-century company, Aegis, Inc. is a dynamic business development firm evolving in the hub of Nashville's health care industry. It embraces next-generation management and customer-service-centered philosophies. ★ This strategic development company offers hospitals and health care providers its trademarked Employer Integrated Network, a business and industry communications system that hospitals provide to companies as a comprehensive, turnkey program for delivery and tracking of employee wellness.

The spirit of empowerment embodies this cutting-edge culture as Aegis employees have shaped the company based on their innovation, knowledge, and energy. Their ease in developing the company's proprietary software, augmenting its Web site on the Internet, working with hospital CEOs, or facilitating wellness programs for individual hospitals and their business community is the anchor for a company on a fast course into the future.

Aegis touts a who's who client list including such hospitals as Columbia, Stanford Medical Center, UCLA Medical Center, and Ohio State Medical Center. Taking advantage of its position in Nashville, one of the country's most influential areas in health care, Aegis is poised for continued success as it moves into the markets of physician practices, independent clinics, health maintenance organizations (HMOs), and occupational health companies. Currently, the firm employs 62 talented individuals and projects growing to 250 employees by the turn of the century.

Roland Wussow, chairman, and Robert Chamberlain, CEO of Aegis, Inc. (top).

Aegis employees have shaped the company based on their innovation, knowledge, and energy (bottom).

Building Strategic Alliances

From education-based print materials in the form of a Health Information Center to its proprietary software called CAPS (Consumer Acquisition and Profiling System), Aegis is a nationally recognized leader in employer development. On behalf of its client hospitals, Aegis creates strategic development systems that are dispersed to a variety of businesses. The Aegis-produced materials explain how the hospital functions as an expert in meeting the health care needs of these businesses, thus establishing a communication bridge between corporate America and health care providers.

"Hospitals want relationships on the outside, but their business is taking care of people on the inside. We help them develop those relationships," says President and CEO Robert Chamberlain, who started the company along with Roland Wussow, chairman, in 1989.

"Although we started as a company offering marketing tactics to hospitals, we are now developing revenue-based strategies,

writing proprietary software, and merging relationships with health care providers and employers. We've added a tremendous database function to our operations," Chamberlain says.

Team Approach to Customer Service

Through its team of professionals, Aegis delivers a soup-to-nuts approach for its hospital clients. An in-house team of market specialists manages the wellness programs and ensures timely delivery of creative materials. Aegis' research and development group provides information and resources for the creative staff to develop attention-getting educational materials. The company's blue-jean-clad technical experts are constantly updating and fine-tuning its database and computer software capabilities. And Aegis' field team of employer development specialists work on-premise at the client hospitals, assisting program development and forging employer relationships.

Chamberlain credits the company's evolution to his employees: "We have evolved because our employees have listened to our customers. Creative solutions, new software applications, marketing, and accountability are a driving force here and our team has shaped a very high standard of work."

Aegis employees' expertise is so keen that the company brings its health care clients in for hands-on training. Hospital administrators get a firsthand view of the capabilities and finesse of the dedicated individuals who represent the heart and soul of Aegis. Clients undergo database training, meet with various individuals who will be supporting their account, and plan out a year of wellness events for its employer partners from blood pressure to breast cancer screenings.

Each event brings hundreds to thousands of participants from area employers. The participants' personal health profiles are entered in the CAPS software, thus providing a thorough database for the hospital and the ability to target risk groups in its myriad programs.

Delivering Accountability

Because the bottom line is important to health care providers, Aegis provides a program that delivers accountability. Rather than a broad-based advertising approach, hospitals use the Aegis Employer Integrated Network as a means to grow hospital revenue. Where the hospital has direct contracts with employers, the program provides additional value through definable cost savings to the employer. It's a win-win situation for all partners and participants. Through its database, Aegis is able to analyze the hospital's investment in each program and provide concrete information on how the hospital spent its money and the results.

"We take a very Zen-like approach to this business by focusing on the day-to-day quality of the work being produced," says Chamberlain. "We believe that profits are the natural consequence of quality and customer satisfaction—not something that drives our vision."

Since its inception, Aegis has assembled a group of dedicated employees who have found deeper meaning in their work. Underneath the day-to-day demands of the workplace, Aegis recognizes that the information being conveyed could result in a life saved. With an indisputable devotion to the client, a feverish work ethic, and a dose of technological wizardry, Aegis, Inc. remains focused on its grand design—strong corporate growth through its commitment to people. According to Chamberlain, "Our true assets go up and down in the elevators each day."

Aegis' technical experts are constantly updating and fine-tuning its database and computer software capabilities.

Aegis provides its clients access to employer worksites through employee-focused health information and education programs.

Cambridge Equity Advisors

Michael Goldston got his start in the investment business early, collecting rare coins when he was eight years old, and he's been collecting profits for his clients ever since. Founder of four investment management companies in Nashville, Goldston is both a treasure hunter in real life and in the investment world.

Drawing upon the early days of his youth, which he spent near Cambridge, England, Goldston has included the Cambridge name in three of his four companies: Cambridge Way Inc., a stock brokerage firm founded in 1987; Cambridge Equity Advisors, Inc., an investment advisory company started in 1989; and Cambridge Rare Coins, Inc., established in 1995, to create and manage rare coin and collectible portfolios. His most recent venture, begun in 1996, is Excalibur Partners, L.L.C., a private, performance-based hedge fund.

Meeting the Needs of High-Net-Worth Investors

These companies manage hundreds of millions of dollars of investment capital for investors located in 45 states and overseas. The combined strength of the companies provides a cohesive unit that is able to react quickly to emerging trends. The companies are large enough to compete favorably in the major financial markets, yet small enough to offer the personal service and attention their clients expect and deserve.

Investing the Cambridge Way

Cambridge Way, Inc. is a full-service broker-dealer founded by Goldston a decade ago to offer independent investment services. The firm began with just two employees—Goldston and Maggie Nuzum, who is now senior vice president—and, combined with Goldston's affiliated money management firm, has grown to 20 employees and almost 1,000 clients.

From the beginning, Goldston's philosophy for success in building an innovative company was to surround himself with high-quality people who shared his vision. The success of the firm is based on internal training of employees and the challenge for them to excel. The success of this endeavor is obvious in the number of long-term employees and low staff turnover.

Excellence in Portfolio Management

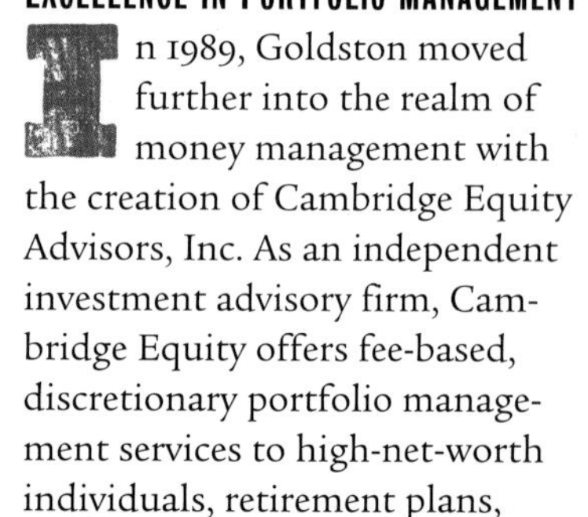

In 1989, Goldston moved further into the realm of money management with the creation of Cambridge Equity Advisors, Inc. As an independent investment advisory firm, Cambridge Equity offers fee-based, discretionary portfolio management services to high-net-worth individuals, retirement plans,

From the beginning, Michael Goldston's philosophy for success in building an innovative company was to surround himself with high-quality people who shared his vision.

corporations, trusts, and 401(k) plans.

Cambridge Equity works with dozens of brokerage firms and banks, offering highly regarded investment advice to a broad client base. In addition, this expertise is available through the major national discount brokerage firms.

There are now more than a dozen investment choices from which to select, including no-load mutual fund portfolios; conservative, blue-chip stock portfolios; asset allocation strategies; and more aggressive, small to mid-size growth stock options. The company has received high accolades for its excellence in portfolio management, including favorable mention and write-ups in dozens of major financial publications, as well as receiving the prestigious Nelson's number one ranking for its mid-cap stock strategy over the past 10 years. The company has grown to be an Inc. 500 recipient as one of the fastest-growing private companies in America.

One common underlying theme in all of these portfolios is the firm's ability to look ahead to spot economic and investment trends and to react quickly before it is obvious to most investors. This ability has enabled Goldston to get into many top-performing stocks ahead of the herd. This clarity of vision is enhanced by the firm's location far from the typical financial centers of the world.

Treasure Hunters

A desire to diversify client portfolios and share a lifelong interest in rare coins and treasure hunting led to the formation of Cambridge Rare Coins, Inc. Protection against the ravages of inflation can be assisted by prudent investments in rare coins. This company specializes in creating rare coin investment portfolios diversified into a variety of rare and scarce gold and silver coins with proven long-term performance.

Goldston's latest discovery? The earliest silver bars ever found in the New World, dated around 1525. These bars were part of Cortés' plundered loot from the Aztecs and were recently discovered in the wreck of a Spanish galleon. These historical artifacts weigh between three pounds and 30 pounds, and are by far the oldest and rarest silver bars ever found in this hemisphere.

The Legend of Excalibur

Whosoever can pull this sword from the stone shall be king of all England" was the chiseled inscription that legend says a young King Arthur read before extracting Excalibur from its rocky home.

The fourth financial weapon to be wielded by Goldston carries the same proud name in its title of Excalibur Partners, L.L.C. This is a private, performance-based hedge fund that is able to invest in a broad range of investment strategies, including going short, using leverage, and buying and selling stock options.

The fund is limited to just 99 investors, including Goldston himself, who also acts as general partner. The goal for the fund is $200 million by the year 2000; its future is the stuff of which legends are made.

Keys to Success: Research, Technology, and Client Service

Cutting-edge technology and innovative research capabilities are an important key to Cambridge's success. Goldston and his team have all the right tools at their fingertips with state-of-the-art information and research systems. A substantial amount of resources are allocated to technology, and the firm is confident that it has all the needed equipment and research capabilities to meet the changing demands of the financial markets.

Above all, there is a commitment to provide each individual client with high-quality, personalized service. From frequent client communications and market updates to ongoing conversations with each client, Cambridge prides itself on delivering the best available client service.

Michael Goldston got his start in the investment business early, collecting rare coins when he was eight years old, and he's been collecting profits for his clients ever since.

Civic Responsibility

Cambridge is also proud to be a responsible member of the community. Beneficiaries of its gifts include the Nashville Chamber of Commerce, Nashville Humane Association, Tennessee Wheelchair Olympics, United Cerebral Palsy, Vanderbilt Children's Hospital, Easter Seals, and Hands on Nashville. In addition, the firm has donated computers to elementary schools, as well as taught classes on the basic principles of investing and finance.

A Vision for the Future

Cambridge has a clear vision of the future of the financial services industry. As a small and innovative group, the companies intend to remain on the cutting edge in terms of high-quality products, excellent service, a continued emphasis on research and technology, and competitive performance.

Cambridge Rare Coins, Inc. specializes in creating rare coin investment portfolios.

GOLD SKIN CARE CENTER

CENTRALLY LOCATED IN THE GREEN HILLS AREA OF NASHVILLE, Gold Skin Care Center provides prompt, one-stop service for all skin care needs. Patients from all over the United States come to Gold Skin Care Center, a noted leader in skin care technology utilizing a combination of dermatology and aesthetics.

DR. MICHAEL H. GOLD IS BOARD CERTIFIED IN DERMATOLOGY AND A MEMBER OF THE AMERICAN BOARD OF DERMATOLOGY, AMERICAN ACADEMY OF DERMATOLOGY, AMERICAN SOCIETY FOR LASER MEDICINE AND SURGERY, AND BOTH THE AMERICAN AND INTERNATIONAL SOCIETIES FOR DERMATOLOGIC SURGERIES (TOP LEFT).

DR. MICHAEL W. BELL IS A BOARD-CERTIFIED DERMATOLOGIST AND PATHOLOGIST FROM CANADA (BOTTOM LEFT).

FACIALS AND MASSAGES ARE POPULAR SERVICES FOR MANY NASHVILLE RESIDENTS (RIGHT).

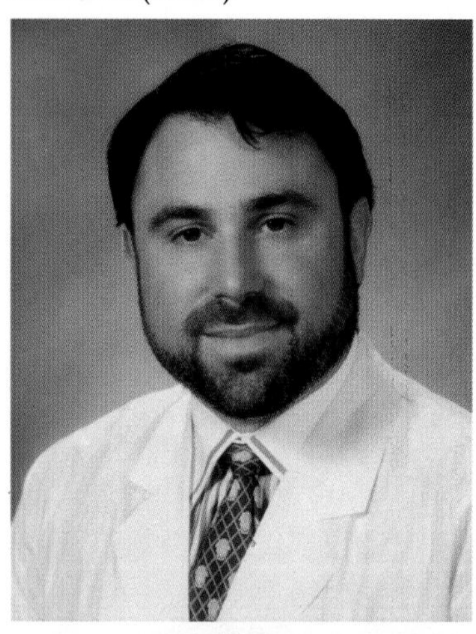

PIONEERS IN RESEARCH AND TECHNOLOGY

Gold Skin Care Center is known for its pioneering research, which has gained widespread national exposure. Dr. Michael H. Gold conducted the first dermatologic trial of a topical silicone gel sheeting—Silastic®, now manufactured as Cica-Care®—to treat scars. The center also served as the pilot test site for the nation's first hair removal laser. As a result, Gold has become a leading authority and highly requested speaker, frequently traveling around the world to lecture on skin care topics.

Thousands of patients have achieved better skin through state-of-the-art laser technology. At Gold Skin Care Center, lasers are used to remove varicose and spider veins, wrinkles and scars, age spots, freckles, birthmarks, port-wine stains, moles, and other skin concerns. Colleagues from the medical community travel to the center from around the globe to learn from Gold's laser experience.

Other procedures performed at Gold Skin Care Center include mole and skin cancer removals, hair transplants, liposuction, sclerotherapy, Endermologie™ (fat massage), soft tissue augmentation, and chemical peels.

ADVANCED AESTHETICS STORE AND SPA

Advanced Aesthetics, the center's cosmetic division, is located next door to the center. Licensed, certified aestheticians, massage therapists, and technicians provide a full line of cosmetic products and professional skin care services, including facials, massages, masques, hand and body treatments, hair removal, makeup consultations, waxing, and nail care services.

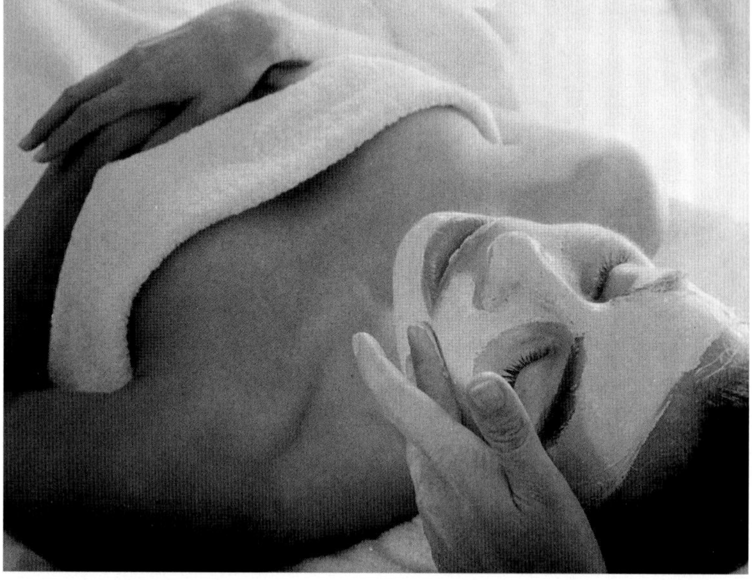

The practice of clinical aesthetics, combining aesthetics and medicine, has been a mainstay at Gold Skin Care Center since its inception. The center's aestheticians are qualified to detect problems with the skin and can immediately consult a board-certified dermatologist if a problem occurs. Under a physician's direction, they consult with patients on products and personal skin care regimens.

MAKING NASHVILLE HOME

Founded in 1990 by Gold, the center is situated in the heart of Nashville's health care mecca. Gold started his practice in Nashville after completing his dermatology residency training at Northwestern University in Chicago.

Gold completed undergraduate studies at Tulane University, obtained his medical degree from the Chicago Medical School, and completed an internship at Emory University. He is board certified in dermatology and a member of the American Board of Dermatology, American Academy of Dermatology, American Society for Laser Medicine and Surgery, and both the American and International Societies for Dermatologic Surgeries.

Gold's associate, Michael W. Bell, MD, is a board-certified dermatologist and pathologist from Canada. He performs in-house lab work and pathologic evaluation, services not commonly found in the Nashville dermatologic market. Bell received his medical degree from the University of Calgary and completed his residency training at McGill University in Montreal. After practicing dermatology for four years, he returned to the University of Toronto and completed a four-year program in anatomical pathology with a subspecialty in skin pathology.

Kyzen Corporation

Many futurists have predicted that environmentally friendly technologies would someday be a major growth industry. Well, the future is now, and it's Nashville's Kyzen Corporation. ★ In 1990, Middle Tennessean Michael L. Bixenman and Oregon-born Kyle J. Doyel began building a company around the business of replacing chlorofluorocarbons (CFCs), the widely used industrial chemicals that have been blamed for damaging the earth's ozone layer. Doyel, an expert on a novel form of alcohol that functions even better than CFCs, became president and chief executive officer. Bixenman, whom Doyel calls "the formulation guru," took the title of chairman. The name Kyzen is from the Japanese *kaizen*, meaning "continuous improvement."

A Tale of Entrepreneurship

In a series of international treaties, governments around the world have affirmed their commitment to eliminating the release of ozone-harming chemicals into the atmosphere. The Clean Air Act of 1990 and other actions by the U.S. government have been aimed at implementing those treaties. Kyzen's founders looked at the environmental quandary posed by CFCs, and they saw opportunity.

Bixenman had been test-marketing a new, environmentally safe paint remover that he had designed. Engineers at General Motors' Delco Electronics were seeking non-CFC materials to clean circuit boards for car manufacturing, and they discovered that Bixenman's material worked better than the CFCs—better, in fact, than any other material they had tried.

Doyel remembers that after those heady days of early discovery, he and Bixenman realized that, in order to take on major players in the CFC business, they would have to prove to the world that they had built a better mousetrap. The larger manufacturers had devised a test to rate CFC replacement formulations based on their cleaning ability, and in 1991, Kyzen became the first non-Fortune 500 company to run its formulation through the test. The procedure was open to observers from industry groups, the Environmental Protection Agency, and competing chemical makers. "We bet the farm on the test," Doyel recalls. When the test was completed, Kyzen had the first perfect score ever registered.

Clean Living

Kyzen's formulas replace CFCs for "any technology application in which the product needs to be cleaned so well that it has high reliability," Doyel says. The applications of the formula are endless. Zenith uses Kyzen's chemistries to clean picture tubes; Intel uses them to clean its state-of-the-art electronic assemblies; and Motorola relies on the formula to clean the inner workings of cellular telephones.

The company custom designs versions of its patented formulations, often different for each application. "What we're selling is not just chemical solutions," Doyel explains. "We're selling solutions to problems."

Today, Kyzen is a publicly held company, growing at a feverish pace. As sales have skyrocketed, its staff has doubled. Additionally, the company is constantly finding new applications for its products. "As electronics and components become more sophisticated and miniaturized, the need to clean increases," Doyel says. Kyzen intends to meet this need, developing environmentally safe formulas for all facets of the technology industry.

The name Kyzen is from the Japanese word for continuous improvement, and the company is living up to its name (left).

Kyzen's formulas replace chlorofluorocarbons (CFCs) for any technology application in which the product needs to be cleaned to ensure its high reliability (bottom).

LifeView Resources

Advancements in medical technology, managed care cost control, and the health care industry's continual need for the latest information, education, and marketing materials have created strong demand for cost-effective video communication products. LifeView Resources has successfully met this challenge by distinguishing itself from competitors through a unique combination of clinical experience and production expertise.

LifeView Resources creates state-of-the-art communications using images that educate, motivate, and inspire an audience.

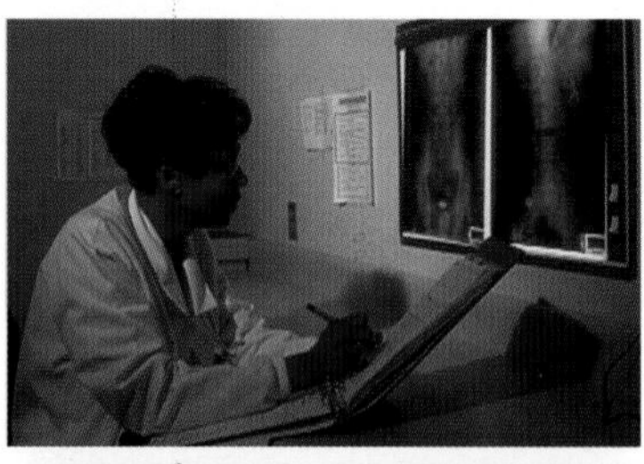

Founded in 1991 under the name Iatro Media (*iatros* is Greek for "physician"), the company initially produced medical-related videos to exclusively fill a niche in the business-to-business health care marketplace. However, company management soon recognized the growing opportunity for products targeted directly to the consumer. In 1997, Iatro Media changed its name to LifeView Resources to better describe the company's expansion into the consumer market.

"Whether the subject targets health care professionals or the general public, we take a great deal of pride in creating state-of-the-art communications that educate, motivate, or inspire the audience," explains Greg Griffith, LifeView Resources cofounder.

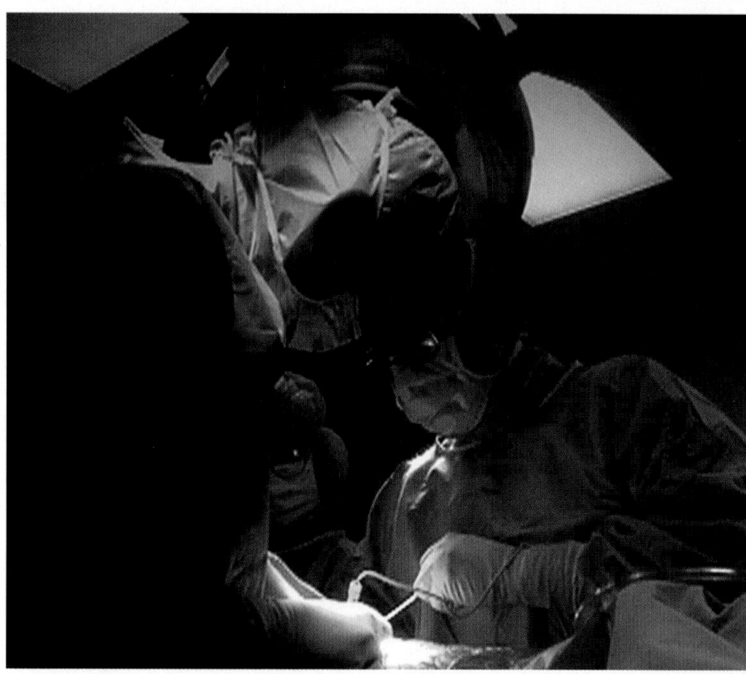

Business-to-Business Clinical Videos

The company works predominately with health care corporations who want to showcase cutting-edge technological breakthroughs, new surgical procedures, or new medical equipment via instructive videos.

In addition to offering state-of-the-art production facilities and in-house editing suites, the company also helps clients promote their finished projects through electronic press kits and marketing and distribution support.

"No matter how complex the clinical procedure or subject matter, we're equally at home in the operating room, physician's office, or studio," says Executive Producer Darren Shipley, regarding the company's track record with an impressive roll call of health care providers, including major corporations such as Columbia, U.S. Surgical, Cook Cardiology, and many more.

Thousands of physicians and health care professionals worldwide have viewed LifeView's clinical video projects, many of which have been translated into multiple foreign languages.

Wellness Products for Consumers

The company's more recent expansion into the consumer market coincides with the nation's growing trend to become more educated and involved in the health and wellness issues that affect people physically and emotionally.

"Our society has become increasingly dependent on electronic media for news and entertainment. The public wants information, and they want it conveyed in an easy-to-understand, convenient-to-access format. Educational video and multimedia packages provide that springboard," says Executive Producer Mike Merryman.

Taking a holistic approach to care, LifeView Resources addresses quality-of-life issues pertinent to the general consumer. The company's introductory self-help project targets the 18 million informal caregivers nationwide who care for a loved one in the home.

"We have a strong desire to help people lead healthier, happier, more stress free lives. So we're currently expanding our media library to include a variety of topics especially pertinent to the aging population," says Griffith.

With the evolving health care environment, advances in medical procedures, and increasing consumer demand for information and education, the future looks exceptionally bright for LifeView Resources. The company plans to continue its diversification strategy by exploring new directions for the fulfillment of its mission—helping people enjoy life to its fullest potential.

Logan's Roadhouse Restaurants

STEAKS AREN'T THE ONLY THINGS THAT SIZZLE AT LOGAN'S Roadhouse Restaurants. The national chain is also known for serving up a good time: It encourages patrons to spin tunes on the restaurant's free-play Wurlitzer jukebox, watch chefs prepare orders over gas-fired mesquite grills, and toss roasted peanut shells on the floor.

A growing chain of 20 restaurants in seven states, the Logan's concept was fine-tuned by President, CEO, and Chairman of the Board Edwin W. Moats, who identified this profitable niche in the steakhouse restaurant business. Since the first location opened in 1991, the publicly held company continues to exceed analysts' projections; 1997 will reap more than $60 million in revenues. Logan's dramatic earnings and revenue growth led *Business Week* to name it one of the Hot Growth Companies of 1996.

Lively Atmosphere

"Our concept is pulled from the American roadhouses that were particularly popular in the 1940s and 1950s," says Moats, describing them as the rough, cinder block buildings that served as hangouts for just about everyone in the community.

The 7,800-square-foot restaurant seats 290, offering less waiting time and an overall good time. Customers dine below lively neon signs and hand-painted murals depicting scenes from American roadhouses of yesteryear. USDA choice steaks, salads, and other items are displayed in the old-fashioned meat counter, and customers can watch cooks prepare their orders. Patrons at the bar can sit back and watch the large-screen television while enjoying their favorite beverages.

Logan's also credits its success to its 2,000-plus, high-energy servers and well-trained managers. The casual, nonregimented atmosphere affords a relaxed environment for employees, and servers are designated to an industry-low three tables each, allowing for a less hectic workload and improved customer service.

Fun Food and Signature Dishes

Steaks are Logan's mainstay, but 30 entrées fill the affordably priced menu. A large variety of seafood, chicken, ribs, and sandwiches round out the offerings. Ample servings of signature dishes like made-from-scratch yeast rolls; brown-sugar- and cinnamon-topped sweet potatoes; and fried green tomatoes draw a loyal clientele for many return visits.

The chain's trademark, though, is the bucket of in-the-shell peanuts placed at each table. While waiting for their entrées, customers can munch on the peanuts and then freely throw the shells on the wooden-planked floor.

Recipe for Success

When Logan's first hit the Nashville scene, it was voted Best New Restaurant in a local newspaper's readers' poll. In addition, the American Academy of Restaurant Sciences has frequently bestowed its Top 10 Steakhouses award on the chain, and the Tennessee Beef Council has given Logan's its Beef Backer Award.

With its founders from Nashville, Logan's makes community involvement a priority. The company hosts an annual golf tournament benefiting the Muscular Dystrophy Association and is frequently involved with fund-raising efforts for the United Way.

Moats intends to slowly grow the chain, realizing the pitfalls of rapid expansion. And he plans to remain true to Logan's appeal to a broad range of consumers, offering generous portions of moderately priced, quality food in a fun, casual setting. These are the ingredients in Logan's Roadhouse Restaurant's recipe for unbridled success.

FROM TOP:

CUSTOMERS DINE BELOW LIVELY NEON SIGNS AND HAND-PAINTED MURALS DEPICTING SCENES FROM AMERICAN ROADHOUSES OF YESTERYEAR.

THE LOGAN'S CONCEPT WAS FINE-TUNED BY PRESIDENT, CEO, AND CHAIRMAN OF THE BOARD EDWIN W. MOATS.

LOGAN'S ROADHOUSE ENCOURAGES PATRONS TO SPIN TUNES ON THE RESTAURANT'S FREE-PLAY WURLITZER JUKEBOX, WATCH CHEFS PREPARE ORDERS OVER GAS-FIRED MESQUITE GRILLS, AND TOSS ROASTED PEANUT SHELLS ON THE FLOOR.

Caterpillar Inc.

Caterpillar Inc. is the world's largest manufacturer of construction and mining equipment, natural gas engines, and industrial gas turbines, as well as a leading global supplier of diesel engines. Cat products help make progress possible around the world. Founded in 1925, Caterpillar is one of only a handful of U.S. companies that lead their industry while competing globally from a principally domestic manufacturing base.

Caterpillar products are sold in virtually every country. The company, based in Peoria, Illinois, delivers superior customer service through its extensive worldwide network of 192 dealers. In Nashville, Caterpillar is represented by Thompson Machinery Commerce Corporation for Cat earthmoving equipment and the Bailey Company for Cat lift trucks. Dealers in North America average more than 50 years of partnership with Caterpillar.

Cat construction machines are used to build, maintain, and rebuild the world's infrastructure.

Caterpillar Financial Products Division

Caterpillar's Financial Products Division is comprised of Caterpillar Financial Services Corporation, Caterpillar Insurance Services Corporation, and Caterpillar Power Ventures Corporation. Serving more than 36,000 customers, the division provides a wide range of financing, leasing, and insurance alternatives for Cat machines, engines, and lift trucks.

In 1991, the division relocated to Nashville, creating a stronger identity for the division in the financial services industry. Today, more than 300 employees work at the Nashville location and hundreds of others staff the division's other locations, which include six U.S. and Canadian regional offices, as well as facilities in South America, Europe, Australia, and Asia. With almost $8 billion in financing, the division offers customers world-class financial products in more than 15 countries.

The financial division adopts the latest networking technology and customized software to improve customer service. One goal is to give salespeople the ability to quote the price of any financial product offered—in seconds—from any location in the world. Optical imaging is also employed to give better service to customers. In this process, documents are transferred to an optical disk that permits easy and efficient access to information through the global network. Improvements like these help the company to manage the growing volume of business, and guarantee prompt and accurate customer service.

Business Excellence

As part of their commitment to business excellence and continuous improvement, employees are encouraged to submit ideas to improve business processes.

Core processes, such as quotation response, credit approval, and document preparation and approval, are continually monitored. Caterpillar knows it is in a business that requires quick turnaround. "Our customers cannot afford delays; neither can we," says James Beard, president of Caterpillar Financial Products Division and vice president of Caterpillar Inc.

Continuing education for employees also contributes to increased efficiency and technical excellence. The Caterpillar Educational Assistance Program has always been a part of the overall strategy of the company. "Caterpillar has long believed that a skilled and knowledgeable workforce is essential to business success. We're committed to education because we live in a dynamic world. The skills and knowledge required to do our jobs are ever changing, and it's important that we create a culture that embraces change," says Beard.

The division is a participant in the Tennessee Quality Award process, sponsored annually by the Tennessee Department of Economic and Community Development. Judged by the same criteria as the acclaimed national Malcolm Baldrige Award—management leadership, monitoring and measuring customer satisfaction, and maintaining continuous improvement in basic processes—this award represents excellence in its most quantifiable form.

Community Commitment

Caterpillar employees participate in several outreach programs in the Nashville community. A supporter of the Adopt-a-School Program, the company became partners with Wharton Arts Magnet Middle School in 1992. Activities include providing transportation and supervision for field trips and working with autistic students. During the holidays, employees provide Halloween treats, and volunteer as Santa and Mrs. Claus and the Easter bunny. In the 1996-1997 school year, the company continued its financial assistance for the POPS program (Power of Positive Students), which encourages students, parents, and faculty to build positive attitudes and life skills.

Volunteer activities for the United Way organization include food collection and distribution for the Second Harvest Food Bank, clothing drives for several United Way projects, and contributions to the Angel Tree Foundation for the Salvation Army. In 1996, some 95.8 percent of employees contributed to United Way programs during the annual employee campaign.

With an intense desire to continually improve business operations and a commitment to making Nashville a better place to live and work, Caterpillar plans to be an enthusiastic participant in Nashville's future. "Our business values and our commitment to the community are seamless," says Beard. "Both Caterpillar and Nashville have a bright future."

Cat Financial's experience in the global marketplace contributes to excellent customer service around the world (left).

Caterpillar Financial is a proud sponsor of the Caterpillar Racing Team in the NASCAR Winston Cup Series (right).

Cat volunteers bring smiles to kindergartners at Wharton Arts Magnet.

Middle Tennessee Motor Cars, Inc.

Imagine winding your way down an open road in the finest built and engineered automobile in the world. Quite probably, you just imagined yourself in a Mercedes-Benz—and Nashville's premier dealership for this premium automobile is Middle Tennessee Motor Cars, Inc. (MTMC). ★ Founded in 1991, MTMC has shown steady increases in sales and customer satisfaction each year. Owner Bruce Burnett and his staff have seen to that success by offering a price/value relationship on thousands of new and previously owned Mercedes.

But success with Mercedes-Benz is nothing new to Burnett. Raised in a family that has owned the Mercedes dealership in Orlando, since 1965, Burnett was weaned on every aspect of the business, from changing a carburetor to selling on the showroom floor.

Burnett's family chose Nashville as its next venture for several reasons. Being from Orlando, they realized that tourism is beneficial to Mercedes dealers. They also recognized Nashville's diversity in areas such as established wealth, expanded health care growth, and a growing manufacturing and industrial base.

Annual gross sales for the Burnett family's automotive enterprises are more than $100 million; MTMC brings in nearly $40 million. Looking ahead for MTMC, the introduction of a new Mercedes-Benz sport utility vehicle should have sales soaring into the new millennium.

Strategic Vision, Business Strategy, and Customer Satisfaction

The overall business strategy of MTMC is to leverage core customer satisfaction with Mercedes products and MTMC sales, service, and support into long-term relationships that result in repeat business over time. "No other luxury automobile manufacturer can offer what Mercedes-Benz can with price value," says Burnett. Within the next few years, as other luxury car manufacturers increase prices, Mercedes-Benz will have 80 percent of its automobiles priced under $50,000.

MTMC is dedicated to taking care of its customers. Sales staff pick up cars needing service, loaner cars are provided, and a Customer Satisfaction Index is used for improvement. At MTMC, roadside assistance takes on a whole new meaning. The company sends out one of its line technicians free of charge within its market area to assist with problems. A toll-free assistance number is available to all owners.

People Making a Difference

MTMC's annual support of the Vanderbilt Children's Hospital and the Un Ete du Vin wine auction for the National Cancer Society is well recognized. Other national organizations benefiting from the Burnett family's generosity include the Alzheimer's Foundation and an eminent scholar chair at the University of Central Florida.

Burnett believes MTMC's greatest asset is its people. The company implements a total quality management council program that gives its employees a chance to make suggestions for the good of the whole. With 65 employees, including salespeople, line technicians, parts experts, and support staff, Burnett believes there is no substitute for ongoing training.

MTMC's total property is located on 6.5 acres, with 46,000 square feet under one roof. Included are the service center and the showroom that house 11 of the most beautiful automobiles money can buy—all of them engineered to take you down that long and winding road with unmatched grace and style.

Founded in 1991, Middle Tennessee Motor Cars, Inc. has shown steady increases in sales and customer satisfaction each year.

Electric Picture Company

FROM MUSIC VIDEOS AND TELEVISION PROGRAMMING TO COMmercials and corporate projects, no two video production jobs are alike. Each has its own creative challenges and budgeting criteria, requiring specific cameras and equipment for its execution. As a result, few production companies can afford to stock every piece of equipment they would ever be called upon to use.

That's where Electric Picture Company (EPC) comes onto the scene. A premier rental house, the company offers high-quality broadcast equipment and accessories to meet the needs of virtually any video project. From recording media and cameras to crew booking, EPC provides a one-stop resource that gives even the smallest production houses and freelancers access to a comprehensive array of high-end gear and supplies.

Industry Innovators

Formed in 1993, EPC has drawn upon its partners' management expertise in production and equipment rental to become a leader in the region's video community. Its solid business approach to each project, coupled with an extensive inventory of state-of-the-art equipment, has earned the company a client roster that reads like a who's who of the entertainment and production industry. Walt Disney Productions, ABC, Turner Broadcasting, HBO, MTV, ESPN, NFL Films, and Warner Brothers are just a sampling of EPC's high-profile clientele from across the country.

"We ask questions and take the time to research a project thoroughly," says company cofounder Steve Roche. "Then we custom-tailor a package of gear and crew that best suits the needs of the client."

The first company in the southeast to own a Sony Digital Betacam DVW-700—a $100,000 video camera that rivals the look of film—EPC has adopted a progressive attitude towards video production. The company took the initiative to teach local videographers how to use the new digital camera, calling in some of the industry's most experienced operators to help conduct an instructive seminar. Based on that success, EPC continues to offer seminars to update and educate production professionals in new technology and production techniques.

EPC and Nashville: A Partnership for Growth

Ranked among the Music City Future 50 by the Nashville Area Chamber of Commerce as one of the area's fastest-growing companies, EPC has been instrumental in promoting Nashville as a site for television programming. Teamed with the Nashville Film Office, the company's partners have exhibited at the National Association of TV Producers & Executives, building Nashville's reputation as a creative media center.

"We look forward to our own future growth, as well as the expansion of Nashville's creative capabilities," says Greg Griffith, cofounder. "We have a vested interest in the development of the local video production community and will continue to work towards advancing its reputation as a site for high-end video production."

As EPC enters the next century, the partners are planning to expand both in size and services offered. Among the first to offer cutting-edge technology such as the high-definition format, EPC will continue to scope out the latest advancements and keep Nashville at the forefront of industry trends.

RANKED AMONG THE MUSIC CITY FUTURE 50 BY THE NASHVILLE AREA CHAMBER OF COMMERCE AS ONE OF THE AREA'S FASTEST-GROWING COMPANIES, ELECTRIC PICTURE COMPANY HAS BEEN INSTRUMENTAL IN PROMOTING NASHVILLE AS A SITE FOR TELEVISION PROGRAMMING.

American Transitional Hospitals, Inc.

ECAUSE THE PATIENTS AT AMERICAN TRANSITIONAL HOSPItals, Inc. (ATH) are critically ill and/or catastrophically injured, staff members are keenly aware of the preciousness of life. As a regional provider of specialty acute care services, ATH not only teaches its patients skills, but instills hope by providing opportunities to help improve their quality of life.

The development of transitional care hospitals stems from the belief that up to 40 percent of medically complex patients in medical, surgical, or rehabilitation units could be treated in less costly settings. Typically, these patients stay in traditional hospitals for extended periods of time with escalating costs. ATH provides a viable alternative, enabling a sophisticated level of nursing, respiratory, and rehabilitative care to these patients at one-third to one-half the cost of traditional acute care inpatient stays.

Founded as American Transitional Care, Inc. in 1987, the company changed its name to American Transitional Hospitals, Inc. in 1992—the same year it moved its headquarters to Franklin, Tennessee, some 20 miles south of Nashville. The move was due, in large part, to the burgeoning health care industry in the area.

As a wholly owned subsidiary of Beverly Enterprises, ATH, under the direction of President and CEO Jerald Moore, owns and operates 12 acute-care hospitals in six states and is on a rapid growth track. ATH opened its Middle Tennessee location in 1995.

ATH Middle Tennessee

s a small, transitional hospital with 40 beds and a dedicated interdisciplinary team approach to acute care, ATH Middle Tennessee is able to make tremendous headway with its patients in a shorter period of time and at less cost than traditional hospitals. "Our patients typically have com-

As a small transitional hospital with 35 beds and a dedicated interdisciplinary team approach to acute care, ATH Middle Tennessee is able to make tremendous headway with its patients.

pleted surgical and diagnostic care at hospitals," says Terri Ann Votava, CEO of ATH Middle Tennessee. "We work with the physicians, case workers, and hospitals to identify patients that could benefit from our care. Our programs and services are designed to complement the care provided by traditional hospitals. We are successful in our efforts because 100 percent of our resources are dedicated to this specialty area."

American Transitional Hospitals has pioneered the hospital-within-a-hospital concept, allowing the company to lease unused space from an existing hospital. Financial resources are highly focused on acute care services—not on bricks and mortar.

From the first day the patient arrives, ATH staff incorporates all health care disciplines into a treatment plan, enabling the patient to transition to a less restrictive and less costly environment at a more rapid pace.

ATH Middle Tennessee has 118 physicians on staff representing a full spectrum of specialties including pulmonology, oncology, internal medicine, infectious disease, cardiology, and neurology. In addition, the hospital provides full therapy services, social services, and 24-hour nursing and respiratory care.

High-Touch, High-Tech

Visitors to ATH Middle Tennessee are likely to hear the sounds of laughter in an open environment supported by a high ratio of staff members to patients. ATH attributes its patient success to an open, positive environment—an environment that is conducive to health, not illness. Open visiting hours encourage family members and children to visit and stay with their loved one. The small size of the hospital facilitates good communication and allows the hospital management team to get very involved with patients and families.

"We are both a high-touch and high-tech facility. The attitude here is very different than at traditional hospitals," adds Votava. "Our ability to put all our resources to make things happen leads to phenomenal outcomes. No one can come close to the clinical outcomes. Our discharged patients are the best testimony to what ATH does.

"In a relatively short time, the health care community in the Middle Tennessee region and beyond has embraced our ability to assist their patients who are high-end users of intensive care units," says Votava. "As we move forward, we are actively redefining acute care services. The hospital within a hospital has had a great impact on how care is delivered."

Founded as American Transitional Care, Inc. in 1987, the company changed its name to American Transitional Hospitals, Inc. in 1992—the same year it moved its headquarters to Franklin, Tennessee.

Celebrating the Little Things

No doubt the hospital's greatest asset is its people—the caregivers who not only help heal the patients, but also help patients and their families adjust to the changes inherent with a post-catastrophic illness or injury. Life-changing success stories occur as a part of ATH's mission. One 16-year-old patient was full of despair and anger, certain his life was confined to bed, hooked permanently to a ventilator. After he was moved into ATH Middle Tennessee, the staff was able to wean the boy off his ventilator in just a few weeks. His anger slowly subsided and his enthusiasm about attending school grew. His remark about ATH: "No one ever told me I could do all these things until I came here."

Whatever the situation, the foremost goal of American Transitional Hospitals is to return each patient to a maximum level of independence while incorporating cost containment by offering innovative approaches without compromising quality of care.

ATH provides a viable alternative to traditional hospitals, providing a sophisticated level of nursing, respiratory, and rehabilitative care to its patients at one-third to one-half the cost.

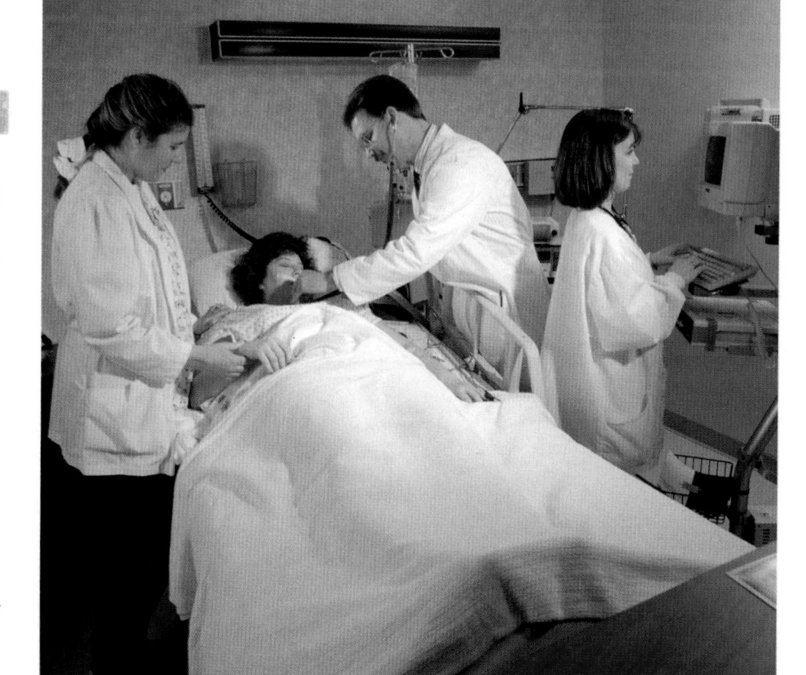

Curb Records

Mike Curb could be called "the power behind the tone." Curb—with a 30-year track record of working with pop and country music greats such as Sammy Davis Jr., Hank Williams Jr., the Osmonds, Lou Rawls, Lyle Lovett, Roy Orbison, Tim McGraw, Merle Haggard, and the Judds—has built Curb Records into one of the most successful independent record labels in the United States.

Curb—songwriter, producer, and record company owner—launched and built his career in Los Angeles. But with an interest in country music, Curb knew he needed to be in Nashville. In 1992, Curb Records moved its corporate headquarters and top executives to Nashville's illustrious Music Row.

Moving to Music City

At the time we moved, Nashville was experiencing the early stages of explosive growth in the country music industry. We knew that to be really successful in the country music arena, we needed to be in Nashville," explains Dennis Hannon, vice president and general manager of Curb Records.

Beginning in 1993, the label started to see success with such artists as McGraw, Hal Ketchum, and Sawyer Brown, as well as considerable success with Wynonna Judd. Just one year later, Curb Records could boast having the number one album on *Billboard*'s Pop Chart and number one album on *Billboard*'s Country Chart for the entire year. McGraw's album also received the Academy of Country Music Album of the Year Award.

Tapping into the pop music industry in 1993, Curb Records brought back the Righteous Brothers' *Unchained Melody*, which went platinum that same year. Also in pop, Curb Records re-released "December 1963 (Oh, What a Night)" by the Four Seasons, which became the longest-running record of all time on the *Billboard* charts.

In mid-1994, the company decided to expand its presence in country music, forming a second label, which signed artists Junior Brown, Hank Williams Jr., Jeff Carson, and LeAnn Rimes, the youngest artist ever to be named American Music Association's New Country Artist of the Year. Rimes' first single, "Blue," spent 27 weeks at number one, and in 1997, Rimes received Grammy awards

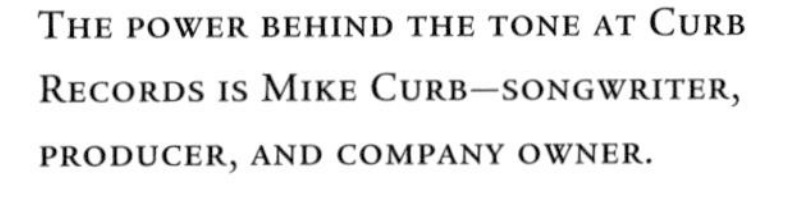

The power behind the tone at Curb Records is Mike Curb—songwriter, producer, and company owner.

Lighting up the charts for Curb Records are artists (clockwise, from top left) LeAnn Rimes, Tim McGraw, Wynonna, Jeff Carson, Hal Ketchum, David Kersh, and Sawyer Brown.

for Best New Artist and Best Female Country Vocal Performance. At the same time, Curb Records also ventured into contemporary Christian music, signing such artists as Whiteheart and Jonathan Pierce. According to Hannon, "The new venture made sense because it fit the personality of the company and the geography—it was all happening in Nashville."

The company's success has continued, as the label had the number one single on *Billboard*'s Singles Chart for the entire year of 1995 with Tim McGraw and the number one video of 1993 on *Billboard*'s Video Chart with Ray Stevens. By the end of 1996, industry trade magazines recognized the Curb group of labels as the third-largest in Nashville—no small feat for an independent record company in Music City.

Independence Breeds Success

But for Curb, success lies far beyond the revenues generated by the company. Curb takes pride in how his company operates within the industry, with a long-term view and commitment toward its artists and employees.

Hannon adds, "We correlate a lot of our success to our move to Tennessee. In a difficult business that demands a lot of creativity, Nashville has the ambience that allows for that state of mind. Everything from lifestyle to employees being happier raising their families has been terrific."

Being independent, Curb Records also attributes its success to its ability to move very quickly in the marketplace, discovering and signing artists, as well as adapting to a volatile industry with regard to promotions and advertising. "That freedom allows us to do things that are directly responsible for the success we've had over the years," Curb notes.

A 30-Year Track Record

Mike Curb began his exceptional career in the mid-1960s at age 20, when he began releasing sound-track albums he composed for motion pictures. His own group, the Mike Curb Congregation, appeared weekly on national television as part of the Glen Campbell show on CBS, and recorded number one hit records such as "Candy Man" with Sammy Davis Jr.

In 1969, Curb merged his company with MGM Records and became president. During his tenure, he turned out hits like "One Bad Apple" by the Osmonds, Lou Rawls' "Natural Man," and "I'm Leaving It All Up to You," by Donny and Marie Osmond. Curb is credited with molding the chart-busting Osmond sound.

After MGM was sold in 1974, Curb went on to build the Curb Music Company and the Curb/Warner label. At one time, the company had five number one songs on the chart, including Debby Boone's "You Light Up My Life," the biggest-selling record of the decade.

In the late 1980s, Curb formed the record company as it is known today. The Curb group of labels, with offices in Los Angeles and Nashville, encompasses a variety of music, but the emphasis for today and the future is on country music.

Curb maintains his company's major contribution to the music industry is in its success with signing, recording, and bringing artists to the marketplace who may not have otherwise had their music presented. "We are very bullish on the music industry in the coming years and see Nashville as continuing to be more of a linchpin in terms of all music. The city will become an entertainment center," says Curb. "However, Nashville will always remain the mecca for country music."

Artists who have helped put Curb Records on the music map include (clockwise, from top left) Lyle Lovett, Junior Brown, Hank Williams Jr., Burnin' Daylight, Jo Dee Messina, Whiteheart, and Jonathan Pierce.

InterMedia Partners

hen InterMedia Partners moved its corporate headquarters from San Francisco to Nashville at the beginning of 1996, company officials vowed that the company would provide state-of-the-art cable television technology and superior customer service and would be an active participant in community affairs. In keeping with the InterMedia slogan, company officials said, "Just You Watch," and proof of these commitments from the multiple-system cable operator was not long in coming.

Just days after the telephones were connected at its new corporate headquarters, InterMedia met with city officials and others to bring NFL football to Music City. InterMedia's support for NFL Yes! was credited by many for raising the awareness needed to support the new stadium, which will be home to the former Houston Oilers.

InterMedia continues on a fast track, integrating itself and its employees firmly in the Nashville community, while overseeing a growing list of cable system acquisitions and facility upgrades to its systems throughout the southeastern United States.

InterMedia made its first foray into Middle Tennessee in 1990. In order to remain competitive in a rapidly changing industry, InterMedia officials saw the need to cluster, that is, to concentrate its systems in one geographic region rather than to be widely distributed throughout the nation. InterMedia chose the Southeast, and specifically Nashville, for its corporate headquarters due to the strong economic growth in the Southeast, familiarity with the region, excellent quality of life, robust business climate, and the fact that Nashville is a good place to raise a family.

InterMedia has experienced rapid-fire growth through the acquisition of more than 10 cable systems in Middle Tennessee, thus becoming the largest cable provider in the state and the 10th-largest cable operator in the country. Through its acquisitions, InterMedia has maintained continuity in investor interest, a further testament to its successful operations.

InterMedia's highly trained technicians constantly maintain the company's cable television systems to ensure superior picture quality and reliability. InterMedia's employees are committed to excellent customer service.

High Technology and High Customer Satisfaction

rue to form, InterMedia has quickly made its mark in Nashville. From an operations standpoint, the company is rebuilding Nashville's cable system, installing the latest in fiber-optic and coaxial cable and digital technology. These advances allow InterMedia to provide such high-technology offerings as high-speed Internet access via cable modem, improved customer service, increased channel capacity, and a high-quality signal. "Our primary commitment is to providing superior customer service by offering top-quality pictures, reliable service, more programming choices, and advanced cable services, all at competitive prices," says COO F. Steve Crawford.

The new network translates to a $40 million investment in Nashville/Davidson County, plus a multimillion-dollar investment in surrounding counties, including Rutherford, Williamson, and Sumner. In a three-year time span, the company plans to spend $300 million to upgrade 17,000 miles of its network and continue building a hybrid fiber-coaxial architecture. Needless to say, skimping on technology and customer service is not in Intermedia's vocabulary.

InterMedia operates under the philosophy that staying on top of advances in technology will allow it to keep pace with customers' changing needs and interests, thereby providing superior service to its customers. Its underlying goal is to provide efficient and high-quality communications services through advanced technology and superior customer service. Each locally operated system is committed to earning the customer's trust every day. Programs such as InterMedia's On-Time Guarantee, which enables customers to count on service technicians to show up when they say they will, exemplify that

commitment. Customers also benefit from expanded walk-in times and 24-hour access to customer service.

Leading by Example

When it comes to corporate citizenship, InterMedia leads by example. Education is at the top of the company's giving list, and it has donated generously to area schools. With a $150,000 investment, InterMedia has committed to provide cable modems for high-speed Internet access to all Davidson and Williamson county schools. Consequently, a school's individual, limited resources and references will not hinder its students from receiving the advantages of high-speed Internet access to such educational Web sites as the Library of Congress and the CNN home page. Additionally, InterMedia's Cable in the Classroom program creates a whole new way of learning by utilizing educational programming on cable and packaging educational products and helpful guides on how to use them for Middle Tennessee teachers.

InterMedia's commitment to the community is reflected in the company's charitable efforts. Its 450 Nashville employees are encouraged to volunteer in local organizations and are recognized for their volunteer efforts through "InterMedia's Good Samaritan" program.

InterMedia is active in each of the communities it serves. One of Nashville's most colorful and popular charitable events is the annual InterMedia Balloon Classic. For several years, InterMedia has underwritten this scenic event, which benefits The EAR Foundation at Baptist Hospital. The company has also sponsored Swing for Sight, a lively golf outing benefiting Prevent Blindness Tennessee.

When funding ran out for the broadcast of the popular Gallatin Green Wave High School football games, InterMedia stepped in and continued to produce and broadcast the games while new sponsors were sought. In Hendersonville, InterMedia became active in Habitat for Humanity, and in rebuilding and maintaining a frequently used community park. In Murfreesboro, InterMedia was an active sponsor and participant in the opening of the Murfreesboro Center for the Arts.

Accelerating into the Future

The finish line isn't even in sight for this young company, which has grown from zero to nearly 1 million subscribers in just nine years. Exponential growth lies ahead for InterMedia, which by 1997, served 600 communities through the 30 local cable systems it owns.

In addition to being an entertainment and education medium, cable services will continue to expand, providing data and information systems. Through continued technological improvements in fiber-optic and digital technology, which allows cable systems to carry a huge amount of information, InterMedia will lead individuals, businesses, government, and educational institutions into the 21st century.

In fact, the first steps for InterMedia include linking all Middle Tennessee cable systems, allowing for efficient and economical operations and giving more customers access to fiber-optic systems. Says Bruce Stewart, InterMedia's executive director of communications, "Our Nashville headquarters, coupled with our growing operation of systems throughout Tennessee and the Southeast, strongly advance InterMedia's objective to be a leader in cable communications services throughout the Southeast."

Clockwise from top left:

The spirit of InterMedia is embodied in the company-sponsored NASCAR race car as it charges toward the finish line.

InterMedia has made its mark on the World Wide Web with its own home page.

The InterMedia Balloon Classic—a spectacular annual event that benefits The EAR Foundation—provides fun and entertainment to Nashville families.

MagneTek, Inc.

THREE YEARS AFTER MOVING TO NASHVILLE FROM LOS ANGELES, MagneTek, Inc. is still attracted to the Music City. From its Century Boulevard headquarters, the electrical equipment manufacturer runs a worldwide business that generates more than $1 billion a year in revenues. ★ To MagneTek, the most important thing isn't whether its brands are household words, as long as its customers' brands are. And they are; among the corporations using MagneTek equipment in their products are Carrier, Caterpillar, IBM, Jacuzzi, Otis Elevator, Trane, and Xerox.

Global Reach

MagneTek operates 24 manufacturing plants in seven countries on three continents, employing 3,500 associates in Tennessee and 13,000 worldwide. Since 1989, the company's stock has been traded on the New York Stock Exchange, and in 1996, MagneTek made it onto the Industry Week 1000 list for the first time, ranking it among the world's largest publicly held manufacturing corporations.

While the company doesn't make consumer products, it does make what makes many consumer—as well as commercial and industrial—products work. MagneTek is a leading manufacturer of energy-saving electrical and electronic devices, including motors, generators, drives, lighting products, and power supplies. It is known as the Energy Engineered™ electrical equipment company because so many of its products save energy, enhance power quality, and improve the efficiency of the systems into which they are installed.

Founded in 1984 in Southern California, MagneTek was created through the acquisition of Litton Industries' Magnetics Group. Ten years later, as part of a corporate consolidation, the company relocated its headquarters to Nashville.

"The purpose of the consolidation was to prune the company back to its core technologies—magnetics and electronics," explains Ronald N. Hoge, MagneTek's president and chief executive officer. "Our greatest strength is our ability to integrate these two technologies into high-quality

Clockwise from top:
MagneTek, Inc. President and CEO Ronald N. Hoge

An estimated 10 percent of all the desktop computers in the world are powered by MagneTek power supplies.

MagneTek electric motors are at work in seven out of 10 homes and circulate the water in half the swimming pools in America.

◄ Marc Solomon

electrical products that solve customer needs quickly at the lowest possible cost."

Leading-Edge Products

Among these products are lighting ballasts, the components that start and operate fluorescent, high-intensity-discharge, and other gas-filled lamps. MagneTek produces both magnetic and electronic ballasts, and is the world's largest maker of electronic ballasts, which are prodigious energy savers.

Other MagneTek products also conserve energy and protect the environment. For instance, MagneTek's Italian subsidiary has developed the industry's first electronic power supplies for electrostatic precipitator air cleaners, which remove particulates from effluent gases and clean the "smoke" created during electricity generation. And MagneTek pioneered the development and marketing of premium efficiency electric motors, which have become the industry norm. Today, the company is taking the next step toward greater energy efficiency with its motor speed controls, which can cut motor electricity consumption by 25 percent. Considering that electric motors consume almost 60 percent of all generated electricity, the positive implications for such a cut in consumption are staggering.

Efficiency of another sort is the mission of MagneTek's drives and systems business. The company supplies electronic, variable-speed drives for factory automation systems, making possible precise control of high-speed production processes. For example, more than 2,000 MagneTek motors and drives are at work in the factories of Intel Corp., the world's leading computer chip maker.

A Green Light to Progress

A recent award recognized MagneTek's progress in making its own manufacturing processes both energy efficient and environmentally friendly. The U.S. Environmental Protection Agency presented its EPAcres award to MagneTek in 1996, lauding the company's performance in the EPA's Green Lights program. Back in 1990, MagneTek was one of the first companies to sign up for Green Lights, under which building owners voluntarily upgrade the efficiency of their lighting based on potential energy cost savings.

To date, according to the EPA, more than 3.5 billion pounds of carbon dioxide emissions have been prevented through Green Lights efficiency upgrades. MagneTek's contribution to the effort? More than 5.5 million pounds of carbon dioxide saved, as well as lesser amounts of other air pollutants. That much carbon dioxide is roughly equivalent to the amount that would be removed from the air by 1,000 acres of trees, qualifying MagneTek for the EPAcres award. And two other local EPAcres winners, Columbia/HCA Healthcare Corp. and Belmont University, used MagneTek ballasts in their lighting upgrades.

Looking to MagneTek's future, Hoge sees a disciplined approach to continuous operational improvement. Says Hoge, "The company will build on its inherent strengths: superior technology, leading-edge products, and talented people committed to our success."

MagneTek electric drives lift and lower approximately four out of five elevators in the United States (top).

More than a third of the office buildings in the United States use MagneTek lighting products (bottom).

Speer Communications, Ltd.

Integrating tomorrow's technology today is the charge of Speer Communications, Ltd., a media and telecommunications conglomerate that opened the doors to its state-of-the-art complex in 1995. ★ Located just north of downtown Nashville, the Speer entertainment complex—a 155,000-square-foot warehouse that has undergone more than $80 million in renovations to become a unique, all-inclusive facility—houses PVS*Speer International, WNAB-TV Channel 58 (Warner Bros.), Speer World-Wide Digital Transmission & Vaulting, and MOR Galleria. These divisions of Speer Communications work in tandem to offer the best in talent and technology available.

The company is the brainchild of Roy M. Speer, the original pioneer of electronic retailing and founder of the Home Shopping Network (HSN), the company that launched interactive shopping on television. Speer's son Richard serves as vice chairman of Speer Communications, and 13-year ABC News veteran Steve Tello is the company's CEO and president.

Speer Communications' master control is the heart of the entertainment complex (top).

PVS*Speer International produces the television series *Sound Station* (bottom).

A High-Tech Arsenal

The Speers' entrepreneurial spirit has inspired them to build the digital facility of tomorrow. Speer Communications employs the most advanced resources available under its PVS*Speer International division, with facilities in Nashville; Washington, D.C.; and Atlanta. The Nashville operation houses one of the country's premier full-service, all-digital complexes. Multiple control rooms, edit suites, "Flame" graphics, AVID nonlinear editing areas, digital mobile units, and a digital recording and duplication media center are all part of Speer's high-tech arsenal. Its eight studios are utilized for everything from filming a 30-second commercial spot to a show with live audience participation.

An adjunct to PVS*Speer International is the Speer Program Development Group, which works with domestic and international clients to develop and produce quality television programming for syndication and other markets.

In keeping with its operating philosophy of integrating cutting-edge technologies, the Speer WorldWide Digital Transmission & Vaulting division offers clients an unparalleled combination of network, security, and storage technologies. The division provides clients with access to a central repository of information throughout the enterprise. Speer's facilities lead the way by offering cost and competitive advantages through network storage rather than discreet physical storage.

Local to Global Broadcasts

Locally, the community benefits from Speer-owned WNAB-TV Channel 58. Nashville's newest full-power broadcast television station and an affiliate of the Warner Bros. Television Network, WNAB-TV provides 24-hour programming with an emphasis on Middle Tennessee sports. Partnering with educational institutions such as the Tennessee Secondary School Athletics Association, Vanderbilt University, Middle Tennessee State University, and Tennessee State University, the station has secured broadcast and cable rights to feature these respective athletic programs to viewers statewide. Utilizing Speer's extensive production resources and mobile satellite field production trucks, WNAB-TV is uniquely capable of offering network-quality broadcasts.

MOR Galleria is Speer Communications' 24-hour cable televi-

sion network. MOR Galleria, formerly known as MOR Music Television, began as the world's first and only music shopping television network.

MOR Galleria informs and entertains viewers with videos, news, and information, as well as offering music-related merchandise. The sheer volume of transactions affords MOR Galleria tremendous buying power and the ability to pass on savings to its customers.

MOR's Internet service (http://www.mormusic.com), marketed to cybervisitors as Club MOR, enables instant access to a library of more than 150,000 music titles. Virtually any music title in print can be purchased through the site or by calling MOR's toll-free number (800-227-5000). The com-pany's telemarketing, distribution, and customer service center is also located in the Speer complex.

PVS*Speer International in Washington, D.C., serves as Speer Communications' international media and production facility, as well as the firm's gateway for international programming and development. The company provides news and postproduction services for many of the world's news agencies as well as Fortune 500 companies.

PVS*Speer International-Washington houses more than 15 broadcasters—some of the most prominent in the industry—on a regular basis, including the British Broadcasting Company, Japan's NHK, European Broadcasting Union, and Irish Television. The Washington company is home to several top-rated international programs, including Japan's *Hidaka Report* and Mexico's *Contrapunto*. The division, which has complete transmission services through Vyvx, fiber, microwave, and satellite capability, can be monitored by Speer Worldwide Digital Transmission & Vaulting through the Nashville facility.

The PVS*Speer International location in Atlanta serves as an AVID Authorized Education Center, offering training to television producers and editors on this state-of-the-art digital editing system. The Atlanta facility also provides AVID, disk storage, and equipment rental, as well as mobile production. The facility links Nashville to the Atlanta market.

From its hub in Nashville and spokes in Washington and Atlanta, Speer's teleport services bring Music City in touch with the world through a new and evolving digital medium of communication. The company's impressive array of satellites located off Nashville's Interstate 65 transmits signals to virtually anywhere in the world.

For a city with its heartbeat in the entertainment industry, Speer Communications' arrival on the Nashville scene was something to sing about. The company cites the talent pool and Nashville's excellent location for satellite capabilities as key reasons for choosing the Music City as the site for its vast entertainment complex.

The future is promising for Speer Communications, as it is geographically and technologically primed to lead the industry in global communications, technology, digital production, and distribution.

Clockwise from top left:
Speer Communications' media center is state-of-the-art.

Sports Talk, with host Greg Pogue, which is broadcast on WNAB-TV 58, is Nashville's only live televised sports talk show.

Julie Tello hosts WNAB-TV 58's "VJ" segments.

Speer Communications' digital, state-of-the-art media and communications facility is located just north of Nashville.

▼ GARY LAYDA

▲ GARY LAYDA

Photographers

Steve Baker is an internationally published photographer who has contributed to more than 100 publications. With a degree in journalism from Indiana University, he is proprietor of Highlight Photography, specializing in assignments for such clients as Eastman Kodak, Nike, Budweiser, the U.S. Olympic Committee, and Mobil Oil, which has commissioned seven exhibitions of his work since 1994. Baker is author/photographer of *Racing Is Everything* and he contributed to another Towery publication, *Indianapolis: Crossroads of the American Dream*. Currently, Baker resides in Indianapolis.

Dan Ball is a Memphis-based freelance photographer who specializes in commercial, editorial, and fine art photography. A regular contributor to the *Memphis Flyer* and *Memphis* magazine, Ball has worked with such clients as AutoZone, International Paper, Nike Inc., and Towery Publishing. Currently, Ball is working on a book of photographs concentrating on the creative counterculture of Memphis. In 1994, he received the Best Feature Cover Photo award from the National News Association.

David Duhl, originally from Fair Lawn, New Jersey, is a freelance photographer who specializes in nature photography, specifically wildflowers, national parks, and endangered species. His images have appeared in *National Geographic World*, *Outside*, and *Tennessee Wildlife*, as well as in several calendars. Duhl teaches advanced techniques in nature photography at Nashville State Technical Institute.

Julie Green, a native of Tulsa, Oklahoma, specializes in equine sports journalism and environmental investigations. Drawing on her education at the University of Missouri School of Journalism, as well as studies with master photojournalist Alex Webb, Green has been published in 42 U.S. and 35 foreign newspapers, 12 books on horses, and *Guitar Player*, *Orion*, *Life*, and *Horse Illustrated* magazines.

Stephen Greenfield is a nationally published, self-taught photographer from Nashville whose areas of specialty include advertising, corporate, and editorial photography. A former police detective, Greenfield has been a professional photographer for 33 years. Currently, he lives in Cleveland, Tennessee.

Steve Jones, a native of Wichita, moved to Memphis in 1987. Specializing in corporate/annual report, sports, location, and music photography, as well as photojournalism, he was a staff photographer for the *Commercial Appeal* from 1987 to 1995. Jones' images can be seen in such publications as *Time*, *Agenda*, the *Washington Post*, and the *New York Times*, as well as in another Towery publication, *Memphis: New Visions, New Horizons*.

Gary Layda is an award-winning photographer who specializes in annual report, stock, public relations, and aerial photography, as well as executive portraiture. Once an instructor of photography at Vanderbilt University's Sarratt Center, Nashville State Technical Institute, and Middle Tennessee State University, he currently is employed by the Metropolitan Government of Nashville. Layda has taken pictures for The Nashville Network, Jack Daniels, Quorum HealthCare, and BellSouth Mobility, and his images can be seen in various national and international publications.

Marianne Leach, a professional dancer for more than 25 years, is a native of Nashville who specializes in theatrical photography, performance and studio work, and special design portraits. Her images have appeared in *Dance Magazine*, *Family Circle*, and *Live Wire*, and her previous clients include the Nashville Electric Service, Nashville Symphony, and Tennessee Repertory Theatre. Leach is the company photographer for the Nashville Ballet and Nashville Opera.

Rich Mays, originally from Charleston, South Carolina, moved to Nashville in 1986. With a bachelor's degree in music from Furman University in Greenville, South Carolina, Mays specializes in corporate, editorial, and fine art photography. His images have been published in numerous magazines, including *Forbes*, *Inc.*, and *Newsweek*. In addition to being a professional photographer, Mays is a certified flight instructor.

Karina McDaniel, an accomplished photographer of celebrity and society weddings, uses techniques of photojournalism to record the sense and emotion of the ceremony while minimizing the usual artificial posing. Since 1986, she has worked with many celebrities, including Johnny Cash, Dolly Parton, and Minnie Pearl. Her images have appeared in such magazines as *Southern Living* and *Southern*, and in the book *Tennessee and the Smokies*. McDaniel owns and operates KARINA—Fine Photography.

Jonathan Postal, born in New York City, lived and worked in London, Sydney, Milan, and New Orleans before settling in Memphis. The creative director of *Eye* magazine, his work has been featured in *Rolling Stone*, *Vanity Fair*, and numerous other magazines. Among his many life experiences, Postal's favorite is the time he was trapped in a 20-foot cage with a 15-foot alligator for 30 minutes.

▶ BOB SCHATZ

David Rogers is owner of D.R. Productions, specializing in panoramic photography. A native of Nashville, Rogers is a member of the American Society of Media Photographers and the National Press Photographers Association.

Bob Schatz, who lives and works in Nashville, specializes in corporate, advertising, and stock photography for such clients as DuPont, IBM, NationsBank, UNISYS, and Service Merchandise. His images have been published in numerous magazines, including *Travel & Leisure*, *Business Week*, *Fortune*, and *Time*, as well as in *Memphis: New Visions, New Horizons*. Schatz is the recipient of numerous Addy awards and recently completed a monthlong assignment in Syria, Jordan, Israel, Greece, and Turkey.

Carol and Dan Thalimer are freelance authors, photojournalists, and photographers who live near Atlanta. Together they have written several guidebooks about the Southeast; contributed to several national and international guides; and written more than 500 magazine and newspaper articles, all of which were illustrated with their own photography. Carol's images were featured in an earlier Towery publication, *Cincinnati: Crowning Glory*.

Ron Volpe is an avid backpacker and hiker whose love of the outdoors has led him to a career in nature photography. Originally from Beaver County, Pennsylvania, Volpe hiked the entire Appalachian Trail, from Maine to Georgia, in 1978. In addition, in one 12-month period, he hiked the Grand Canyon, Yellowstone National Park, and Glacier National Park. Currently, Volpe is an interim teacher with Davidson County School District and operates a small business marketing his photographs to corporate clients.

Aubrey Watson, a Nashvillian by birth, is a graduate of the New York Institute of Photography. His nature and travel images have been published in *USA Today*, *Parade*, *Southern Living*, *Outdoor Life*, and *Better Homes & Gardens*. He is coauthor of *The Outdoor Photographer's Bible*, published by Doubleday & Co., and the winner of numerous industry awards.

David Wright, a native of Booneville, Mississippi, is a freelance photographer who specializes in historic architectural, landscape, and wedding photography. His images have been published in *Victorian Homes*, *Heartland USA*, and *Home & Away*, and he has worked with such clients as Holiday Inns and the Nashville Convention & Visitors Bureau. Wright, who currently lives in Nashville, spends his free time traveling the back roads of Tennessee, searching for unspoiled vistas and picturesque settings.

Other photographers and organizations that have contributed to *Nashville: City of Note* include Tim Campbell, John Chiasson, the Country Music Hall of Fame, and Les Leverett.

Acknowledgments

Special thanks to Jim Sherraden of Hatch Show Print for designing the *Nashville: City of Note* poster, assisting with the book jacket photo shoot, and supplying the letterpress alphabet that was used for the drop caps in this book.

Thanks also to Manuel's for supplying the cowboy hat and jacket used in the photo on the book jacket.

◆ GARY LAYDA

◆ DAVID WRIGHT PHOTOGRAPHY

Index of Profiles

BOB SCHATZ